# THE HOUSING PROBLEM: A REAL CRISIS?

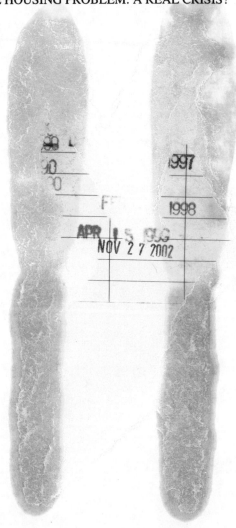

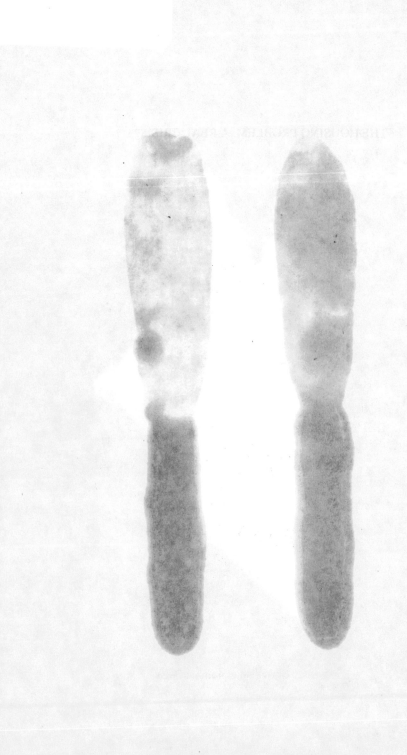

# THE HOUSING PROBLEM
## A Real Crisis?

### A PRIMER ON HOUSING MARKETS, POLICIES, AND PROBLEMS

MICHAEL A. GOLDBERG

University of British Columbia Press

Vancouver

# THE HOUSING PROBLEM: A REAL CRISIS?

*A Primer on Housing Markets, Policies and Problems*

This book has been published with the
assistance of the Canada Council. The research upon
which it is based was supported by the
Economic Council of Canada

**Canadian Cataloguing in Publication Data**

Goldberg, Michael A., 1941-
  The housing problem

Bibliography: p.
ISBN 0-7748-0173-5

1. Housing. 2. Housing - Canada. 3. Housing -
Prices. 4. Housing policy. I. Title.
HD7287.G64        333.33'8         C83-091000-X

INTERNATIONAL STANDARD BOOK NUMBER 0-7748-0173-5

*Printed in Canada*

# Contents

# Tables

# Tabl

# Preface

This monograph has had a long gestation period. It was undertaken originally at the request of the Economic Council of Canada in the aftermath of the Anti-Inflation Board (AIB) of the mid-1970's. As a successor to the AIB the Economic Council created the Centre for the Study of Inflation and Productivity (CSIP) with the purpose of informing Canadians specifically about inflation and productivity, and more generally about the functioning of the Canadian economy. In an attempt to communicate its work to the Canadian public the Centre issued a periodical, *The Monitor,* which noted in its first issue in October, 1978, that the Centre's

> basic thrust will be to use its analytical and educational capabilities to promote a better understanding of major issues concerning the nature and sources of inflation, productivity, and performance on the part of public and private decision-makers as well as the general public.

Housing was an issue which was of particular concern both to the Centre and to the Canadian public after the dramatic increase in house prices that occurred in the 1972-75 period, and which was soon after followed by a period of dormancy from 1976 to 1979. Accordingly, the Centre wanted someone to develop a monograph on the workings of the housing market in Canada that would be simultaneously rigorous and rooted in sound academic research while being comprehensible to the interested but technically untrained "average" Canadian.

In the summer of 1978 I was approached to put together such a monograph. The monograph was completed by the spring of 1979. However, for a variety of reasons, including the demise of the Centre, the monograph never appeared. The Centre and the Economic Council of Canada did graciously grant permission for me to develop the manuscript as I saw fit and to seek its publication elsewhere, with the understanding that the contents in no way reflected the views past or present of the Economic Council of Canada, which I duly note here. While completely absolving CSIP and the Economic Council of any association with the contents, I do want to acknowledge their role in getting this manuscript off the ground.

Much of the original material remains, though it has benefited from the input of several anonymous readers, from considerable editing to develop a consistent and easily readable style, and from my own involvement in a number of housing policy issues since the initiation of this project. Perhaps most importantly it has benefited from the passage of time itself. The period since the summer of 1978 has been a particularly chaotic one for housing markets in Canada. From the doldrums of 1978 came the frenetic boom of 1980 and early 1981. No sooner had consumers begun to learn to cope with soaring prices and staggering interest rates which climbed into the 22-23% range in 1981, than they had to learn to deal with plummeting housing prices, rising unemployment, declining income and persistent high levels of inflation and interest rates.

All of this forced me to reevaluate much of what I had written earlier, to place it in the broad context of volatile market behaviour, and to key the discussion to market forces and away from the current boom-bust cycle. The result is intended to serve the interested reader both in boom times and in depressed market conditions and to provide a sound understanding of market forces that wil[1] enable the reader to comprehend the specific market condition of the present.

Given the evolution of this monograph several expressions of thanks are due to various helpers who lent a hand at several stages of its development. Ruth Calder and Claire Brown were involved in the initial effort. Ruth Calder in particular helped with the annotations in the bibliography and with keeping the prose readable. The second iteration benefited considerably from the assistance of Sara Bennett in updating tables and reorganizing the text, tables and appendices. Most recently, Karen Eng has brought the tables up to date to include the most recent complete year data from 1981. Lastly, Jane Fredeman, Senior Editor of the U.B.C. Press, the two anonymous referees upon whom she called for critical evaluation of the manuscript, and Brian Scrivener provided constructive and needed criticism. Finally, the staff of the Word Processing Centre of the Faculty of Commerce did absolutely heroic work in helping me to meet impossible publication deadlines.

To all, my sincere thanks. Despite their best efforts, the present monograph inevitably suffers from having to cover so much material in such a brief space. It also suffers from my own ignorance of much of the housing literature, particularly the social and cultural perspectives. Notwithstanding these, it is my hope that the resulting product does advance understanding of and knowledge about the functioning of Canadian housing markets and of the housing policies adopted by governments to deal with the numerous complexities of the "housing issue" in its most elaborated form.

# 1

# Introduction

An earlier version of this monograph written in June 1981, began with the following:

> After three or four years of dormancy, housing is again coming to the fore as an important political issue. Simultaneously, one reads about the lowest level of housebuilding activity in Canada in more than a decade and the wildest house price boom in recent memory in British Columbia. The public is understandably confused. Is the housing "crisis" one of boom or bust? People in sluggish markets are concerned about protecting their equity in their housing unit. People in British Columbia are concerned about the prospect of "ever again" being able to afford to buy suitable housing.

The recent experience in British Columbia conjures up memories of the house price spiral that struck most of Canada's urban areas during the 1972-75 period and threatened "the Canadian dream" of homeownership. The recent house price surge in British Columbia is captured in the following example. A relatively modest three-bedroom bungalow in Vancouver's Kerrisdale area which sold for $99,500 in February 1979 was selling for $145,000 in February 1980 and for $245,000 in February 1981. This represented an increase of 150% in just two years. Price increases in other parts of British Columbia were no less staggering.[1] The same Kerrisdale bungalow was selling for an estimated

$185,000 in July 1982, a decline of nearly 30% from an April 1981 peak of $255,000. The public is understandably stunned and unable to make sense out of such dramatic short-term increases and decreases.

There have been periodic "hot spots" and housing price spirals throughout much of Canada's first century. The only claim of the present British Columbia situation is its recency. It is certainly not the first boom of its kind, nor is it likely to be the last. It is neither the biggest nor most dramatic increase.[2] Similar increases undoubtedly loom in the near future for other regions of Canada, particularly those subject to periodic and dramatic spurts in economic activity, though even more stable areas are not immune from short-run surges in real property prices.[3]

Given the recurrent nature of these housing cycles and the continued confusion of the general public vis-à-vis housing matters, a primer on housing and housing markets appears called for to help citizens come to terms with housing issues in an informed manner. The present volume is intended to provide the non-technical reader with a range of important ideas and "facts" relating to housing and housing markets so that such phenomena as British Columbia's recent price explosion are understandable.

Housing markets as we will see are highly localized markets. They are also very prone to periodic disruption because of the volatility of demand and the relative sluggishness of supply in the short run. Their periodic and localized nature makes them somewhat unusual in the economic literature. However, if we as a society are to make appropriate and effective decisions to deal with housing markets we must understand how these markets function. An understanding of the operation of essentially local housing markets can assist us and the policymakers in governments acting on our behalf. Armed with a sound conceptualization of how housing markets operate, we can try to avoid making counterproductive short-run policies (such as rent controls and land banking) that have longer-run adverse effects.

This then is our agenda:

i. To survey what is known about housing markets and housing affordability, primarily in Canada but elsewhere as well when relevant.
ii. To identify and discuss some of the relationships between the rising preferences of consumers and rising incomes and housing prices.
iii. To pose the following question, and provide the best answer possible from our current knowledge: "What do high and rising or low and falling housing prices really mean, and what do they imply for the future of Canadian society as we currently know it?"
iv. Lastly, to explore a range of policies designed to improve the responsiveness and efficiency of housing markets and to identify classes of policies that are likely to be counterproductive and thus should be avoided in future.

To achieve these and other related objectives, a number of important elements will be studied. First, we will review the role of housing in both the national economy and in the economy of Canadian households. Brief mention is also made of the importance of housing from a social perspective, vis-à-vis social problems and social policy.

In Chapter 3 the question of housing affordability is reviewed in some detail. First, housing prices and rents are examined over the past two decades to determine their longer-term trends. Then the components of housing costs are examined. These include mortgage costs and availability, recent and likely future innovations in mortgage lending, costs and availability of residential land, property taxes, housing maintenance and repair expenditures, and the costs of buying and selling houses. Finally, changes in these various prices and costs are compared with changes in income levels, in order to zero in on the exact nature of the affordability question, its breadth, depth, anticipated duration, and its causes and cures.

After a review of a range of data on housing prices and costs and their importance to the well-being of the nation, Chapter 4 provides a non-technical survey of the basic tools of housing market analysis. This will enable the reader to analyse a range of possible and proposed remedies to perceived and existing housing problems. Since the focus of this book is economic, the emphasis in Chapter 4 is placed upon economic tools. The social issues that result from economic policies are very important and will be alluded to, but they will be treated as of secondary importance here. For example, the questions of affordability (and rising prices generally) are basically economic questions and will be treated as such here, although they do have significant social implications, which will be mentioned but not addressed in detail.

Given these fundamentals of economic analysis, Chapter 5 moves on to examine housing policy issues: who makes housing policy and why; and what are the economic implications of many past and proposed solutions to housing problems? Federal, provincial and local policies which affect housing and housing markets are surveyed in this section.

. The book closes with a discussion of some of the difficult, and possibly unresolvable, issues which loom ahead. Will people begin to move from the suburbs to more central locations? Will the people who were born during the postwar baby boom finally begin to have their own children, thereby creating a mini baby boom? How will poor people who are on fixed incomes cope with rising housing costs? In short, for whom is there and for whom will there be a genuinely serious housing crisis? Present economic conditions provide an excellent chance to reflect on housing markets since there is no crisis surrounding the issue currently. This respite should allow us to gain an understanding of these markets before they become active again. Let us begin.

# 2

# Why is Housing so Important?
## An Introduction to "The Problem"

Accommodating the housing needs and desires of the Canadian public has presented governmental policymakers with an array of challenges since well before the passage of the first Dominion Housing Act in 1935. The character of these challenges has changed considerably as we have moved from the economic depression of the 1930's to the economic boom of the early 1970's and back to the depression of the early 1980's. During the depression and postwar era, policymakers attempted to improve housing conditions through the provision of mortgage credit. More recently, government policy has shifted to stimulating homeownership and upgrading the level of housing that Canadians can afford, through such programmes as the Assisted Home-Ownership Program and the Residential Rehabilitation Assistance Program. In 1981, the federal government (through the Canada Mortgage and Housing Corporation) spent $1,007 million.

When provincial policies and tax subsidies to homeowners and rental housing investors are added, the sum is rung into many billions of dollars.[1] Accordingly, the housing question must be looked at in considerable detail. These large sums of government monies for housing indicate that housing is important. The question is, just *how* important is it to the Canadian economy, to the provinces, to the municipalities and, of course, to individual Canadian households?

A BRIEF SUMMARY: PRICES, COSTS, RENTS AND INCOMES

In this section a range of important elements in housing prices and rents have been considered. Information has been presented on:

  i. housing prices and rents on new and existing residential units;
 ii. mortgage cost and availability, and sources of mortgage lending;
iii. residential land availability and cost;
 iv. property taxes and operating costs;
  v. transaction costs;
 vi. construction costs.

The picture that emerges from these data is a consistent one: the prices of housing and rents, and the associated costs of building and operating housing of all types, have all risen dramatically since 1961. However, this represents only one side of the picture. It is also necessary to look at the trends in income levels before beginning to talk about a housing affordability crisis.

A look at the changes in income levels since 1961 in Table 4 reveals an offsetting trend. Since 1961, per capita income in current dollars (unadjusted for inflation) rose by 605%. Household incomes through 1980 rose by 400%. This compares with a 405% increase in the average multiple listing sale (MLS) and only a 326% increase in the average price of houses financed under the National Housing Act (both through 1981). These data do not substantiate the claim that housing is beyond the financial reach of the average Canadian family. After all, approximately two-thirds of Canadian households already own their housing units.

This public concern over house prices and rents needs to be resolved. One hypothesis is that there are essentially two quite distinct housing crises in Canada. The first is a crisis in expectations, whereby the expectations of the *average* Canadian household have risen regarding what constitutes a minimum quality home. People now want houses that they cannot easily afford owing to continued increase in what is deemed to be minimal housing.

The second is closer to the traditional housing crisis: there are some people who just cannot afford to purchase or rent suitable accommodation. These lower income households are suffering from a genuine affordability problem: they simply cannot afford to rent or purchase housing of a reasonable standard and in a reasonable location at a reasonable proportion of their income and with reasonable security of tenure.

In order to discuss these housing issues further we need to get a better understanding of the mechanisms by which house prices and rents are determined and by which they increase over time. In other words, it is necessary to acquire some basic tools of economic analysis before proceeding to a more detailed discussion of affordability and the public policies which are needed in order to solve the existing affordability problems.

# 4

# Housing Market Analysis — Some Economic Tools

In order to make sense of the world people tend to break it up into digestible conceptual pieces. Economists find it useful to break the economy into smaller pieces, in order to study it more effectively.[17] The most traditional breakdown is between that of the whole economy and the that of various decision-making components that comprise the economy. The analysis of the economic system as a whole is called *macroeconomics:* it focuses on questions of government spending, consumption, investment, international trade, and government tax policy (called *fiscal policy*). Macroeconomics also deals with financial variables such as the amount of money (paper currency, coins, and chequing and savings accounts), stocks and bonds, and the prevailing rates of interest. The government policies which influence these financial or monetary variables are called *monetary policy*.

In contrast to this top-down view is the bottom-up view of the economy which is provided by studying the numerous decision-making units in the economy. This component-oriented approach which focuses on smaller economic units, as opposed to the whole economic system, is called *microeconomics*. The microeconomic decision-making units are the *firms* which produce the goods and services on which society depends, and the *households* (or *consumers*) that purchase these goods and services and also provide the savings and labour which enable the goods and services to be produced.

Housing, as we have seen, is a very important element in terms of the national economy and in terms of individual households. Accordingly, any economic analysis of housing must look at both macroeconomic and microeconomic aspects. It now makes sense to look at the various components of national economic activity in order to see the relationship between housing and the other components in the economy. To measure economic activity, economists have created the concept of gross national expenditure (GNE), which is the sum of various annual expenditures by major groups in the economy.

| (GNE) Gross National Expenditure | (C) = Consumption (spending by consumers) | (I) + Investment (spending by business, government, & households) | (G) + Government (spending on on current programmes) |
|---|---|---|---|
| | | (E) + Exports (to consumers, businesses, & governments abroad) | (M) - Imports (by Canadian businesses, governments, & consumers) |

This can be expressed by the formula:

$$GNE = C + I + G + E - M$$

By using the data provided by Statistics Canada in the National Income and Expenditure Accounts this equation can be reconstructed using the data for 1979 (in millions $):[18]

GNE = C(1981) + I(1981) + G(1981) + E(1981) - M(1981)
    - residual error
328,501 = 190,025 + 81,743 + 66,192 + 98,999 - 107,177 - 1,274

Housing constitutes an important part of GNE because it is a large component of both consumption (C) and investment (I). For instance, in 1981 housing construction, repair, and maintenance amounted to $19.3 billion and represented 5.9% of GNE and, more importantly, 23.6% of all investment. Furthermore, consumer (household) expenditures on heat and light and other housing-related consumption amounted to $46.6 billion in 1980 (the most recent year with complete data) or 16.2% of 1980 GNE and 27.9% of total 1980 consumption.

By placing the figures presented earlier in the context of the GNE equation it begins to come clear how macroeconomists treat housing as an important element in macroeconomic policy. It is the general goal of economic policy at the national level to increase GNE while maintaining both price stability (that is, little or no inflation) and maintaining reasonably full employment (traditionally taken as being 4% unemployment or less). Returning to the GNE equation it can be seen that the policies which increase C, I, G, or E and decrease M will all lead to increases in GNE. The main task which confronts the macroeconomist is that of identifying the various policies and factors which influence the components of GNE, so that economic policies can be formulated which will lead to increases in GNE per capita (that is, the average amount of gross national expenditure per man, woman, and child in Canada). These increases have to be constrained, though, so that prices and unemployment do not rise to levels which are socially and politically unacceptable.

Of more concern to most Canadians than the relationship between housing and the national economy are the microeconomic considerations of house prices and rents. Accordingly, we will now shift our attention away from GNE, consumption, investment, and government spending and focus upon the determinants of house prices and upon the supply of and demand for housing in specific housing markets.

It is necessary to focus on specific local markets because housing is not a *national* economic good. Houses are largely fixed in location and a study of house prices means a study of specific local housing markets, since that is where the economic forces of supply and demand concentrate. Unlike stocks and bonds, which can be transported easily, housing cannot be moved, and the services it provides must be consumed at the location of the housing unit. Therefore, it is necessary to explore the special supply and demand factors for housing in order to understand better how house prices are determined and also to understand what can be done to influence these prices.

DEMAND AND SUPPLY: INFORMING OUR INTUITIONS

As cited in most introductory texts, economics is the study of how society "allocates scarce resources among competing uses to produce goods and services."[19] Of prime importance in this allocation is the price of a given good or service, the general notion being: the higher the price, the less the use; the lower the price, the higher the use.

The utility of studying microeconomic relationships can already begin to be seen. Government policies, for instance, which affect housing prices will also affect how the society allocates its scarce housing resources among its citizens. If the government suddenly started giving each purchaser of a *new* house a $20,000 cash bonus, then the effective price to the consumer of new houses would initially drop by $20,000, which would stimulate greatly the demand for new houses. Simultaneously, however, the demand for existing houses would drop. Society as a whole, therefore, would divert increasing quantities of scarce resources, such as serviced land, labour, and construction materials, into the production of new housing and away from other sectors and from the mainte-nance of existing housing. Therefore, by studying the microeconomics of hous-ing markets it is possible to analyse the effects of a broad range of housing and housing-related policies.

Figure 1 below indicates the relationship between the price of a good or service and the quantity of that good or service which is demanded by con-sumers at each price. The vertical axis represents the price of a good or service, while the horizontal axis represents the quantity of that good or service which is demanded by consumers. The curve slopes downward to the right, illustrating the idea that as prices fall we demand more. Similarly, as prices rise (that is, move up the curve to the left) the demand declines.

**FIGURE 1**

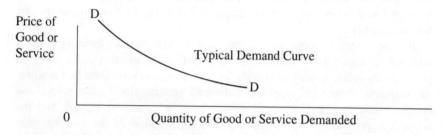

The demand curve depicted here relates the price of any good or service to the quantity of that good or service demanded by the consuming public. It should be noted that demand as studied by economists is different from desire or need, precisely because it is related to price, and therefore to the ability to pay. As a result, economists speak of effective demand, which is really desire or need tempered by the ability to pay. Thus, in strictest economic terms, poor people do not represent a very significant demand for goods and services because they do not have the necessary ability to pay for them. Their needs are no less than the needs of those who can afford clothing, food, shelter, and luxuries, but the effective demand of the poor is minimal because their ability to translate their needs and desires into purchasing power is small. This is not to imply that this is a desirable state of affairs, but just that this is the way it is. This distinction between effective demand and actual needs and desires is of great importance in understanding the housing issues we discuss later.

One other basic concept of microeconomics has been particularly important to people studying housing, and that is the concept of price elasticity. The idea is quite a simple one and is firmly rooted in sound intuition. Essentially, a good is defined as having a price-elastic demand if a change in price leads to a relatively larger change in quantity demanded. For example, assume that the price of apples *increases* from $.25 to $.30 apiece (that is a 20% increase in price). If such a price increase leads to a 25% *decrease* in the quantity of apples demanded by the public, then we would say that the demand for apples is price elastic, since the percentage drop in quantity demanded exceeded the percentage increase in price. If, on the other hand, the 20% price increase led to only a 5% decrease in demand for apples, we would say that the demand in these circumstances is price inelastic, that is, the demand for apples is not very responsive to changes in price, since the percentage drop in quantity demanded was less than the percentage increase in price. Intuitively, elastic demand is where small changes in price lead to large (and opposite) changes in quantity demanded. Inelastic demand, on the other hand, is sluggish and does not respond greatly to small changes in price.

In an analogous fashion we can speak about elasticity of supply with respect to price. Supply that is very responsive to price change is elastic, whereas supply that is unresponsive is called inelastic. The supply of housing is quite inelastic in the short run (for instance one to three years), since it takes a long time to gear up housing production and as a result most of the housing supply is represented by houses that are already built. The supply of these existing houses is quite unresponsive to price change, since they exist and have virtually no alternative use in the short run.

The concept of demand and supply elasticities with respect to price is a central one in housing economics, and the empirical estimation of these elasticities allows policymakers, in theory at least, to trace through the effects of various demand and supply and pricing policies on quantities ultimately demanded and supplied in the housing markets of Canada.[20] The estimation and use of these elasticities has occupied a great deal of the housing economics literature because of the importance of the concept in making and implementing housing policy.

These are the basics of the demand curve, but there is more to economics than just the basics. The demand curve pictured above assumes that the demand for all other goods and services in the economy remains constant, and also that incomes and prices remain constant. If we now consider the fact that incomes have been rising, then we can see that instead of there being a constant and unchanging demand curve such as that pictured above, there is a shifting demand curve. Take as an example the demand for furniture. Assume that the demand (that is, the relationship between price and quantity demanded) is given by the Figure 1 demand curve. Consider now what would happen if incomes were increased, for example, by cutting taxes and adding additional dollars to paycheques. It could now be expected that, since people have more money to spend, they will buy more furniture at every price than they did before. This situation may be illustrated using demand analysis by drawing a new demand curve which reflects greater purchasing power resulting from the tax cut (Figure

2). In essence, the additional income has served to shift the entire demand curve upward, which is another way of saying that at each price there will be a greater demand for furniture. Other changes could affect the demand for furniture. For example, increased numbers of previously dependent children leaving home to establish their own households would lead to a dramatic change in the number of households in Canada. This increase in the number of households would have the effect of shifting the demand curve upward, reflecting the fact that there are now more households looking to buy furniture.

**FIGURE 2**

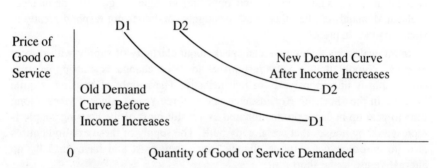

It is possible to trace through the effects of such things as tax cuts and population changes on the demand for a given good or service. In general, the more money or people that can be attracted into a given market, the higher will be the demand curve. However, this also works in reverse. Declines in income or population can lead to declines in demand — witness the declining demand for teachers and schools as the number of school age Canadian children drops.

Supply is in many ways the reverse of demand.[21] Higher prices act as deterrents to demand but as stimulants to supply. Thus, producers will produce more of any given good or service the higher its price rises. What usually happens is that as prices rise additional entrepreneurs are coaxed into the marketplace to take advantage of the high prices and the possibility of high profits. Pocket calculators provide a good example. Initially, these space-age by-products were very expensive to buy and were highly profitable to the people who produced them. However, the high profit attracted increased competition, and so the supply expanded. The higher the price, the higher the profits and the greater the number of calculators offered for sale. The supply curve that is sketched out in this way has the characteristic that at higher prices ever greater quantities of goods or services are offered for sale (see Figure 3). At lower prices, lower quantities are offered (the reverse of the demand situation). In the case of demand, limited purchasing power, which is a consequence of constant income and population, results in this trade-off between price and quantity. In the supply case, limited profit and entrepreneurship serve to force the trade-off.

## FIGURE 3

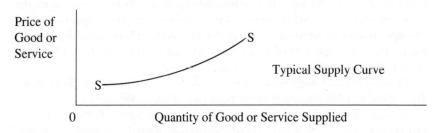

Price of
Good or
Service

Typical Supply Curve

0          Quantity of Good or Service Supplied

If, as in the demand example, the false assumption is dropped that everything must remain constant (for example, prices of all other goods, costs of production, and the state of technology), then it is possible to shift the supply curve outward. For example, if someone suddenly develops a way to produce calculators using cheaper raw materials and cheaper production methods (as in fact happened), then profits will rise, and at each price, manufacturers using these new techniques will be willing to produce more calculators than before. This has the effect of shifting the supply curve out to the right, which is a graphic way of depicting the increased willingness to produce calculators at each given price. Also, if the costs of production rise (through scarcity of a key ingredient, such as labour), then the supply curve can be expected to shift backward. This means that under these conditions of scarcity, producers would have to be offered higher prices for the same amount of goods or services, since the higher cost of production reduces their profits. These situations are represented below:

## FIGURE 4

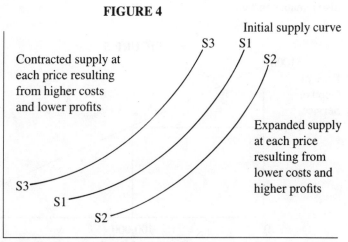

Price of
Good or
Supply

Initial supply curve

S3    S1

S2

Contracted supply at
each price resulting
from higher costs
and lower profits

Expanded supply
at each price
resulting from
lower costs and
higher profits

S3

S1

S2

Quantity of Good or Service Supplied

To sum up, demand responds negatively to prices, so the higher the price the lower the demand. As well, supply responds positively to price; the higher the price, the higher the level of supply. We are now in a position to put both these concepts to work to determine the price that the goods and services demanded by the public and supplied by the entrepreneurs will trade for in the market, and also to see the quantity of goods demanded/supplied.

Two hypothetical numerical examples will serve to demonstrate these ideas. The following table illustrates the hypothetical demand for dishwashers among the households of Edmonton (roughly 200,000 households). If the price were low enough, say $5, then every household would want a dishwasher. Alternatively, if the price were high enough, say $1,000, then virtually no one would want a dishwasher. If the price were about $400, then approximately half of the households would want dishwashers.

| Price Per Dishwasher | Number of Dishwashers Demanded (i.e., Number of Households Willing to Buy Dishwashers) |
|---|---|
| $5 | 200,000 |
| $400 | 100,000 |
| $1000 | 0 |

The above information can be represented on a demand curve. The price per dishwasher is given on the vertical axis and the quantity of dishwashers demanded is given on the horizontal axis. Economists construct these curves by observing actual prices and quantities for individual goods and services, and then use statistical techniques to measure the demand curve. However, the demand curve is only relevant if the prices of all other goods and services besides dishwashers remain constant, and if incomes, populations, and tastes also remain constant.

**FIGURE 5**

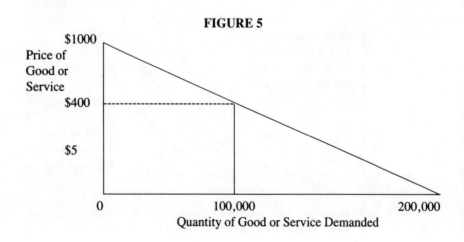

If the assumption of constant population, for example, is now dropped, the demand curve may move even if income per capita and preferences for dishwashers remain unchanged. Assume that there is a massive increase in the number of households, such as the one we have recently experienced in Canada: a result of immigration, the setting up of new households by postwar baby-boom people, and rising incomes which allow young adults to leave home and establish new households. These factors result in the number of households growing by 50%, so that instead of 200,000 households there are now 300,000 households. It is assumed that these additional households have the same preference for dishwashers as the original 200,000 households had, and that they have the same income pattern. Under these assumptions a new demand schedule can be constructed:

| Price Per Dishwasher | Number of Dishwashers Demanded |
| --- | --- |
| $5 | 300,000 |
| $400 | 150,000 |
| $1000 | 0 |

The corresponding demand curve (which lies above the old demand curve) is shown below:

**FIGURE 6**

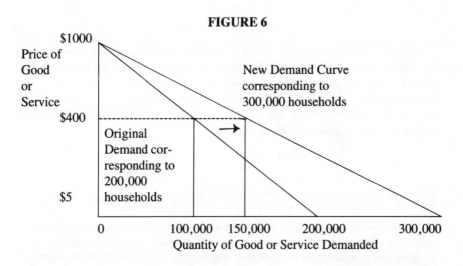

Lastly, a decline in the number of households through outmigration could be imagined, such as was experienced through most of the post World War II period in the Atlantic Provinces. Such outmigration would reduce the number of households and would therefore shift the demand curve to the left. In the case of rising demand, consumers will purchase more dishwashers at every price since there are now more consumers. A similar result could be obtained with a constant number of households but with higher incomes, or a change in taste favouring dishwashers, or any number of other events which lead to a greater demand for dishwashers at each and every price.

The case of declining demand is pictured below:

## FIGURE 7

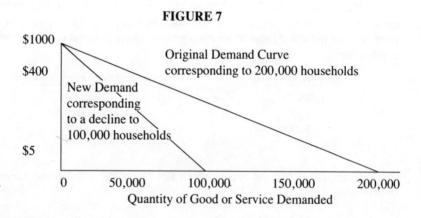

Quantity of Good or Service Demanded

An analogous set of curves could be constructed for supply and analogous hypothetical numerical examples could be developed to illustrate how changes in technology, or labour costs, or any other costs, influence the supply and demand together: this would enable us to determine the price at which dishwashers will actually trade in the marketplace, and the number of dishwashers that will be sold (and supplied) at that price.

THE MARKET: DEMAND AND SUPPLY TOGETHER

Unfortunately, the supply or the demand curve taken separately only indicates the various combinations of price and quantity at which suppliers will produce and consumers will consume. Separately, they cannot tell us anything about the price and quantity of dishwashers (or any other goods or services) actually traded, since each curve represents an infinite number of combinations of price and quantity. To determine market price and quantity it is necessary to combine the supply and demand curves on one diagram in order to see where they intersect. At the intersection supply and demand are equal and the market

will be in balance.[22] This situation, called *equilibrium* by economists, is
depicted below:

**FIGURE 8**

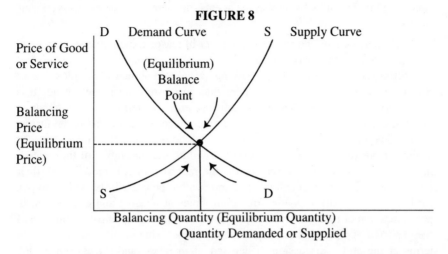

Balancing Quantity (Equilibrium Quantity)
Quantity Demanded or Supplied

For prices higher than the balancing price, suppliers are willing to supply
more goods (dishwashers or houses) than consumers are willing to purchase.
There is thus pressure to lower prices to eliminate surpluses and to stimulate
demand, so that exactly the quantity supplied is consumed. Goods which are
below the balancing price are bargains, so consumers are willing to consume
more than producers are willing to produce, and there is a condition of excess
demand. This excess demand causes prices to rise, which in turn encourages
producers to produce additional goods so that supply and demand eventually
achieve equilibrium again.

This, then, is the basic mechanism by which markets set prices. Prices are set
where demand and supply are equal, for only at that price is the total quantity of
production consumed (that is, there are no surpluses) and the total quantity of
demand (consumption) satisfied by production. These basic tools of supply and
demand may now be applied to a very special commodity, housing. By applying
these economic tools to the housing market a range of policies may be analysed
in order to see the effect that they are likely to have on both the price and
quantity of housing.

THE ECONOMICS OF HOUSING MARKETS: AN INTRODUCTORY ANALYSIS OF
MARKET ELEMENTS — CONSUMERS, PRODUCERS, REGULATORS AND MARKET-
MAKERS

In order to study the behaviour of housing markets, it is necessary to understand the motives and behaviours of the principal actors in the housing market-

place. Accordingly, we shall discuss consumers (buyers and renters), producers (developers and investors), regulators (governments and other regulatory institutions), and market-makers (real estate agents, financial institutions, lawyers, and others).

Consumers demand housing for a number of reasons, including shelter, prestige, investment, and proximity to jobs, recreation, schools, and other services and activities. The demand for housing is an exceptionally complex matter because housing embodies much more than just a roof over one's head. It is useless to look at mere quantity of housing, either in terms of the number of housing units available or in terms of square footage. Location and social factors are of equal importance. Although people seek housing to satisfy their needs for shelter or prestige, their *effective demand* will be the translation of these needs into a dollar bid (either for rent or for the purchase price), modified by their income, wealth and expectations. The amount that people will be willing to pay for housing is in part a function of the attributes of housing and its location, in part a function of their ability to pay for these attributes, and in part a function of the expected appreciation (or depreciation) in the value of the housing unit. In terms of the above discussion of demand, if incomes (and prices) remain the same but if houses are produced that have more of the attributes wanted by consumers than previous houses, then these houses will be more highly sought after and will be purchased (or rented) first: more desirable housing will be demanded over other similarly priced but not similarly prized units. As incomes rise, consumers are able to afford housing with those attributes which had been previously denied to them through income restrictions (assuming of course that prices have not risen faster than their incomes). Therefore, houses with such attributes should rise in price, that is, large housing units or housing units with such luxuries as saunas and swimming pools should become more popular as incomes rise.

On the producer side of the market, the situation is somewhat simpler because producers (and investors) generally supply housing if and only if it is profitable for them to do so. Profitability is determined by such factors as the price that consumers are able and willing to pay, the costs of land, materials, labour, and financing, and the difficulty involved in bringing together land, labour, materials, and capital (that is, government and institutional constraints). The higher the expected profit the greater the number of housing units produced. Both rising prices and falling costs will stimulate supply, assuming that, in the first instance, costs do not rise faster, and, in the second instance, prices do not fall as well. Under these circumstances, profits can be expected to increase, attracting more development. Any events that increase profitability and yet do not make housing development or investment any riskier will generally increase production. Events that make housing less profitable compared with other sectors of the economy can be expected to reduce the housing output (that is, falling rents, rising interest rates, and cumbersome development appoval processes). This also applies to the existing stock of houses. Rising profits can coax the owners of existing housing to sell or rent their units, thereby increasing the effective supply of housing units on the market.

So much for consumers (demand) and producers (supply). As noted earlier, a market price will be established where suppliers and demanders can get together to settle on an agreed market price and quantity. Therefore, the rules governing how buyers and sellers can get together are very important in determining price. The government plays the largest role in setting the rules for real property transactions. Under the British North America Act (Section 92), the provinces were granted exclusive control of local property markets. Provincial governments have in turn delegated much of their constitutional responsibility to their municipalities. Therefore, it is the provinces and the municipalities that primarily influence local housing markets. For example, in order to build new housing, a developer must either have a vacant, properly zoned parcel of land, or a developed and properly zoned property. If the land is not properly zoned, then the developer must have the land rezoned, either through municipal government action or through provincial government action (if the land lies outside an incorporated area), or in many instances through both levels, as is often the case in Ontario. However, it should be kept in mind that even with properly zoned and serviced land development still may not occur if national economic policy and national economic climates are poor. The circumstances in the fall of 1982 of high interest rates and low employment discouraged development despite ample zoned and serviced land.

In the simpler case, with properly zoned vacant land, the developer must obtain a building permit from the municipality of the province, as well as obtaining necessary inspections for wiring, plumbing and fire protection, again from either or both the provincial or the local government. If the land has a building on it which is to be demolished, then a demolition permit must be issued before any of the preceding steps can be carried out. And, once the housing is completed it must be sold or leased in conformity with — at the minimum — provincial real estate and land registry laws.

Provincial and local governments, therefore, are vitally involved in housing markets. Through their regulatory roles they greatly affect the cost and quantity of new housing (that is, the location of the supply curve). To a lesser extent the federal government is also involved, primarily as a provider and/or guarantor/insurer of mortgage funds rather than as a regulatory agent, although the National Building Code is a federal code enforceable at local/provincial option. Federal economic policies also interact with mortgage policies to influence the demand for housing: the federal government can move the demand curve quite dramatically through fiscal and monetary policies. Specifically, federal tax shelters, such as the recently ended Multiple Unit Residential Building (MURB) programme, increase the demand for development by making residential buildings attractive investments to high income earners. In the 1972 tax changes single family homes became exempt from capital gains, making homeownership more attractive and stimulating demand for homeownership. Conversely, recent monetary policy of high interest rates has slowed demand for homeownership and for investment in rental housing.

So far we have reviewed buyers' and sellers' motives as well as the regulatory functions of government. The remaining actors in the housing market are those professionals and institutions who help bring buyers and sellers together, most notably real estate agents, lawyers, notaries, and financial institutions. By exposing the supply of housing units to the greatest number of prospective buyers, real estate agents act in the interests of their clients (the sellers) to sell the units as quickly as possible and at the highest price. Buyers are also served by such advertising activities, as it brings to their attention the full scope of housing available at different prices and in different locations. Since housing is usually too expensive to purchase without any credit, financial institutions provide the necessary credit in the form of mortgage loans which enable interested buyers to purchase the desired housing (that is, to translate desires into effective demand). Finally, lawyers and/or notaries provide the necessary legal expertise to make sure that the buyers' legal interests are registered and in order, and that the sellers' obligations are fully discharged.[23]

## TOWARD A PRELIMINARY ANALYSIS: AN INTRODUCTION TO THE ECONOMICS OF HOUSING MARKETS

Housing, and, more generally, real property, possesses a number of economic characteristics which are sufficiently unusual to require a careful application of the basics of demand and supply analysis. These unusual characteristics include the following:

1. *Housing services,* not housing units, are demanded by consumers. People live in housing units, which are identifiable durable physical entities, but what is really valued is the range of services provided by the unit, including such services as shelter, prestige, and capital appreciation for homeowners. In evaluating housing problems and housing policies, it is essential that we consider the services provided by housing units, and not just the physical condition of the units themselves. For example, it is now generally accepted that many of the substandard inner city housing areas in both Canada and the United States provide vital services in the form of a sense of community and belonging, despite the fact that they are in substandard physical condition. Thus, in evaluating housing conditions it is necessary to explore the full range of services provided by the housing unit and its neighbourhood before reaching any conclusions about the overall adequacy of the housing stock. The range and quality of

services that flow from the stock of housing units should not be confused with the range and quality of the housing units themselves.

2. Housing is a *durable good* lasting many decades, and the implications of this characteristic are two-fold. First, it is important to keep in mind the long-term consequences of short-run housing decisions, since we will have to live with the effects of these decisions for decades, or, in some cases, for centuries. Second, since housing units do not disappear after they are built, a stock is built up over time which is ordinarily thirty times as large as the flow of new housing built in any given year. Thus, the stock of existing housing is an important element in determining housing prices and conditions.

3. Housing is *fixed in location* and cannot simply be moved to areas of highest demand. The implication of this characteristic is straightforward: housing markets are localized. This is important because it makes a national housing policy difficult even to conceptualize. During the past several years we have seen a variety of local housing markets heat up while others have been relatively cool. In the early 1970's Vancouver and Toronto in particular were struck by house price increases. As the boom ebbed in Vancouver and Toronto, Saskatoon and then Edmonton and Calgary experienced rapidly rising prices. While this high demand was being focused on the foregoing cities, other (generally smaller) cities were experiencing prolonged periods of no-growth, slow growth or even decline, as happened in the Atlantic Provinces. The "hot" spots in 1980 and early 1981 were Vancouver and St. John's, Newfoundland (because of pending oil discoveries offshore). But both have cooled considerably. Indeed, Vancouver prices have fallen back in late 1982 to pre-boom 1979 levels. The principal point is that since housing is not movable, excess units from the Maritimes or other slowly growing or declining communities cannot be moved to the areas of rapid growth. The housing "problem" is in fact a series of local problems, each of which has to be examined within the context of its own market area and the forces that give rise to the boom. The price discrepancies between different markets are demonstrated by Table 20 below.

4. In housing and other real property markets it is the *rights* that go with the property that are basically of value. This central idea in real estate economics explains why homeownership is valued, especially during inflationary times, more highly than renting. Homeowners have the right to unlimited tenure in their unit — no one can cancel their lease, with the infrequent exception of expropriation by the Crown. In addition to this *right* of possession, they also have the right to any capital gain that might accrue to the property. They also have the right to renovate or otherwise maintain and improve their house. Renters have none of these rights, which is why identical units (as happens now in condominium developments) can be sold for one price and rented for another, with ownership typically being significantly more costly than home-rental.

TABLE 20
## HOUSE PRICES IN SELECTED CANADIAN CITIES
(house prices and taxes are given in thousands of dollars)

| Housing Market | Burnaby, B.C.  House 1/House 2 | Kerrisdale, B.C. (Vancouver)  House 1/House 2 | Lethbridge, Alta.  House 1/House 2 | Petrolia, Alta. (Edmonton)  House 1/House 2 |
|---|---|---|---|---|
| June 1978 Price | 73/112 | 97/156.5 | 64/103 | 81/121.5 |
| Oct. 1978 Price | 73/112 | 97/156.5 | 64/103 | 83.5/128.5 |
| Taxes | 1.1/1.5 | 1.55/2.15 | .6/.97 | .865/1.05 |
| Feb. 1979 Price | 73/115 | 99.5/160 | 66.5/105 | 116/135.5 |
| % Change June 1978 to Feb. 79 | 0%/2.7% | 2.6%/2.2% | 3.9%/1.9% | 8%/11.5% |
| Feb. 1980 Price | 80/128 | 145/220 | 70.2/112 | 92.5/143.5 |
| June 1980 Price | 95/135 | 160/250 | 78.5/118 | 95/1.05 |
| Taxes | 1.2/1.6 | 1.7/2.32 | .75/1.28 | .75/1.05 |
| Oct. 1980 Price | 98/138 | 185/275 | 78/123.5 | 96/143.5 |
| % Change Feb. 1980 to Oct. 80 | 29.9%/7.8% | 27.6%/25% | 11.8%/10.3% | 3.8%/0% |
| July 1981 Price | 145/175 | 227/340 | 87/152 | 103/152 |
| Feb. 1982 Price | 140/169 | 210/300 | 87/52 | 100/145 |
| July 1982 Price | 115/150 | 185/265 | 81/150 | 100/141 |
| Taxes | 1.4/1.8 | 1.9/2.6 | 7.5/1.5 | .98/1.3 |
| % Change Feb. 1982 to July 1982 | -17.8%/-11.2% | -11.9%/-11.7% | -6.8%/-1.3% | 0%/-2.7% |

* Lot servicing costs are not prepaid; these costs are recovered through taxation.
"House 1" above refers to a detached three-bedroom bungalow of approximately 1,200 square feet on a fully serviced lot of approximately 5,500 square feet. It is five to eight years old, and has 1½ bathrooms. It is situated in an average residential urban neighbourhood.

**TABLE 20 (continued)**
**HOUSE PRICES IN SELECTED CANADIAN CITIES**
(house prices and taxes are given in thousands of dollars)

| Housing Market | Mt. Royal, Alta. (Calgary) House 1/House 2 | Southdale, Man. (Winnipeg) House 1/House 2 | Saskatoon, Sask. House 1/House 2 | Halifax, N.S. House 1/House 2 |
|---|---|---|---|---|
| June 1978 Price | 105/165 | 57/85 | 58/92 | 56/98 |
| Oct. 1978 Price | 105/165 | 60/90 | 61/97.5 | 56/98 |
| Taxes | .865/1.3 | 1.0/1.8 | .75/1.3 | .84/1.5 |
| Feb. 1979 Price | 116/176 | 60/90 | 62.5/100 | 56/98 |
| % Change June 1978 to Feb. 1979 | 10.5%/6.7% | 6.3%/5.9% | 6.8%/8.7% | 0%/0% |
| Feb. 1980 Price | 139.5/200 | 64.5/96 | 72/110 | 61/105 |
| June 1980 Price | 144/235 | 67.5/98 | 72/115 | 64.5/114.5 |
| Taxes | .96/1.54 | 1.35/2.025 | .85/1.5 | 1.15/1.9 |
| Oct. 1980 Price | 160/245 | 67.5/98 | 73/119 | 68/120 |
| % Change Feb. 1980 to Oct. 80 | 14.7%/22.5% | 4.7%/2.1% | 1.4%/8.2% | 11.5%/14.3% |
| July 1981 Price | 190/300 | 74.2/110 | 72/126 | 100.8/129 |
| Feb. 1982 Price | 190/300 | 74.3/110.5 | 74/131 | 108.9/138.9 |
| July 1982 Price | 185/280 | 75.5/112 | 74/131 | 108.9/182.6 |
| Taxes | 1.1/1.7 | 1.5/2.1 | 1.1/1.9 | 1.33/1.85 |
| % Change Feb. 1982 to July 1982 | -2.6%/-6.6% | 1.6%/1.3% | 0%/0% | 0%/31.5% |

"House 2" above refers to a detached four-bedroom house of approximately 2,000 square feet on a fully serviced lot of approximately 6,500 square feet. It is five to eight years old, and has 2½ bathrooms. It is situated in a prime residential urban neighbourhood.

*Sources: Royal Trust Survey of Canadian House Prices* (Toronto: Royal Trust Co., 1978 to 1980, 1982).

**TABLE 20 (continued)**
**HOUSE PRICES IN SELECTED CANADIAN CITIES**
(house prices and taxes are given in thousands of dollars)

| Housing Market | Beaconsfield, P.Q. (Montreal) | St. Foy, P.Q. | Ottawa, Ont. | Toronto, Ont. |
|---|---|---|---|---|
| | House 1/House 2 | House 1/House 2 | House 1/House 2 | House 1/House 2 |
| June 1978 Price | 39/65 | 50/91.5 | 62.2/90.25 | 81.6/133 |
| Oct. 1978 Price | 41/68.5 | 52.5/91.5 | 61.7/89.95 | 81.6/133 |
| Taxes | 1.07/*1.85 | *1.42/*2.9 | 1.27/1.64 | 1.05/1.92 |
| Feb. 1979 Price | 42.5/72 | 55.5/93.5 | 61.6/88.9 | 81.6/133 |
| % Change June 1978 to Feb. 79 | 9%/10.8% | 11%/2.2% | -1.6%/-1.5% | 0%/0% |
| Feb. 1980 Price | 47.2/79.5 | 54.5/89 | 62/91 | 93/152.5 |
| June 1980 Price | 53/88 | 56/91.6 | 62.8/89.5 | 98/157 |
| Taxes | *1.075/*1.85 | *1.14/*1.98 | 1.3/1.8 | 1.15/2.2 |
| Oct. 1980 Price | 61.3/104.9 | 58.3/95.55 | 63/91.5 | 102/163 |
| % Change Feb. 1980 to Oct. 80 | 29.9%/31.9% | 7%/8% | 1.6%/0.5% | 9.7%/6.9% |
| July 1981 Price | 73.5/126.9 | 61.5/99.5 | 73.1/109.5 | 115.4/160.3 |
| Feb. 1982 Price | 63.5/110 | 61.5/98.6 | 75/120 | 108.5/151.6 |
| July 1982 Price | 57/98 | 62.5/— | 84/124 | 108.5/151.6 |
| Taxes | 1.4/2.4 | 1.3/2.3* | 1.4/1.8* | 1.2/1.7 |
| % Change Feb. 1982 to July 1982 | -10.2%/-10.9% | 1.6%/3.4% | 12%/3.3% | 0%/0% |

5. In examining housing markets one should focus on both the *stock* of existing units and on the *flow* of new units onto the market. It is not enough to be concerned merely with the cost of new construction as the determinant of house prices, since there are many more existing homes for sale or rent at any period of time than there are new homes. Thus, it is necessary to look at the total supply of housing units, which comprises both new and existing homes. This distinction between the existing stock and the new flow is essential to an understanding of the behaviour of housing prices.

Armed with these preliminaries it is now possible to apply supply and demand analysis to current housing market issues. We shall begin with supply, because unlike most other economic goods the housing supply is comprised both of new production and of past production (existing housing units).

As was noted previously, the stock of housing grows through new production over time. As long as new production exceeds demolition and destruction of units in each year, then the stock will grow. The result of this growth over time is that after many years the accumulated stock greatly exceeds new production in any given year. For instance, in Canada in 1976 there were 7,166,090 occupied housing units out of a total stock of 7,550,900 units. In that same year there were 273,203 new units started and 236,249 units completed. These starts represented a mere 3.8% addition to the occupied stock (only 3.6% of total stock), while the completions were only 3.5% of occupied stock and 3.1% of total stock. Moreover, the 273,203 units that were started during 1976 represented a record high figure which has yet to be exceeded.[24] In contrast, there were a paltry 177,793 units started in 1981, a figure artificially bloated by late-year starts on MURB's to meet the December 31, 1981 termination date for the MURB programme. The 1981 starts were only 2% of the 1981 stock. Table 21 below presents data concerning dwelling starts in Canada from 1970 to 1981.

This situation can be expressed graphically by drawing the supply curve to reflect the fact that supply (new plus existing units) cannot change very dramatically in any given year, or over any period of time much shorter than three to five years. Where the earlier supply curve sloped upward to the right, the housing supply diagram is almost vertical, reflecting the fact that the supply is *inelastic,* it cannot change much in response to price or anything else, since the total supply is so heavily dominated by the standing stock of existing structures.

**FIGURE 9**

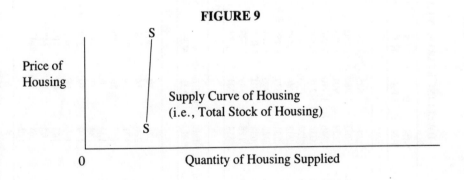

## TABLE 21
### DWELLING STARTS, IN CANADA, BY TYPE, BY REGION AND PROVINCE, 1970-1980 (DWELLING UNITS)

| Period Annee | Nfld. T.N. | P.E.I. I.P.E. | N.S. N.E. | N.B. N.B. | Atlantic Atlantique | P.Q. P.Q. | Ont. Ont. | Man. Man. | Sask. Sask. | Alta. Alb. | Prairies | B.C. C.B. | Canada |
|---|---|---|---|---|---|---|---|---|---|---|---|---|---|
| | | | | | | **Single-Detached** | | | | | | | |
| 1970 | 2,204 | 625 | 3,132 | 2,091 | 8,052 | 16,234 | 21,577 | 3,068 | 1,552 | 6,575 | 11,195 | 13,691 | 70,749 |
| 1971 | 2,783 | 1,285 | 4,565 | 3,054 | 11,687 | 20,665 | 31,088 | 3,719 | 2,932 | 10,258 | 16,909 | 17,707 | 98,056 |
| 1972 | 3,229 | 901 | 3,218 | 3,931 | 11,279 | 26,453 | 37,932 | 4,889 | 3,945 | 12,182 | 21,016 | 18,890 | 115,570 |
| 1973 | 4,246 | 1,970 | 3,696 | 4,889 | 14,801 | 28,194 | 42,751 | 5,816 | 4,838 | 13,839 | 24,493 | 21,313 | 131,552 |
| 1974 | 4,037 | 1,208 | 3,570 | 4,174 | 12,989 | 31,708 | 33,886 | 5,405 | 6,390 | 13,511 | 25,306 | 18,254 | 122,143 |
| 1975 | 3,727 | 733 | 3,604 | 4,752 | 12,816 | 32,089 | 33,669 | 4,334 | 7,416 | 14,989 | 26,739 | 18,616 | 123,929 |
| 1976 | 4,233 | 746 | 4,432 | 4,860 | 14,271 | 37,449 | 32,252 | 4,726 | 7,603 | 17,765 | 30,094 | 20,247 | 134,313 |
| 1977 | 2,531 | 577 | 3,755 | 3,433 | 10,296 | 29,511 | 27,899 | 4,193 | 6,705 | 14,298 | 25,196 | 15,501 | 108,403 |
| 1978 | 2,322 | 990 | 3,181 | 4,409 | 10,902 | 23,363 | 27,949 | 3,999 | 5,864 | 19,757 | 29,620 | 18,195 | 110,029 |
| 1979 | 2,658 | 801 | 3,047 | 4,721 | 11,227 | 22,069 | 28,261 | 2,944 | 6,758 | 20,066 | 29,768 | 17,792 | 109,117 |
| 1980 | 3,128 | 341 | 2,729 | 2,544 | 8,749 | 15,594 | 18,693 | 1,623 | 3,682 | 16,780 | 22,085 | 22,600 | 87,721 |
| 1981 | 2,354 | 201 | 3,131 | 1,896 | 7,573 | 14,231 | 24,440 | 2,473 | 3,189 | 17,972 | 23,634 | 19,193 | 89,071 |

| Period Annee | Nfld. T.N. | P.E.I. I.P.E. | N.S. N.E. | N.B. N.B. | Atlantic Atlantique | P.Q. P.Q. | Ont. Ont. | Man. Man. | Sask. Sask. | Alta. Alb. | Prairies | B.C. C.B. | Canada |
|---|---|---|---|---|---|---|---|---|---|---|---|---|---|
| | | | | | | **Semi-Detached and Duplex** | | | | | | | |
| 1970 | 76 | 50 | 363 | 296 | 785 | 2,399 | 4,624 | 889 | 63 | 897 | 1,849 | 1,169 | 10,826 |
| 1971 | 286 | 38 | 239 | 326 | 889 | 2,245 | 7,395 | 884 | 111 | 1,007 | 2,002 | 1,220 | 13,751 |
| 1972 | 171 | 24 | 268 | 267 | 730 | 1,754 | 8,237 | 852 | 88 | 1,170 | 2,110 | 818 | 13,649 |
| 1973 | 189 | 50 | 386 | 351 | 976 | 1,789 | 7,950 | 448 | 174 | 997 | 1,619 | 901 | 13,235 |
| 1974 | 134 | 6 | 180 | 222 | 542 | 1,421 | 6,058 | 617 | 298 | 1,037 | 1,952 | 1,050 | 12,023 |
| 1975 | 34 | 22 | 581 | 249 | 886 | 1,415 | 8,543 | 555 | 424 | 2,015 | 2,994 | 1,565 | 15,403 |
| 1976 | 119 | 59 | 238 | 174 | 590 | 1,795 | 8,502 | 574 | 751 | 1,955 | 3,280 | 1,723 | 15,890 |
| 1977 | 140 | 16 | 162 | 91 | 409 | 2,138 | 10,364 | 834 | 520 | 2,573 | 3,927 | 1,535 | 18,373 |
| 1978 | 143 | 45 | 110 | 40 | 338 | 3,112 | 8,607 | 1,423 | 716 | 4,362 | 6,501 | 1,374 | 19,932 |
| 1979 | 65 | 18 | 148 | 14 | 245 | 3,221 | 7,899 | 234 | 568 | 3,349 | 4,151 | 780 | 16,296 |
| 1980 | 78 | 33 | 42 | 22 | 175 | 2,427 | 4,628 | 34 | 278 | 2,618 | 2,930 | 989 | 11,149 |
| 1981 | 112 | 2 | 76 | 14 | 204 | 2,419 | 5,533 | 47 | 413 | 1,907 | 2,367 | 1,245 | 11,768 |

**TABLE 21 (Continued)**
**DWELLING STARTS, IN CANADA, BY TYPE, BY REGION AND PROVINCE, 1970-1980 (DWELLING UNITS)**

Row

| Period Annee | Nfld. T.N. | P.E.I. I.P.E. | N.S. N.E. | N.B. N.B. | Atlantic Atlantique | P.Q. P.Q. | Ont. Ont. | Man. Man. | Sask. Sask. | Alta. Alb. | Prairies | B.C. C.B. | Canada |
|---|---|---|---|---|---|---|---|---|---|---|---|---|---|
| 1970 | 184 | 5 | 162 | 183 | 534 | 3,456 | 8,130 | 935 | 12 | 2,422 | 3,369 | 1,566 | 17,055 |
| 1971 | 201 | 14 | 344 | 230 | 789 | 1,491 | 7,602 | 823 | 100 | 3,051 | 3,974 | 1,803 | 15,659 |
| 1972 | 167 | 74 | 526 | 307 | 1,074 | 2,159 | 8,811 | 435 | 112 | 2,027 | 2,574 | 2,362 | 16,980 |
| 1973 | 59 | 47 | 688 | 226 | 1,020 | 1,360 | 11,977 | 93 | 250 | 1,090 | 1,433 | 1,501 | 17,291 |
| 1974 | 561 | 101 | 394 | 112 | 1,168 | 770 | 9,518 | 303 | 128 | 1,305 | 1,736 | 1,740 | 14,932 |
| 1975 | 1,064 | — | 225 | 129 | 1,418 | 1,183 | 12,212 | 268 | 478 | 2,904 | 3,650 | 3,300 | 21,763 |
| 1976 | 691 | — | 204 | 135 | 1,030 | 1,129 | 17,918 | 1,105 | 605 | 8,626 | 10,336 | 3,263 | 33,676 |
| 1977 | 85 | 10 | 376 | — | 471 | 702 | 13,782 | 884 | 490 | 7,168 | 8,542 | 3,124 | 26,621 |
| 1978 | 123 | 51 | 107 | 7 | 288 | 502 | 9,703 | 1,035 | 290 | 6,504 | 7,829 | 2,687 | 20,379 |
| 1979 | 88 | 28 | 73 | — | 189 | 459 | 5,745 | 363 | 237 | 4,263 | 4,863 | 1,993 | 13,249 |
| 1980 | 180 | — | 113 | 10 | 303 | 841 | 3,826 | 151 | 108 | 4,230 | 4,489 | 2,249 | 11,402 |
| 1981 | 278 | — | 62 | — | 340 | 485 | 4,863 | 23 | 220 | 4,853 | 5,096 | 4,741 | 15,525 |

Apartment and Other

| Period Annee | Nfld. T.N. | P.E.I. I.P.E. | N.S. N.E. | N.B. N.B. | Atlantic Atlantique | P.Q. P.Q. | Ont. Ont. | Man. Man. | Sask. Sask. | Alta. Alb. | Prairies | B.C. C.B. | Canada |
|---|---|---|---|---|---|---|---|---|---|---|---|---|---|
| 1970 | 172 | 104 | 2,221 | 612 | 3,109 | 25,029 | 42,344 | 4,053 | 116 | 6,357 | 10,526 | 10,890 | 91,898 |
| 1971 | 388 | 26 | 2,160 | 1,320 | 3,894 | 27,381 | 43,895 | 5,279 | 417 | 11,286 | 16,982 | 14,035 | 106,187 |
| 1972 | 334 | 80 | 1,152 | 1,853 | 3,419 | 25,380 | 47,953 | 5,892 | 700 | 7,124 | 13,716 | 13,247 | 103,715 |
| 1973 | 337 | 55 | 2,964 | 1,769 | 5,125 | 28,207 | 47,858 | 5,174 | 1,124 | 5,051 | 11,349 | 13,912 | 106,451 |
| 1974 | 179 | 19 | 1,864 | 1,353 | 3,415 | 17,743 | 36,041 | 2,427 | 868 | 3,155 | 6,450 | 10,376 | 74,025 |
| 1975 | 517 | 92 | 1,956 | 1,853 | 4,418 | 20,054 | 25,544 | 2,688 | 2,187 | 4,799 | 9,674 | 10,671 | 70,361 |
| 1976 | 666 | 37 | 2,596 | 1,603 | 4,902 | 28,375 | 26,010 | 2,934 | 4,184 | 10,425 | 17,543 | 12,494 | 89,324 |
| 1977 | 963 | 221 | 3,202 | 784 | 5,170 | 25,229 | 26,085 | 3,499 | 5,110 | 14,036 | 22,645 | 12,198 | 92,327 |
| 1978 | 277 | 124 | 1,455 | 711 | 2,567 | 16,694 | 26,081 | 5,664 | 2,657 | 17,302 | 25,623 | 6,632 | 77,327 |
| 1979 | 188 | 221 | 1,270 | 286 | 1,965 | 15,981 | 14,982 | 2,231 | 4,179 | 12,269 | 18,679 | 6,780 | 58,387 |
| 1980 | 462 | 94 | 1,011 | 70 | 1,637 | 10,624 | 12,980 | 787 | 2,182 | 8,403 | 11,374 | 11,714 | 48,329 |
| 1981 | 475 | — | 446 | 278 | 1,199 | 12,510 | 15,325 | 281 | 2,150 | 13,738 | 16,169 | 16,406 | 61,609 |

*Sources:* *Canadian Housing Statistics* (Ottawa: CMHC, 1979) Table 10; *Canadian Housing Statistics* (Ottawa: CMHC, 1980) Table 10; *Canadian Housing Statistics* (Ottawa: CMHC, 1981) Table 10.

Although the *supply* of housing is relatively fixed in any given year, this is certainly not true of housing *demand*. Because housing markets are highly localized and local areas are subject to significant inflows and outflows of population and income, the demand for housing can change rapidly. If the possibility of dramatically changing income and population levels is combined with even more volatile behavioural considerations (such as housing investment behaviour), the possibility of wide fluctuations in demand increases greatly. For example, during the great boom in housing prices that occurred in Canada during the early 1970's many people decided to become active participants in the housing market to get "a hedge against inflation." By so doing they greatly increased the normal demand for housing by adding a speculative demand based on their expectations that housing would soon become too expensive. This behaviour, in fact, did cause prices to rise appreciably, and the increases were fueled even further by rapidly rising incomes.[25] Sometime during the mid-1970's the bubble burst and consumer behaviour changed, cooling the housing market across Canada, with the exception of one or two local hot spots such as Edmonton and Calgary. The 1980-81 boom and bust in Vancouver's housing market provides a more current reminder of the volatility of demand. Thus, in the longer run, demand patterns stabilized and fell into line with longer run population and income growth.

The foregoing demand situation can be presented in a diagrammatic form which enables us to show not just one but a series of demand curves which may shift in the short run as a result of population changes.

**FIGURE 10**

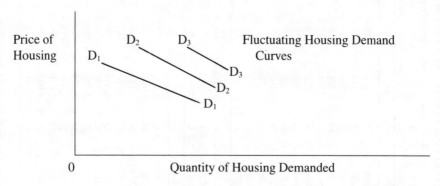

Supply and demand can now be put together in order to determine the price where supply and demand are equal. Because supply is relatively fixed in the short run, only the price is left to be determined: the supply is primarily determined by the standing stock of housing. This situation is depicted in Figure 11 below.

**FIGURE 11**

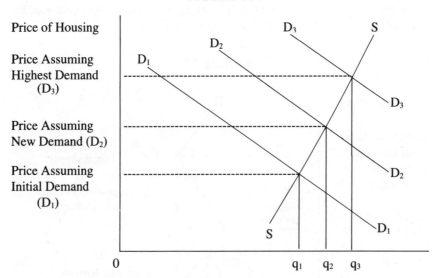

Quantity of Housing Demanded or Supplied

In the short run, the price of housing will be determined mainly by a level of demand which can often be volatile. The supply of housing is relatively fixed in the short run, and therefore the point at which demand and supply intersect (that is, are equal or in equilibrium) is the point at which we find the market price.

This conception of the housing market is a useful start, but it has a number of drawbacks which should be mentioned. To begin with, this is a rather short run and static view of the world. Although the housing supply is fixed in the short run and the demand for housing is volatile in the short run, in the longer run, the supply of housing can expand significantly and demand patterns stabilize into longer run population and income trends. Also, in the short run the costs of new housing are not of primary importance in determining overall house prices, because the new housing in any given year represents such a small proportion of the total housing stock. But over periods of time of about five to ten years, the cost of providing new housing plays an important role in determining housing prices.

Therefore, it appears that in the long run it is necessary to switch to a more traditional demand and supply model, where supply behaves normally and slopes upward to the right and demand slopes downward to the right as is shown in Figure 12. Here, if production costs are rising, the supply curve will shift upward from $S_1$ to $S_2$ (reflecting greater costs at each level of output), and prices can be expected to rise (from $P_1$ to $P_2$), unless demand falls by a greater amount than production costs have risen.

In the short run we are essentially working with fixed supply and variable demand, and we need one kind of analytical tool (Figure 11).

**FIGURE 12**

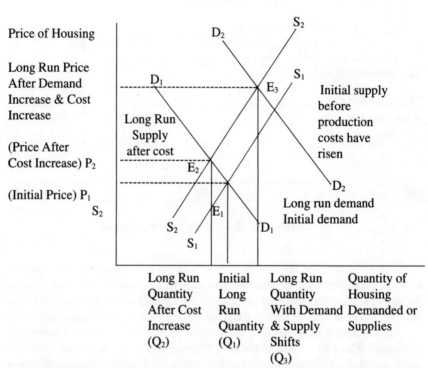

In the longer run we use a more standard analysis in which supply slopes upward to the right (Figure 12). In deciding which type of analysis to use, each situation must be carefully assessed in order to ensure that the assumptions implicit in each method of analysis are met by the facts of the situation to be analysed (that are we dealing with a short-run or longer run issue).

We are now at the point at which we can proceed to explore some current housing issues using the tools developed above. Since the interest here lies in the area of analysing problems and policies, the following is concerned with the policymaking process as it relates to housing issues in Canada, and with the specific policies brought forward under the aegis of this process to solve our perceived or actual housing "problems."

# 5

## Governments and Affordability:
## Some Intended and Unintended Impacts of
## Housing Policy on Housing Prices and Rents

WHO MAKES HOUSING POLICY IN CANADA AND HOW DO THEY DO IT?

*Who makes policy in Canada?*

Under Section 92 of the British North America Act provincial legislatures were assigned exclusive responsibility for "all matters of a merely local or private nature in the province" (Section 92(16)), as well as for "municipal institutions in the province" (Section 92(8)), and finally for "property and civil rights in the province" (Section 92(13)). The Federal Parliament of Canada was assigned to deal with national and international issues (Section 91). But because housing is an important element in the Canadian economy there are a number of powers that the House of Commons has at its disposal which enable it to influence housing and related urban issues. The Parliament of Canada has responsibility for "the regulation of trade and commerce" (Section 91(2)) for "currency and coinage" (Section 91(14)), for "banking, incorporation of banks, and the issue of paper money" (Section 91(15)), and for "interest" (Section 91(19)). The Canadian federal government can own property in urban areas and through its spending power significantly influence cities and local housing and mortgage markets.

Federal housing policy has generally been implemented through the ability of the House of Commons to influence interest rates, the money supply, the cost of credit, and other aspects of the economic system. On the other hand, urban' policy (which covers much more than merely urban housing) has been left to the provinces through their control of municipal institutions and property rights. Provincial governments in turn have delegated to municipalities the powers to regulate land use and subdivision activity, and to control the type of urban development within each municipality. It is significant that the recently enacted *Canadian Charter of Rights and Freedoms* did not alter these allocations. It is also significant that property rights, a provincial power, were explicitly not included in the Charter.[26]

Viewed from this perspective, the question of who makes housing policy in Canada is far from straightforward. The Government of Canada exercises considerable initiative in the housing policy area, but ultimately this initiative must be tempered by provincial and municipal input because the provinces and their municipalities determine just how and where houses are to be built, serviced and marketed.

The primary authority for federal housing policy in Canada is derived from the National Housing Act, 1953-54, as amended. This was "an act to promote the construction of new houses, the repair and modernization of existing houses, and the improvement of housing and living conditions." The Act was also designed to create jobs and stimulate the economy. It was not intended to regulate cities. The emphasis is on new and other construction, a role fully consistent with the federal responsibility for national economic management, since housing, as we saw earlier, is a major component of the national economy.

The National Housing Act and its amendments were originally and continue to be implemented and monitored by the Canada Mortgage and Housing Corporation (known as the Central Mortgage and Housing Corporation prior to 1979), which is a Crown Corporation created by an act of Parliament in 1945. Federal housing policy is primarily brought about through the National Housing Act, the Canada Mortgage and Housing Corporation, the provision of federal guarantees of mortgage loans by approved lenders, the subsidization of interest rates to certain needy and non-profit groups (such as senior citizens and co-operatives), and occasionally the direct lending of mortgage funds to Canadians who have been turned down by other sources of mortgage money. The federal government also has indirect influence over housing through its control of the money supply and its influence on interest rates. Federal taxing powers also greatly affect housing preferences and supplies because capital gains on principal residences are not taxable and because significant tax advantages are given to investors in rental housing from time to time. The deductibility of mortgage interest and property taxes for income tax purposes also falls within federal jurisdiction: such a policy was introduced (though not enacted) by the Progressive Conservative government in 1979, and despite its tax cost in the billions of dollars it is always politically attractive. CMHC estimated that "tax expenditures" (foregone taxes) for housing amounted to more than $6.4 billion in 1979, compared with only $446 million for direct housing subsidies.

Provincial governments have generally allowed the municipalities to regulate land use, subdivision and urban development, though Ontario and Quebec, for instance, have become involved in the large-scale provision of public housing.[27] Most of the other provinces have also provided housing assistance in the form of subsidized first or second mortgages or grants for downpayments. However, because of the potentially massive cost of such policies, provincial governments usually prefer to let the federal government use its much greater financial resources for such subsidy programmes. In response to the staggering increases in West Coast house prices, the British Columbia provincial government did introduce a range of land servicing and mortgage subsidy programmes in late 1980 in order to try to ease the burden on first-time home purchasers, but these programmes were introduced only because the housing situation was so serious: provincial governments do not generally take such drastic action lightly. It should also be noted that the British Columbia programmes built on their existing cost-sharing servicing programmes and increased the size of these programmes to reflect higher land and housing prices.

Municipal housing policies are virtually nonexistent. The great cost of housing programmes largely precludes all but the largest and richest cities, such as Toronto, from providing housing or housing subsidies, though many (almost twenty now) larger municipalities have created non-profit housing corporations to avail themselves of CMHC subsidies and to serve lower income households. But municipalities have an important role to play because it is their responsibility to grant approval for subdivisions so that land can be made available for housing. These local governments also control the zoning of land, and thus they control the density at which housing is built. The municipalities also have the authority to set standards through subdivision and zoning powers, and they can significantly affect both the rate and the price at which housing is provided. The City of Vancouver, for example, tied a portion of the development of its False Creek area to non-market (that is, subsidized) housing which was paid for with the profits made from the market housing. This sort of policy may well be useful in other Canadian municipalities which are experiencing short-run surges in demand.

Governments are elected to carry out political decisions and are generally swayed by political rather than economic considerations, but the political good and the economic good often coincide. Housing is a unique good which possesses many social as well as economic characteristics. Many Canadians put a high value on homeownership as a measure of security, status, wealth, and general well-being. Social reformers have long contended that the poor must be well housed before they can break out of the poverty cycle. Housing policy is thus also a crucial component of social policy. Therefore, it is to be expected that there will be considerable political pressure on all levels of government to put homeownership within the financial reach of most Canadians. Additional political pressure comes from the companies which build and sell housing: businesses exercise considerable political clout from the supply side (builders, organized labour, agents, mortgage lenders and lawyers/notaries) as well as from the demand side (citizen consumers).

Housing has often been used by the central governments as a tool of social welfare policy and as a means of redistributing wealth to lower income groups, as was the case in Canada during the 1970's.[28] The public's demand for affordable housing and for wealth redistribution are two primary types of political pressure on all levels of government, and a great variety of housing programmes have been designed to deal with these pressures. Because of the present level of unemployment, employment creation is also an important factor in Canadian housing policy.

## HOW DO GOVERNMENTS SEEK TO AFFECT HOUSING DEMAND, SUPPLY AND PRICES?

### Federal demand-oriented housing policies

Most federal housing policies are demand-oriented and are intended to provide additional income or mortgage credit to Canadian consumers so that they can afford more and/or better housing. At the national (macroeconomic) level, the standard economic dichotomy between fiscal and monetary policy can be employed to categorize federal demand-oriented housing initiatives. With monetary policy, federal economic policymakers have a dilemma on their hands. During times of inflation, the monetary authority (the Bank of Canada) usually restrains credit and takes some of the steam out of the economy as it was doing, for instance, over much of the 1980-82 period. The result is a higher interest rate and a restriction in the availability of credit. This makes it more difficult and more expensive to borrow, which in times of rising prices makes it particularly difficult to buy housing. However, if the Bank of Canada were to make credit easily available it would cause further inflation and would push house prices even higher. The demand and supply diagrams illustrate how the federal monetary policy can have this effect.

When the federal monetary policy eases credit and thereby increases the effective demand for housing, it has the short-run effect of increasing the price of housing. Credit policies which lead to increases in demand are depicted by moving the demand curve from $D_0$ to demand curve $D_1$. Supply increases only modestly from $q_0$ to $q_1$, but the price, in the *short* run (roughly three years or less), rises quite sharply from $p_0$ to $p_1$.

**FIGURE 13**

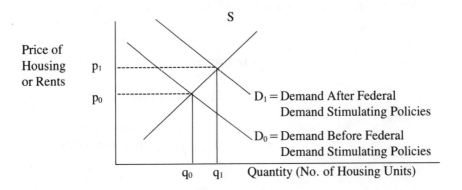

The upward impact on prices of expansionary monetary policies is not unique to housing. The above supply and demand diagram represents the effects of a number of policies all ostensibly aimed at making housing more affordable by giving the public more money for housing. Ironically, in the short run, such policies have the effect of raising demand and thereby raising house prices.

A number of policies have been proposed or recently implemented which are designed to ease the financial burden of homeownership in particular and also of renting secondarily. The most important of these policies are as follows:

i. allowing the deductibility of mortgage interest and property taxes from gross income in the calculation of taxable income (as is already allowed in the U.S.); (proposed by Progressive Conservative Party, among others)

ii. broadening the Registered Home Ownership Savings Plans; (proposed)

iii. keeping the capital gains on principal residences non-taxable, all other assets remaining subject to capital gains tax; (present Canadian policy)

iv. providing rent subsidies or grants, or mortgage subsidies or grants, such as the Assisted Home Ownership Program (AHOP) and Shelter Allowances and the graduated payment mortgage; (proposed, and some like AHOP were implemented and then stopped during 1970's)

v. lowering the cost of intra-urban transportation, thus freeing more income for housing (actually done in most parts of Canada through subsidizing freeways and public transportation).

Each of the above demand-stimulating policies can be represented by the demand and supply diagram given in Figure 13. In the short run such demand stimulants will lead to higher prices and to lower affordability, but in the longer run these higher prices will encourage additional supply, thus moving prices back toward their original level. Whether or not prices get back to their original level over time depends primarily on the costs of providing new housing units and on the level of demand. The longer run situation is presented below in

Figure 14: the increase in supply (which is depicted by shifting the supply curve to the right) causes an eventual decrease in price.

**FIGURE 14**

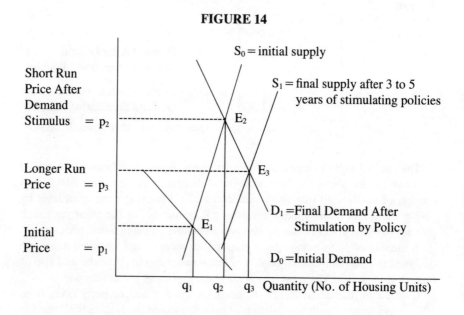

*Federal supply-oriented housing policies*

Although federal housing policies can alter the demand for housing very quickly, it takes several years to make much difference to the supply of housing. Stimulation of supply is slow even when there is an abundance of available properly zoned residential land: it takes time to build housing units and to make them ready for occupancy. This is particularly true for large multi-family units which require long lead times for approvals and planning, financing, and construction. If the federal government simultaneously stimulated both demand and supply, it should lead to increased prices in the short run followed by gradually declining prices as new housing units come onto the market. The ultimate equilibrium price will depend on the level of demand and on the costs of putting the new supply on the market.[29] The previous demand and supply diagram represents just such a situation in which both demand and supply are stimulated. The case of supply stimulation by itself is represented by the portion of the preceding diagram which shows supply expanding from $S_0$ to $S_1$. In this situation the demand curve remains unchanged.

Some of the more important recent supply-oriented housing policies are as follows:

   i.  the Assisted Rental Program, whereby builders get interest and tax subsidies which enable them to construct rental units which can then adhere to the rent limits set by the federal government;

  ii.  allowing artificial accounting losses from Multiple Unit Residential Buildings to be used as tax shelters, which stimulates the supply of such residential buildings by making them more attractive as investments than they otherwise would be;

 iii.  federal land-banking and servicing programmes which provide additional supplies of serviced land for residential development;

 iv.  federal cost-saving programmes, such as the removal of federal sales tax on building materials and the subsidization of land assembly and subdivision;

  v.  non-profit and co-operative programmes which provide interest reduction and planning and development cost assistance;

 vi.  public housing, now largely dormant but which typically shared construction costs and rent supplement subsidies with the province.

These programmes can all be expected to have their desired effects eventually, but their success cannot be measured in the short run because these are necessarily longer run programmes. Public impatience with the federal government is often based on a misunderstanding both of the means by which housing prices and rents are determined and of the inherent nature and timing of the various demand and supply programmes. If the public's demands for quick action were met, the result would be rapidly increasing price spirals, because although demand can be increased almost immediately, housing supplies can only expand relatively slowly. And the government could not reasonably be blamed for such effects, because they would be the result of the normal operation of the housing market.

*Provincial and local housing policies*

Most of the power for regulating housing markets and for controlling urban development lies with provincial and municipal governments. The provincial powers are derived primarily from Section 92(8) ("Municipal Institutions in the Province") and Section 92(13) ("Property and Civil Rights in the Province") of the BNA Act. Only a few examples from the enormous range of provincial housing policies will be mentioned here.

Provincial and municipal governments have implemented many policies designed to stimulate demand and/or supply. Because of their constitutional power to control local land use and urban development, provincial and local governments have an additional policy tool which the federal government lacks, namely that of controlling directly the potential supply of housing.

*Provincial and local government stimulation of housing demand*

One result of the high cost of housing subsidies is that on the local government level these efforts have been confined mainly to occasional public housing or non-profit housing developments in one of the larger cities, such as Montreal, Toronto, London, and Vancouver, which is supply-side intervention. But, the provincial governments, with their larger financial resources, have become more directly involved. Subsidies have been applied to mortgage rates and/or property taxes, and various kinds of cash grants have been given. For example, in British Columbia as of 1966, the Provincial Home Acquisition Act provided a $500 cash grant to first-time housing purchasers who had resided in the province for at least one year. Eventually, the programme was escalated to provide a grant of $1,000 or a second mortgage loan of up to $5,000 at highly subsidized mortgage rates for the purchase of a new home. People buying existing homes could receive $500 or a second mortgage loan of up to $2,500. As of October 1, 1982, British Columbia also provides for up to $60,000 of mortgages to be written down to an effective interest rate of 12%. The Province of Ontario introduced a similar programme in 1974, providing a $1,500 cash grant to first-time home purchasers, regardless of their income level or of whether or not the house was new. The Ontario Home Ownership Made Easy (HOME) Plan introduced a programme supplement in 1967, whereby the province subsidized the interest rate on first and second mortgages on land which had been subdivided by the province and leased such land to purchasers at favourable rates.

Another stimulant to homeownership is provided by the B.C. Provincial Home Owner Grant Act of 1957, according to which the province will underwrite a significant portion of residential property taxes for owner-occupied housing. The province currently provides a $380 grant to all homeowners and an additional $100 grant to homeowners over 65 years of age who occupy the home they own. In British Columbia, renters over 65 years of age are also given grants, which range up to $100 per year. Also, the SAFER programme (Shelter Allowances for Elderly Renters) provides additional rental subsidy for needy elderly people.

The economic effect of these grants and subsidies is that of increasing demand. They put more money in the hands of the public — money which can be spent on housing. This causes an increase in the aggregate demand for housing, which in turn eventually produces an increase in the supply of housing.

*Provincial and local government stimulation of supply*

These programmes, generally carried out in conjunction with federal supply expansion programmes, take a variety of forms. They include: promoting the servicing and subdivision of residential land (such as the HOME plan in Ontario); various forms of public housing, limited dividend housing, and co-operative and non-profit housing, the costs of which are usually shared with the federal government; and such programmes as the British Columbia's Home Conversion programme which encourages the conversion of single-family dwelling units into multi-family rental units. The effects of these and similar supply expansion policies can be analysed using supply-demand diagrams, wherein the supply curve shifts to the right in order to lower prices by offsetting increases in demand with increases in supply. However, it should be remembered that such policies take several years to produce noticeable effects. Such programmes must be regarded as longer term efforts to meet growing and changing housing demands.

MARKET CONTROLS

It is generally through the use of various control measures that the provinces and municipalities exert their greatest impact on housing demand, supply, and price. A few examples will serve to illustrate this point.

*Rent control*

Rent control establishes limits on rent levels and/or rent increases. The effect of rent control is analysed in Figure 15 below.

**FIGURE 15**

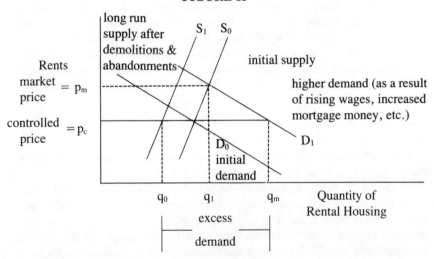

Two negative consequences result from the imposition of rent control following demand-stimulated higher rents. The first consequence is that in the short run, rents are prevented from achieving their market level, $p_m$, by being kept to an artificially low level, $p_c$. At market levels there is no excess demand, because supply and demand are exactly equal, but at the artificially low level, $p_c$, there is significantly more demand for housing than landlords are willing to supply at those rents. Thus, artificially low rents result in higher demand at a time when demand already exceeds supply. The second consequence is even more destructive. Over the longer run, landlords and investors will regard rental housing as being an unattractive investment if rents are not allowed to rise sufficiently to cover the costs of operating and maintaining the rental units. New rental construction will therefore be discouraged, and in extreme cases (in New York City, for instance) rental units will be allowed to deteriorate until they are abandoned by landlords.[30] In this situation, the excess demand gets much worse since supply *decreases* (the supply curve moves to the left) as rental units are abandoned and demolished. A short-run solution, rent control, to a short-run problem, excess demand, can thus become a chronic long-term problem, with low-income families usually being the hardest hit (it is low-cost housing which is generally demolished or abandoned). A number of wary policymakers have devised control programmes which allow rents to rise as landlords' costs rise, but such programmes are difficult to administer, and they involve additional costs to landlords. The existence of rent controls, even of those with cost escalation, usually creates an unfavourable investment climate for rental housing construction and discourages the supply of new rental units, thereby adversely affecting the long-term supply of rental housing.

One last point also needs to be made about rent control, and that relates to its inequity. Rent control represents a "blind" subsidy from landlords to tenants on the implicit assumption that landlords can afford to give subsidies and tenants need subsidies. This overlooks the fact that many landlords have their retirement savings tied up in their rental buildings. It also ignores the fact that many tenants can afford higher rents. Finally, it only subsidizes tenants in rent-controlled buildings, disadvantaging tenants in uncontrolled units (usually newer units).

*Land use controls*

Land use controls which limit the size and type of buildings that can be built on any given site, or in any given sector (zone) of a municipality, have the effect of restricting the supply of housing. This is of little consequence in the short run, for as was seen earlier, housing supply is relatively fixed for any period of up to approximately three years. The negative consequences of land use controls are therefore not felt immediately, but they are felt as the housing market attempts to expand and is inhibited by land use controls. This is illustrated in Figure 16 below in which supply curve, $S_m$, represents the longer-run supply curve that would result in the absence of land use controls. Supply curve, $S_c$, to the left of $S_m$, is the supply curve that results from the imposition of land use controls. If demand is assumed to be constant, the result of restricting housing densities is a smaller quantity of housing and therefore higher prices. Such an outcome is often an intended result of zoning, as it is frequently the desire of residents of some communities to restrict housing supplies in order to make their own houses more valuable or to protect their communities from change. But even when such exclusionary motives are not at work, the result is similar; both well-intentioned and ill-intentioned land use controls will eventually restrict the housing supply and raise house prices. It is when many, or most, municipalities impose such land use controls that the aggregate effect on house prices all over the country becomes significant. Higher prices and reduced supply are typical symptoms of the widespread use of restrictive land use controls.[31]

**FIGURE 16**

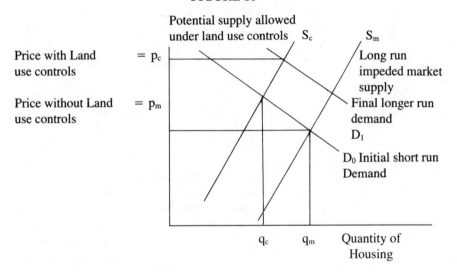

Potential supply allowed under land use controls $S_c$    $S_m$

Price with Land use controls   $= p_c$

Price without Land use controls   $= p_m$

Long run impeded market supply
Final longer run demand
$D_1$
$D_0$ Initial short run Demand

$q_c$   $q_m$   Quantity of Housing

OVERREGULATION: MUNICIPAL RED TAPE

It has commonly been believed that high servicing costs and municipal requirements were at the root of the house price boom of the early 1970's. It was also widely held that municipalities created, or worsened, this state of affairs through their requirements of high quality servicing for subdivisions, and that their sluggish approval processes added months or years to the development process and therefore ultimately added to housing prices. This issue can be analysed in terms of supply and demand, with the supply curves now being shifted upward and to the left as a result of the higher costs being imposed by municipalities. The result is, of course, that new units cost more and therefore fewer new units are produced. While the result makes sense, it is necessary to question the use of a supply-demand situation where supply is viewed as being so responsive in the short run. Because the short-run supply of housing is relatively fixed, increases in the cost of producing new units only affect house prices very gradually. The appropriate supply-demand diagram in the short run is one in which supply is relatively fixed, as shown in Figure 17.

**FIGURE 17**

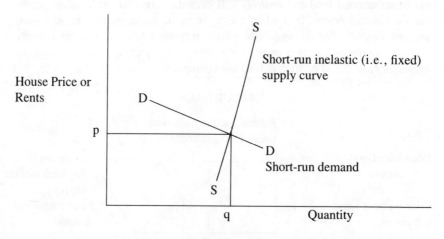

**FIGURE 18**

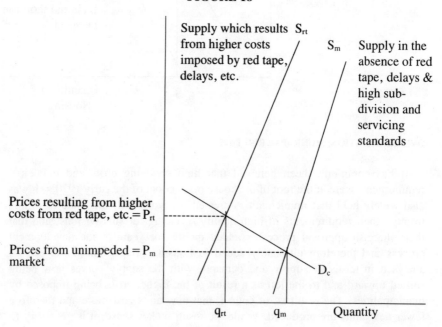

This example illustrates an important lesson: one's analytic tools must not only be good, but they must also be the appropriate tools if one is to get useful answers. In this case, the supply-demand diagram which implicitly assumes that supply is responsive to changes in price is not appropriate in the short run. The appropriate diagram is the one in which the supply is inflexible. Thus, municipal policies that raise production costs cannot, in the short run, affect housing prices because housing prices are primarily determined by demand, not supply. However, the continued imposition of higher servicing standards and long approval processes will eventually lead to higher priced new housing, and higher priced new housing will ultimately result in higher priced housing generally, as new houses constitute a larger proportion of the overall housing. The foregoing are also the findings of the Greenspan Report.[32]

# 6

# The Future of Housing Prices and Rents

In this final section, we shall examine some of the factors that are likely to affect the demand and supply, and therefore the price and quantity, of housing in Canada over the next several decades. The problems facing Canadian policy-makers are presented so that interested citizens can better assist their government in identifying and selecting appropriate housing policies for the future.

UNDERSTANDING THE BEHAVIOUR OF MARKET PARTICIPANTS

Behavioural uncertainties are perhaps the most difficult problems which confront the forecasters of housing costs and availabilities. A brief inventory of the most important questions regarding market participant behaviour includes the following:

*Consumers* — Will the traditional family (two parents plus at least two children) become the norm again? Will divorce rates remain high? Will people marry earlier or later? Will they have fewer or more children? Will the trend toward two or more income earners per household increase, continue, or decline? Will households prefer more central housing locations to suburban ones, and will this hold for family households as well as non-family households? Will people continue to prefer living in metropolitan areas?[33]

*Producers* — Will housing continue to provide an attractive production opportunity to builders? Will rental units be attractive investments? Will mortgage funds be sufficiently abundant and inexpensive to enable developers and investors to invest in housing?

*Governments* — Will the federal government extend various forms of housing subsidy, such as non-taxation of capital gains on principal residences? Will widespread homeownership continue to be an important goal of all levels of government? Will local governments continue to impose land use controls, thereby regulating housing supplies? Are high servicing and subdivision standards going to remain popular with local governments? Will other provincial governments take over greater responsibility for urban development, as they already have in Ontario and British Columbia?[34]

There are a large number of unanswered questions here, and there are many more than those mentioned above. Housing policy for a strong city centre will be dramatically different from housing policy for non-metropolitan areas. Housing policy where the private sector finds housing an attractive investment opportunity is going to be very different from housing policy where private risk capital is not readily forthcoming. Housing policy for smaller non-family households will be very different from housing policy directed toward satisfying the needs of families in terms of its size, amenities and location. And to complicate matters even further, housing policies during times of economic prosperity will be very different from those during times of economic hardship, high unemployment, slow economic growth, and high and variable rates of inflation. Under a depressed economic scenario we can expect minimal government intervention, given lower tax revenues. We can also expect dramatic declines in demand and in housing consumption per household. This all means that the values, tastes, and behaviour of the major market participants will be significant determinants of the kinds of housing policy needed to provide high quality housing services to the Canadian public. In the very volatile economic times of the early 1980's, we can expect major changes in participant behaviour, changes which are central to housing market functioning, yet which are exceedingly difficult to forecast.

THE FUTURE USABILITY OF THE STANDING STOCK OF HOUSING

The uncertainties discussed above are relevant primarily to the new housing that will be built in Canada during the next few decades. But an equally important question concerns the stock that is already in place. Even if there are no demolitions and the growth rate of housing stock is 3% per year, it will take over twenty-three years to double the supply of housing. Thus, even after twenty-three years *half* of the housing stock will be housing that was already built by 1982. After forty-six years, *one-quarter* of housing stock will be constituted by pre-1983 housing. It follows from this that the usability of the current housing stock will be of great importance in the future. Accordingly, there are a number of questions that must be asked concerning the current stock of housing.

*Demand* — What sorts of factors influence the demand for the standing stock of housing? Are these factors likely to change, and if so how? How responsive is this demand to various policies such as income and property tax manipulations, subsidies, grants, and historic preservation and neighbourhood improvement programes?

*Supply* — What factors influence the supply of services from the existing stock? How will the supply of these services change during the next few decades? What role do housing demolitions play in removing the standing stock from the supply of housing? How important are conversions, renovations, repairs and maintenance, and the general upgrading and adaptation of the existing housing stock? What latitude is there for government policy to influence reinvestment behaviour in ways that will prolong the life and utility of the housing stock?[35]

AFFORDABILITY, ONCE MORE: SOME POLICY OPTIONS

In the light of the above information, it is not possible to arrive at precise answers concerning the future of housing prices and the effects that these prices will have on the ability of Canadian households to afford the housing of their choice. We must take a closer look at the affordability issue again to provide a basis for informed government policy in the future.

*What About "Poor" People: Affordability I*

The definition of precisely who falls into the low-income category varies from year to year, from family size to family size, and from location to location. Table 22 below provides the low-income definitions for 1976, 1978, and 1980. Families with five members who lived in an urban area with more than 500,000 people were classified as low-income families if they earned less than $10,121 in 1976, less than $11,909 in 1978, or less than $14,316 in 1980. But the same sized family living in a rural area was classified as low income if it had an income of less than $7,363 in 1976, less than $8,663 in 1978, or less than $10,413 in 1980. The differences in Table 22 reflect the fact that it costs more to live in a large urban area than it costs to live in a rural area. One factor which is not captured by the data in Table 22 is the regional variation in cost of living among equal size urban areas. High cost areas are traditionally found in certain locations in British Columbia, for example, and low cost areas are found in Ontario and Quebec.

**TABLE 22**
**LOW INCOME CUT-OFFS OF FAMILY UNITS,[1] 1976**

| Size of Family Unit | Size of area or residence | | | | |
|---|---|---|---|---|---|
| | 500,000 and over | 100,000- 499,000 | 30,000- 99,999 | Less than 30,000[2] | Rural areas |
| 1 person | $ 4,117 | $ 3,853 | $ 3,742 | $ 3,442 | $ 2,992 |
| 2 persons | 5,966 | 5,587 | 5,425 | 3,442 | 4,341 |
| 3 persons | 7,613 | 7,130 | 6,920 | 6,369 | 5,537 |
| 4 persons | 9,054 | 8,478 | 8,230 | 7,573 | 6,584 |
| 5 persons | 10,121 | 9,476 | 9,201 | 8,467 | 7,363 |
| 6 persons | 11,111 | 10,404 | 10,102 | 9,293 | 8,080 |
| 7 or more persons | 12,184 | 11,405 | 11,075 | 10,188 | 8,859 |

**LOW INCOME CUT-OFFS OF FAMILY UNITS, 1978**

| Size of Family Unit | Size of area or residence | | | | |
|---|---|---|---|---|---|
| | 500,000 and over | 100,000- 499,999 | 30,000- 99,999 | Less than 30,000 | Rural areas |
| 1 person | $ 4,844 | $ 4,534 | $ 4,404 | $ 4,050 | $ 3,520 |
| 2 persons | 7,020 | 6,574 | 6,384 | 5,871 | 5,108 |
| 3 persons | 8,957 | 8,390 | 8,142 | 7,494 | 6,516 |
| 4 persons | 10,654 | 9,976 | 9,684 | 8,910 | 7,747 |
| 5 persons | 11,909 | 11,149 | 10,826 | 9,963 | 8,663 |
| 6 persons | 13,074 | 12,241 | 11,886 | 10,935 | 9,507 |
| 7 or more persons | 14,336 | 13,419 | 13,031 | 11,987 | 10,424 |

**LOW INCOME CUT-OFFS OF FAMILY UNITS, 1980**

| Size of Family Unit | Size of area or residence | | | | |
|---|---|---|---|---|---|
| | 500,000 and over | 100,000- 499,000 | 30,000- 99,999 | Less than 30,000[2] | Rural areas |
| 1 person | $ 5,822 | $ 5,450 | $ 5,293 | $ 4,868 | $ 4,231 |
| 2 persons | 8,438 | 7,902 | 7,674 | 7,057 | 6,140 |
| 3 persons | 10,767 | 10,085 | 9,788 | 9,008 | 7,833 |
| 4 persons | 12,807 | 11,992 | 11,640 | 10,711 | 9,312 |
| 5 persons | 14,316 | 13,402 | 13,014 | 11,976 | 10,413 |
| 6 persons | 15,716 | 14,714 | 14,287 | 13,145 | 11,428 |
| 7 or more persons | 17,232 | 16,130 | 15,664 | 14,409 | 12,530 |

[1] This table represents the revised cut-offs. For information on the original levels see: J. R. Podoluk, *Incomes of Canadians,* Queen's Printer, 1968. For information on the revised cut-offs, an unpublished paper "Revision of Low Income Cut-offs" is available on request. It should be noted that the revised low income cut-offs are being presently reviewed and a further revision is under consideration.

[2] Includes non-metropolitan cities (with a population between 15,000 and 30,000) and small urban areas (under 15,000).

*Source:* Statistics Canada, Catalogue 13-206.

According to these definitions, 720,000 families were classified as low-income families in 1979 (that is, approximately 11.2% of the total of 6,027,000 Canadian families). Of the 2,510,000 unattached individuals In 1979, 861,000, or 34.3%, were classified as being low income. In other words, in 1979 almost one household out of every six or 18.5% of all households suffered from insufficient income. This indicates a slight improvement since 1975. In 1975, 681,000 families out of a total of 5,610,000 (11.8%) were classified as low income. And there were 832,000 low-income unattached individuals in 1975 out of 1,352,000 (38.1%).

Table 23 below presents some of the data from the 1974 Survey of Housing Units which was conducted by Central Mortgage and Housing Corporation in the twenty-two Census Metropolitan Areas and in Charlottetown, P.E.I. (The 1976 Census does not provide information on housing quality.) Traditionally, households are expected to spend no more than 25% of their income on housing (that is, rent or homeownership, and all maintenance and mortgage expenses).[36] Of the 2,953,000 units surveyed, 702,000 spent 25% or more of their incomes on housing. This means that roughly 24% of all Canadian households in 1974 were experiencing difficulties in paying for shelter.[37]

Another way to get at the situation is to look at the proportion of lower-income households (that is, those in the lowest 20%). Of the households with annual incomes of less than $6,000, 79% were experiencing difficulty in paying for shelter. Of the households in this low-income group, 55% had to spend more than 35% of their income on housing.

According to these data, a significant proportion of Canadian households experienced difficulty in paying for housing services. It should be remembered, though, that these are the figures for twenty- three specific housing areas, not for the whole of Canada. Another difficulty with applying the 25% shelter-cost-to-income rule is that there are some households which voluntarily spend more than 25% of their income on housing (households, for instance, which anticipate a rapid rise in their income). Young families often spend more than 25% of their income on housing when they buy their first home. Accordingly, it is necessary to distinguish between households which voluntarily encumber themselves with higher shelter-cost-to-income ratios and households which are forced to do so. In order to account for households which voluntarily spend more than 25% of their income on housing CMHC created Table 24 below, which is based on the idea that "*Households in need* are those who ought to have their separate, adequate, suitable dwelling unit, but who are not in a position to exercise effective demand for this unit at 25% or less of their income."[37] To implement this concept, CMHC calculated the prevailing normal market rent or cost of ownership, and then used this figure (rather than that of actual shelter costs) to calculate shelter- cost-to-income ratios. According to this adjusted calculation, instead of 702,000 households experiencing shelter-cost-to-income ratios over

**TABLE 23**

**ACTUAL SHELTER COST TO INCOME RATIOS BY HOUSEHOLD CHARACTERISTICS, CMHA'S ONLY, 1974, ALL TENURES**

| Characteristics | All Households | | Households paying (row percentage in brackets) | | | Households in inadequate housing and paying (row percentage in brackets) | | | |
|---|---|---|---|---|---|---|---|---|---|
| | No. in 1,000's | % of All HH | Over .25 | Over .30 | Over .35 | Over .25 | Over .30 | Over .35 | Any Ratio |
| **Characteristics** | | | | | | | | | |
| All Households | 2,953 | 100% | 702(24%) | 480(16%) | 344(12%) | 103( 4%) | 78( 3%) | 57( 2%) | 393(13%) |
| Owners without mortgage | 608 | 21 | 85(14%) | 61(10%) | 48( 8%) | 12( 2%) | 9( 2%) | 7( 1%) | 64(11%) |
| Owners with mortgage | 959 | 33 | 223(23%) | 134(14%) | 87( 9%) | 17( 2%) | 10( 1%) | 8( 1%) | 79( 8%) |
| Renters | 1,387 | 47 | 394(28%) | 284(21%) | 209(15%) | 73( 5%) | 58( 4%) | 43( 3%) | 251(18%) |
| (Other and excluded) | (329) | — | — | | | — | | — | — |
| **Income Quintiles** | | | | | | | | | |
| 1st:  1500-6000 | 460 | 16 | 366(79%) | 309(67%) | 253(55%) | 72(16%) | 61(13%) | 46(10%) | 99(21%) |
| 2nd:  6001-10400 | 612 | 21 | 195(32%) | 108(18%) | 60(10%) | 22( 4%) | 13( 2%) | 9( 2%) | 108(18%) |
| 3rd:  10401-14400 | 614 | 21 | 23(14%) | 42( 7%) | 23( 4%) | 7( 1%) | 3( 1%) | — | 72(12%) |
| 4th:  14401-19900 | 624 | 21 | 42( 7%) | 16( 3%) | 5( 1%) | — | — | — | 63(10%) |
| 5th:  19901 + | 643 | 22 | 16( 3%) | 5( 1%) | 2( 0%) | — | — | — | 51( 8%) |
| **Age Group** | | | | | | | | | |
| –35 | 979 | 33 | 245(25%) | 152(16%) | 107(11%) | 36( 4%) | 26( 3%) | 20( 2%) | 140(14%) |
| 35-59 | 1,382 | 47 | 241(17%) | 160(12%) | 106( 8%) | 33( 2%) | 25( 2%) | 16( 1%) | 168(12%) |
| 60 + | 592 | 20 | 216(37%) | 168(28%) | 130(22%) | 34( 6%) | 27( 5%) | 21( 4%) | 85(14%) |
| **Family Type** | | | | | | | | | |
| Fam. no child | 745 | 25 | 149(20%) | 101(14%) | 72(10%) | 15( 2%) | 11( 1%) | 9( 1%) | 82(11%) |
| Fam. with child | 1,395 | 47 | 229(16%) | 136(10%) | 87( 6%) | 26( 2%) | 17( 1%) | 10( 1%) | 166(12%) |
| Single parent — Male | 25 | 1 | 5(20%) | 4(16%) | 3(13%) | — | — | — | 5(22%) |
| Single parent — Female | 117 | 4 | 53(45%) | 42(35%) | 31(26%) | 12(10%) | 10( 9%) | 8( 7%) | 27(23%) |
| 1 Ind. — Male | 175 | 6 | 57(33%) | 41(23%) | 28(16%) | 13( 7%) | 10( 6%) | 8( 5%) | 34(19%) |
| 1 Ind. — Female | 296 | 10 | 156(53%) | 119(40%) | 96(32%) | 25( 8%) | 20( 7%) | 15( 5%) | 41(14%) |
| 2 + Ind. — Male Head | 105 | 4 | 23(22%) | 15(15%) | 10(10%) | 6( 6%) | 5( 5%) | 3( 3%) | 23(22%) |
| 2 + Ind. — Female Head | 91 | 3 | 29(32%) | 22(24%) | 18(20%) | 4( 5%) | 4( 4%) | 3( 4%) | 15(17%) |

* Excluded are: Incomes below $1,500, non-cash renters, subsidized renters.

TABLE 23 (continued)

ACTUAL SHELTER COST TO INCOME RATIOS BY HOUSEHOLD CHARACTERISTICS, CMHA'S ONLY, 1974, ALL TENURES

| | All Households | | Households paying (row percentage in brackets) | | | Households in inadequate housing and paying (row percentage in brackets) | | | |
|---|---|---|---|---|---|---|---|---|---|
| | No. in 1,000's | % of All HH | Over .25 | Over .30 | .35 | .25 | .30 | .35 | Any Ratio |
| **Crowding I** | | | | | | | | | |
| <1 Person Per Room | 2,818 | 96 | 679(24%) | 466(17%) | 334(12%) | 97( 3%) | 74( 3%) | 54( 2%) | 357(13%) |
| >1 Person Per Room | 125 | 4 | 23(18%) | 14(11%) | 9( 8%) | 6( 5%) | 4( 4%) | 3( 2%) | 36(29%) |
| **Crowding II** | | | | | | | | | |
| Sufficient Area | 2,682 | 91 | 638(24%) | 434(16%) | 311(12%) | 85( 7%) | 64( 2%) | 48( 2%) | 319(12%) |
| Insufficient | 261 | 9 | 65(25%) | 46(17%) | 33(13%) | 18( 7%) | 14( 5%) | 10( 4%) | 74(28%) |
| **Adequacy I** | | | | | | | | | |
| Has bath, toilet, hot water | 2,844 | 98 | 681(24%) | 465(16%) | 332(12%) | 87( 3%) | 66( 2%) | 49( 3%) | 348(12%) |
| Lacks/shares | 58 | 2 | 21(36%) | 15(26%) | 11(19%) | 16(27%) | 12(20%) | 8(14%) | 43(77%) |
| **Adequacy II** | | | | | | | | | |
| No major repairs needed | 2,551 | 87 | 599(24%) | 402(16%) | 286(11%) | | | | |
| Major repairs needed | 393 | 13 | 103(26%) | 78(20%) | 57(15%) | 103(26%) | 78(20%) | 57(15%) | 393(100%) |
| **Mover Status** | | | | | | | | | |
| Moved in last 3 years | 1,364 | 46 | 400(29%) | 264(19%) | 186(14%) | 50( 4%) | 39( 3%) | 29( 2%) | 178(13%) |
| Did not move | 1,586 | 54 | 302(19%) | 216(14%) | 158(10%) | 52( 3%) | 39( 3%) | 28( 2%) | 216(14%) |
| **Sex of Head** | | | | | | | | | |
| Male | 2,372 | 81 | 442(19%) | 282(12%) | 187( 8%) | 57( 2%) | 40( 2%) | 28( 1%) | 300(13%) |
| Female | 572 | 19 | 260(46%) | 198(35%) | 157(27%) | 46( 8%) | 38( 7%) | 29( 5%) | 93(16%) |
| **Children in HH** | | | | | | | | | |
| Yes | 1,549 | 53 | 289(19%) | 184(12%) | 122( 8%) | 40( 3%) | 28( 2%) | 19( 1%) | 200(93%) |
| No | 1,401 | 48 | 413(30%) | 290(21%) | 222(16%) | 63( 5%) | 50( 4%) | 38( 3%) | 193(14%) |

**TABLE 23 (continued)**

**ACTUAL SHELTER COST TO INCOME RATIOS BY HOUSEHOLD CHARACTERISTICS, CMHA'S ONLY, 1974, ALL TENURES**

| | All Households | | Households paying (row percentage in brackets) | | | Households in inadequate housing and paying (row percentage in brackets) | | | |
|---|---|---|---|---|---|---|---|---|---|
| | No. in 1,000's | % of All HH | Over .25 | Over .30 | Over .35 | Over .25 | Over .30 | Over .35 | Any Ratio |
| **Location** | | | | | | | | | |
| Atlantic | 92 | 3 | 26(28%) | 17(19%) | 12(13%) | 5( 5%) | 3( 4%) | 2( 3%) | 14(15%) |
| Quebec | 850 | 29 | 170(20%) | 119(14%) | 86(10%) | 41( 5%) | 33( 4%) | 24( 3%) | 176(21%) |
| Ontario | 1,251 | 43 | 299(24%) | 200(16%) | 142(11%) | 29( 2%) | 22( 2%) | 17( 2%) | 113( 9%) |
| Man. and Sask. | 234 | 8 | 58(25%) | 40(17%) | 28(12%) | 12( 5%) | 8( 4%) | 5( 2%) | 41(18%) |
| Alberta | 277 | 9 | 69(25%) | 46(17%) | 32(12%) | 7( 3%) | 5( 2%) | 4( 1%) | 26(10%) |
| British Columbia | 247 | 8 | 80(33%) | 58(23%) | 43(18%) | 10( 4%) | 7( 3%) | 5( 2%) | 23( 9%) |
| **Household Category** | | | | | | | | | |
| O, < 35, F- | 70 | 2 | 15(21%) | 9(12%) | 4( 7%) | — | — | — | 4( 6%) |
| O, < 35, F+ | 215 | 7 | 58(27%) | 28(13%) | 17( 8%) | 5( 2%) | 2( 1%) | 1( 1%) | 22(10%) |
| O, < 35, SP | 4 | — | 3(70%) | 2(57%) | 2(53%) | — | — | — | — |
| O, < 35, IND | 12 | — | 4(34%) | 3(24%) | 2(17%) | — | — | — | 2(20%) |
| O, 35-59, F- | 131 | 4 | 15(11%) | 9( 7%) | 5( 4%) | — | — | — | 10( 8%) |
| O, 35-59, F+ | 703 | 24 | 96(14%) | 58( 8%) | 39( 6%) | 6( 1%) | 4( 1%) | 3( 0%) | 49( 7%) |
| O, 35-59, SP | 34 | 1 | 11(31%) | 8(22%) | 5(16%) | 2( 5%) | — | — | 6(18%) |
| O, 35-59, IND | 48 | 2 | 14(29%) | 10(22%) | 7(15%) | 2( 3%) | — | — | 7(15%) |
| O, 60+, FAM | 260 | 9 | 52(20%) | 36(14%) | 27(11%) | 4( 1%) | 3( 1%) | 2( 1%) | 24( 9%) |
| O, 60+, IND | 90 | 3 | 41(46%) | 33(36%) | 25(28%) | 9(10%) | 7( 8%) | 5( 6%) | 18(20%) |
| R, < 35, F- | 201 | 7 | 30(15%) | 19(10%) | 13( 7%) | 4( 2%) | 3( 2%) | 3( 2%) | 27(13%) |
| R, < 35, F+ | 192 | 7 | 36(19%) | 22(12%) | 15( 8%) | 8( 4%) | 5( 3%) | 3( 2%) | 36(19%) |
| R, < 35, SP | 27 | 1 | 16(58%) | 13(48%) | 11(42%) | 4(13%) | 3(13%) | 3(11%) | 6(23%) |
| R, < 35, IND | 259 | 9 | 85(33%) | 57(22%) | 42(16%) | 14( 5%) | 11( 4%) | 9( 3%) | 42(16%) |
| R, 35-59, F- | 83 | 3 | 13(16%) | 8( 9%) | 5( 6%) | — | — | — | 13(15%) |
| R, 35-59, F+ | 196 | 7 | 28(14%) | 20(10%) | 11( 6%) | 6( 3%) | 5( 3%) | 3( 1%) | 46(24%) |
| R, 35-59, SP | 51 | 2 | 23(46%) | 19(37%) | 13(25%) | 6(12%) | 5(11%) | 4( 8%) | 15(29%) |
| R, 35-59, IND | 133 | 5 | 41(31%) | 28(21%) | 21(16%) | 10( 7%) | 7( 6%) | 4( 3%) | 22(16%) |
| R, 60+, FAM | 119 | 4 | 42(36%) | 33(28%) | 23(20%) | 7( 6%) | 5( 4%) | 4( 3%) | 22(19%) |
| R, 60+, IND | 124 | 4 | 81(66%) | 66(54%) | 54(44%) | 14(11%) | 12(10%) | 10( 8%) | 22(18%) |

*Source:*  Adapted from *Shelter Cost to Income Ratios* Gerd M. Doepner (Ottawa: CMHC, 1978), pp. 7-9.

25%, there are now only 424,000 households in that category, representing only 14.4% of the households as opposed to 24% previously. But the burden still falls very heavily upon the 20% of Canadian households which have the lowest incomes. This bottom 20% includes 348,000 households (or 75.7% of the households in the bottom 20%) which are in need of financial help to pay for their housing.

Moreover, these lowest-income households represented over 82% of the households who need shelter assistance to obtain adequate housing. Unfortunately, there is every reason to believe that the low-income households of 1974 are no better off today: inflation has risen at least as rapidly as their incomes have risen.

It appears, then, that at least one out of every seven Canadian households is experiencing difficulty in affording adequate housing. But these households also experience affordability problems with respect to the other necessities of life. An often suggested solution for this problem is to provide lower-income households with subsidized housing, but this solution is not one that I, or most economists, favour. What the poor generally need is additional income, not additional housing. Housing subsidies constitute an indirect and economically inefficient way to provide lower income-households with the additional income that they need. However, housing subsidies do have great appeal to the donor groups (that is, that portion of the Canadian population which is above the poverty line) because the donors can exercise considerable control over the nature of the gift. There is a widely held fear that, if left to their own devices, the poor would spend any additional income on less "wise" purchases than housing. This fear is assuaged somewhat by the practice of specifying exactly what commodity the subsidy or grant is to be spent on.

Such a solution to the housing/income problems of poor households has two major disadvantages. First, it forces such households to spend the subsidy on housing and thus possibly to distort their preferred expenditure patterns: housing may well not be the first thing that they would choose to purchase with an additional $1,000 in income. (This has recently been demonstrated by U.S. experiments.[38]) This distortion of preferences is also socially undesirable, because it is patronizing to those with low incomes. It also causes additional problems. If poor households are given subsidies which they have to spend on housing, then the effective demand for housing will be increased. Any increase in the effective demand causes an upward shift in the demand curve, and when there are only a few housing vacancies (as has been the case historically in many cities in Canada) this leads to higher-priced housing. Thus, housing prices and rents could quickly rise if these additional housing expenditures were made on behalf of the poor.[39] This in turn should attract additional housing development. The end result would be that more housing would be built than would have been if there had been no intervention in the housing market. This is desirable *if and*

## TABLE 24
### HOUSEHOLDS IN NEED*, CMA'S ONLY, 1974
(In 1,000, incidence among need households in brackets)

| | All Households Regardless of Deed | | Core Need Households Current Problem | | | |
| --- | --- | --- | --- | --- | --- | --- |
| | No. in 1,000's | % of All HH | Total Number (= 100%) | Currently inadequate a/o unsuitable | Currently inaffordable | Currently inaffordable and inadequate a/o unsuitable |
| **Crowding I** | | | | | | |
| < 1 Person Per Room | 2,818 | 96 | 396 | 41(10%) | 253(64%) | 101(26%) |
| > 1 Person Per Room | 125 | 4 | 28 | 13(46%) | 2( 6%) | 13(48%) |
| **Crowding II** | | | | | | |
| Sufficient Area | 2,682 | 91 | 338 | 23( 7%) | 255(75%) | 61(18%) |
| Insufficient Area | 261 | 9 | 86 | 31(37%) | | 54(63%) |
| **Adequacy I** | | | | | | |
| Has bath, toilet, hot water | 2,884 | 98 | 393 | 42(11%) | 252(64%) | 98(25%) |
| Lacks/Shares | 53 | 2 | 31 | 12(37%) | 3(10%) | 17(66%) |
| **Adequacy II** | | | | | | |
| No major repairs needed | 2,551 | 87 | 308 | 15( 5%) | 255(83%) | 38(12%) |
| Major repairs needed | 393 | 13 | 116 | 39(34%) | 65(53%) | 77(66%) |
| **Mover Status** | | | | | | |
| Moved in last 3 years | 1,364 | 46 | 220 | 29(13%) | 133(59%) | 64(28%) |
| Did not move | 1,586 | 54 | 198 | 25(12%) | 122(62%) | 51(26%) |
| **Sex of Head** | | | | | | |
| Male | 2,372 | 81 | 255 | 38(17%) | 126(56%) | 61(27%) |
| Female | 572 | 19 | 199 | 16( 8%) | 129(65%) | 54(27%) |
| **Children in HH** | | | | | | |
| Yes | 1,549 | 53 | 143 | 29(20%) | 72(50%) | 42(29%) |
| No | (1,601) | 18) | 281 | 25( 9%) | 183(65%) | 73(26%) |

**TABLE 24 (continued)**
**HOUSEHOLDS IN NEED\*, CMA'S ONLY, 1974**
(In 1,000, incidence among need households in brackets)

| | All Households Regardless of Deed | | Core Need Households | | | |
| | | | Current Problem | | | |
| | No. in 1,000's | % of All HH | Total Number (= 100%) | Currently inadequate a/o unsuitable | Currently inaffordable | Currently inaffordable and inadequate a/o unsuitable |
|---|---|---|---|---|---|---|
| **Location** | | | | | | |
| Atlantic | 92 | 3 | 17 | 2(13%) | 10(55%) | 6(32%) |
| Quebec | 850 | 29 | 157 | 36(23%) | 59(44%) | 52(33%) |
| Ontario | 1,251 | 43 | 127 | 6( 5%) | 93(73%) | 28(22%) |
| Man. and Sask. | 234 | 8 | 36 | 4(11%) | 22(60%) | 10(29%) |
| Alberta | 277 | 9 | 41 | 3( 7%) | 30(74%) | 8(19%) |
| British Columbia | 247 | 8 | 45 | 2( 5%) | 31(69%) | 11(25%) |
| **Household Category** | | | | | | |
| O, < 35, F- | 70 | 2 | 5 | — | 3(58%) | 2(37%) |
| O, < 35, F+ | 215 | 7 | 2 | — | — | — |
| O, < 35, SP | 4 | — | | — | — | — |
| O, < 35, IND | 12 | — | 2 | — | 2(87%) | — |
| O, 35-59, F- | 131 | 4 | 17 | 2( 9%) | 11(67%) | 4(24%) |
| O, 35-59, F+ | 703 | 24 | 4 | — | 3(83%) | — |
| O, 35-59, SP | 34 | 1 | 3 | — | 2(79%) | — |
| O, 35-59, IND | 48 | 2 | 27 | 2( 8%) | 22(81%) | 3(11%) |
| O, 60+, FAM | 260 | 9 | 27 | — | 19(67%) | 8(28%) |
| O, 60+, IND | 90 | 3 | 21 | — | 14(67%) | 6(27%) |
| R, < 35, F- | 201 | 7 | 33 | 8(24%) | 15(44%) | 11(32%) |
| R, < 35, F+ | 192 | 7 | 15 | 2(12%) | 8(55%) | 5(33%) |
| R, < 35, SP | 27 | 1 | 62 | 4( 7%) | 40(64%) | 18(29%) |
| R, < 35, IND | 259 | 9 | 11 | 3(28%) | 7(60%) | — |
| R, 35-59, F- | 83 | 3 | 32 | 13(42%) | 10(31%) | 9(28%) |
| R, 35-59, F+ | 190 | 7 | 21 | 2(12%) | 11(54%) | 7(34%) |
| R, 35-59, SP | 51 | 2 | 32 | 3(10%) | 18(57%) | 11(34%) |
| R, 35-59, IND | 133 | 5 | 34 | 4(11%) | 21(62%) | 10(28%) |
| R, 60+, FAM | 119 | 4 | 74 | 7( 9%) | 47(64%) | 20(27%) |
| R, 60+, IND | 124 | 4 | | | | |

*Source: Shelter Cost to Income Ratios*, Gerd M. Doepner (Ottawa: CMHC, 1978), pp. 27-29.

*only if* housing is at the top of society's shopping list, but if housing is not society's highest priority, then housing subsidies will lead to an unwanted over-production of housing, and to a significant expenditure which society might not otherwise have made.[40] Such inefficiency is serious because of the enormous expense involved in building housing units. The question remains: "aren't there less expensive and more efficient ways to help low-income households?" I think that the answer is yes, the basic problems could be solved by the simple expedient of providing lower-income households with additional income and allowing them to spend it as they saw fit. The administrative cost of providing such funds need not be high: there could be a *negative income tax* for low-income households which would provide them with additional funds each month. This alternative would also have the advantage of keeping the expenditure decisions in the hands of the recipients rather than in the hands of the government or the taxpayers.[41] Low-income households still will face problems of security of tenure and rents; but a sizable step would have been made toward solving their housing and income problems.

An alternative solution would be to provide the poor with subsidies which were specifically earmarked for housing, but to leave the decision to the recipients as to what types of housing would be rented or purchased with the subsidy. This would eventually cause an over-production of housing, but it would be more financially efficient and less socially unacceptable than expensive public housing schemes are. These shelter allowances would also be acceptable to the Canadian taxpayer (who would, of course, have to donate the money for subsidies).[42]

Whatever means are taken to alleviate the serious housing problems of low-income households, it is clear that something needs to be done.[43] But there is also a feeling in Canada that housing is becoming less affordable even for the solidly middle-income households. This second type of affordability problem needs to be examined in detail. I shall refer to this type as Affordability II.

## Is Housing Really Becoming Unaffordable?: Affordability II

Since 1972, when house prices began rising rapidly in Canada, it has not been unusual to hear people state that fewer than 20% of Canadian households can afford a home. Such statements reflected the general feeling that it would soon be nearly impossible for the typical Canadian household to afford to buy a typical new house. Affordability II of this sort is quite different from the affordability problem of the poor discussed above, and a number of preliminary observations should be made. In 1981, 63% of Canadian households already owned a house, up from 60% in 1971. This clearly belies the claim that only 10 to 20% of Canadians can afford the average priced new or existing home. House prices rise only because people are willing and able to purchase the houses. As was seen earlier, house prices, in the short run, are largely determined by demand forces because the housing supply takes a long time to grow and is therefore relatively inflexible. Thus, rising prices reflect rising demand, and rising demand is a result of rising household incomes and an increase in the affordability of housing. During the period in which house prices rose most rapidly in Canada (1971-75), the MLS Canadian house price average rose 86.6% from $24,581 to $45,878, but the median family income rose 60.2% from $10,368 to $16,613, and the per capita income rose 74.8% from $3,435 to $6,005. Thus, even during those four years in which house prices did rise faster than incomes, the discrepancy was still not very large. And if we take the 1970's as a whole, we can see from Table 4 earlier that incomes during that decade increased more than house prices and rents. For example, from 1971 to 1981 the prices of CMHC new houses increased by 186.8%, the MLS Canadian average house price increased by 191.3%, and the CMHC rent index rose by 54.8%, but household incomes increased by over 226% and per capita incomes rose by more than 228%.

One of the most frequent claims that is made concerning Affordability II is that, while housing may not be that unaffordable for the average household, it is completely out of reach for younger households, particularly those starting families. Once again, available evidence does not support this claim. The average age of buyers of new NHA homes fell from 33.1 years in 1970 to 31.7 years in 1981. In fact, only in 1979 and 1981 did the average age rise from the previous year. Moreover, the proportion of household income that goes to service NHA mortgages has remained essentially unchanged since 1979, according to data available from CMHC.[44] All of this hardly supports the case that there is any real Affordability II problem evident in Canada.

It is even more difficult to substantiate the existence of Affordability II problems when one considers that these data refer to averages: there are no data specifically on the incomes of people who are purchasing houses. From the rise in house prices we can infer that the incomes of house purchasers also rose, and that they rose at least as fast as house prices. The alternative hypothesis is that people are spending increasingly larger portions of their incomes on housing, a hypothesis which is not supported by the evidence from the 1974 Survey of Housing Units and the previously cited data from CMHC. The furor in Canada during the early 1970's over the alleged existence of Affordability II problems was followed by a major battle which took place in the United States during the latter half of the 1970's. The U.S. debate has raged over two major technical issues, namely how one should measure the income of the typical American household, and how one should measure the typical house price. Different studies have led to quite different conclusions regarding Affordability II depending upon what is considered typical (either income or house price). The debate has not taken account of the points noted above, which apply as much in the

U.S. as in Canada.[45] It also overlooks the fact that the *typical* house is not the legitimate focus of this housing debate. The discussion should focus on minimally suitable new or existing housing units and whether or not *they* are affordable. The difficulty with focusing on typical houses is that such houses have become increasingly luxurious: they now include as standard many features which were previously regarded as optional. The result is that the typical house of 1983 is vastly different from the typical house of 1971: North American families have come to expect increasingly luxurious homes. Thus, it is not possible to compare the costs of typical houses over time, because the public definition of "typical" has changed so significantly.

In general, Canadian households have not suffered declines in their ability to afford adequate housing. Average incomes and average house prices have risen together, even over the 1971-75 period. Affordability II does not appear to be a genuine problem given the above data. But what about the future? Will the typical single-family home become unaffordable for the typical Canadian household? Single-family houses are becoming more expensive as land prices rise as a proportion of house prices.[46] This means that single-family housing will tend to be on smaller lots and may more frequently take the form of completely attached row- or town-housing. It is reasonable to expect household incomes and house prices to continue to keep pace with one another, though we should also expect brief "crisis" periods of local rapid price appreciation or depreciation followed by periods of rather slow growth in house prices, such as has been the experience over the past several years in Canada as a whole (see Table 15 above). It should be noted, though, that it is likely that there will continue to be problems in distributing this growing income among all Canadian households. Although middle-income Canadians should continue to be able to afford housing, lower- and fixed-income households are likely to experience real Affordability I problems. Looking far into the future to the turn of the twenty-first century, one could envisage a scenario in which single-family houses are in excess supply as the Canadian population ages and moves out of single-family houses into more suitable and smaller housing.[47]

Turning to our southern neighbour for comparisons and guidance is not likely to be fruitful in dealing with our Canadian housing issues. For example, between 1972 and 1975, when Canada was experiencing rapid increases in house prices, the U.S. housing market was experiencing low levels both of housing production and of housing purchase. During this period, therefore, there was a marked discrepancy between house prices in Canadian cities and house prices in American cities. Many people assumed that either the government or the private sector in Canada was fiddling with the market and thus creating these dramatic differences in price. In 1971, for instance, the average house cost $26,431 in Vancouver, and $26,343 in Seattle. In 1976 the MLS average house in Vancouver cost $62,476, whereas the average Seattle house cost only $35,200. But by

1978, the MLS average for Vancouver had risen to only $67,103, while the average house sold in Seattle had risen dramatically to $59,447. The price discrepancy that was so marked in 1976 was largely eliminated by 1978. The point to remember is that short-term comparisons between U.S. and Canadian housing markets are not particularly helpful. House prices in Vancouver in 1981, for example, which were thought to be so outrageously high, nevertheless appeared to be quite reasonable when they were compared with prices in such U.S. markets as Southern California, the San Francisco Bay Area, and the Baltimore-Washington region in the same year. Comparison with Tokyo, Hong Kong, and Zurich should provide comfort to house shoppers in Canada. If one chooses a sufficiently short period, one can convince oneself that there is a serious Affordability II problem. But a longer-term view of the Canadian and the U.S. housing markets reveals that housing is no less affordable to middle-income families today than it was a decade ago: even short-run building and demand cycles must be viewed from a longer-term perspective.[48] The 1982 "bust" in Vancouver house prices did much to realign prices with falling real incomes and rising unemployment, just as an economic analysis using the tools provided in Chapter 4 would have predicted.

## THE LAND-AVAILABILITY QUESTION AGAIN

This issue of land-availability relates closely to the concern that land prices are rising more rapidly than incomes. Blame is generally laid either at the feet of the developers, who are accused of monopoly practices, or at the feet of politicians and bureaucrats, who are accused of being inexcusably inefficient. These rising costs were caused by the increased competition between developers and prospective homeowners for sites in, or near to, Canadian cities.[49] Once again we must remember that the demand for land is derived from the value of the uses to which it can be put. High house prices lead to high land prices, not vice versa.

When reviewing the findings of the Greenspan Report, it was shown that no shortage of land exists or is likely to exist in and around any city in Canada during the foreseeable future. It was suggested that municipalities have acted responsibly in regulating urban development and in passing the costs of growth on to those who made this growth necessary (that is, on to new residents). Under the BNA Act the federal government is prohibited from intervening directly in the affairs of local governments. Local governments operate on a pay-as-you-go basis and can only afford those expenditures that will be tolerated by local residents who pay taxes and who vote. Local governments will not want to impose costs of growth on existing residents who vote, but will rather impose such costs on future residents who do not yet vote.

The tradition of leaving growth and subdivision to local control has had a number of benefits. And there is enough land in and around Canadian cities that land availability should not become a serious issue or pose any long-term obstacle to the orderly growth and development of urban areas in Canada.[50] Short-term and localized shortages and surpluses should still be expected, given the lags involved in the approval and construction processes.

SOME CONCLUDING OBSERVATIONS

The evidence seems to lead to the conclusion that there is no substantial housing crisis in Canada today: nor does it seem that there will be one, in the near future. The overall quality of the Canadian housing stock has improved dramatically during the last three decades. Indices of crowding, housing quality, and housing amenities have improved significantly and continue to improve. Over 90% of the occupied houses in Canada today are of an adequate or above adequate standard. The Canadian housing stock, then, is good and is improving. Thus, the housing problem is not one of substandard or overcrowded structures.

The data presented in previous sections should help dispel the idea that housing prices are getting beyond the financial reach of ordinary Canadians. The question remains whether or not Canadians really do want lower priced housing. Perhaps they do not, as recent Vancouver experience highlights. Over 60% of the households in Canada own their housing units, and they have a vested interest in house prices continuing to rise. Of the 38% of the households who rent, about half would probably prefer to own their housing units. Thus, at least 60% of Canadian households favour rising house prices, since they already own their units, and only about 20% do not own their units but would like to do so. Practical politics dictate that governments will continue to make the policies necessary to prevent house prices from declining because three times as many households benefit from such policies as would benefit from declining prices. The 1981 and 1982 record mortgage interest rates called forth public outrage precisely because high rates led to lower prices as households adjusted their housing expectations downward.

What is desired ideally, of course, is low prices for new entrants and high prices for existing homeowners' units. This is no more realistic than wanting high wheat prices for farmers but low bread prices for the consuming public. This is clearly not possible, so the pressure will remain for housing prices to increase and with it the call for subsidized mortgages, aid to first time housepurchasers, and the like.

Rising house prices (in real terms, that is, net of general inflation) are explained by the growing scarcity of centrally located land and the rising costs of capital, construction, and transportation. High prices reflect the value that

Canadians place on good housing in stable and conveniently located neighbour-hoods. Rather than expensive housing being regarded as a curse, it can equally well be viewed as a blessing, because it indicates the existence of healthy residential neighbourhoods in healthy cities. Very few Canadians want declining neighbourhoods and the accompanying declines in house prices. Steadily increasing house prices are a measure of our success at building and maintaining liveable cities: they are not necessarily an indication of failure.[51]

Rising house prices have not posed any serious problems for the average Canadian household over the past decade, and it is unlikely that prices and rents will outstrip average incomes in the future. Thus, Affordability II is primarily the problem that the average Canadian household consistently expects more and more housing and does not feel happy paying any extra for it. Such expectations are unrealistic: if the average household wants more and more luxuries it will have to allocate extra dollars of its income in order to pay for them. The well-equipped "average" housing units of 1983 should not be expected to cost as little as the less luxurious "average" houses of 1970 cost.[52] So the average Canadian household can afford good quality housing, though the housing may be less opulent or well located than is hoped for.

Households on fixed, inadequate, and interruptible incomes do face serious Affordability I problems. They often have little chance of obtaining adequate shelter at costs that they can afford. Moreover, given the relatively fixed and/or uncertain nature of their incomes, their financial situation is precarious whether we experience worse and worse inflation or significant disinflation accompanied by high unemployment. The inflation in housing prices and rents that was so beneficial to the majority of Canadian households was a great burden to low-income households. There is a serious need for government action to assist in providing supplementary incomes so that these households can obtain the neces-sities of life, including adequate shelter.

However, for the Canadian middle class the only housing crisis is the fact that their unrealistic expectations have led to rising demands, which in turn have caused house prices to rise even further. This may make life slightly more difficult for some middle-income households, but it is not an affordability crisis such as that which is being experienced by low-income households. These frustrated middle-income households should accept that quality housing is a dimension of life which is worth pursuing, but which is in relatively short supply. Analyses in terms of supply and demand have clearly demonstrated that highly valued things which are in relatively short supply are certain to be expensive.

Most Canadians, then, are well housed in healthy neighbourhoods in healthy cities. For the vast majority there is essentially only a crisis in expectations. Approximately 20% of Canadian households have a real affordability problem, and it is on this affordability problem that policymakers should be concentrating.

*A Postscript about the future*

We began by raising some questions about the future of urban form, about people's housing preferences and changes in these preferences, and more generally about the future of housing markets in Canada. We were not alone in asking such questions, and researchers have devoted a great deal of attention to such issues as the future of the traditional family, the role of working women, child-rearing and household-forming behaviour, and the like. While it is hazardous in the best of times to suggest the future course of such behavioural decisions, we can at least report here some of the more recent evidence.

In July of 1981 a symposium was held at the University of British Columbia with the title, "The Future of North American Housing Markets into the 21st Century." That symposium brought together leading academics and policymakers from both Canada and the United States to explore future trends in housing and mortgage markets. Several general conclusions emerged with which it is fitting to close this book.[53]

First, looking at housing demand, it was agreed that later marriage, smaller families, continued high participation rates of women in the labour force, and volatile immigration (both international and internal) would characterize demographic events into the next century. Continued uncertainty and volatility in the economy, particularly with respect to inflation and mortgage interest rates, would also likely be a reality over the foreseeable future. These two factors together augured poorly for housing demand over the remainder of the present century. Demand should slow fairly continuously after the late 1980's, implying significant reductions in new construction activity in the 1990's and beyond. However, even this consensus view was clouded by the possibility that marriage and fertility rates could turn around, and there could be a mini baby boom shortly. Furthermore, high rates of international immigration could greatly increase the size of the Canadian population and add considerably to housing demand. Finally on the demand side, even if the slow demographic growth scenario unfolds, it is still highly likely that there will be pockets of intense housing activity reflecting the continued redistribution of economic activity and of people within Canada away from the heartland regions of central Canada, Ontario and Quebec.

Looking at the supply side, there was widespread agreement that there would continue to be areas of excess supply (slowly growing and declining regions, again usually in central Canada but also in parts of Atlantic Canada and the Prairies) and other areas where supply constraints would be faced. Chief among these constraints were land use and urban development controls and the inflexibility of much of the standing stock of housing. However, here too, the general consensus was tempered by the acknowledgment that careful maintenance and renovation of the existing stock and building at higher densities (that is, removing some of the present institutional constraints) could ease the flow of new stock onto the market and adapt the old stock to changing needs of a changing Canadian population.

Innovations in development forms (such as mixed-use developments, town- and row-housing, smaller residential lots, and mixing of density and housing types in small areas) are likely to continue over the coming decades to provide greater choice in style and location. Moreover, the emerging smaller household, often without children, is much freer in its ability to experiment with new housing types and locations. In this vein there is every reason to believe that the recent perceived repopulation of central city areas should continue, both in renovated and new housing.

In short, the gains made by Canadians on the housing front should continue over the closing decades of the twentieth century. New housing forms and choices should evolve. Slower population and household growth should provide the opportunity to expand choice without greatly raising costs and prices for the vast majority of the Canadian populace. The removal of demand pressures and the slower pace of housing markets (despite periodic local hot spots) should also enable housing and social policymakers to progress in their efforts to obtain appropriate housing with reasonable security of tenure for those lower-income households who have had to bear the brunt of much of the volatility of the past housing booms and busts.

Whatever course of action is to be followed, both for market and non-market participants, a sound understanding of market function is at the heart of effective housing market operation and housing policies in the future. With this knowl- edge can all help guide the course of housing in Canada into the next century and beyond.

# Notes

1. *C.M.H.C. Annual Report* (Ottawa: CMHC, 1981) provides an excellent source of information on housing in Canada each year. CMHC estimated in 1977 that there were an additional $64.6 billion in "tax expenditures" from untaxed capital gains on houses and nontaxation of imputed rents in owner-occupied housing. See CMHC, Background Document on Social Housing (Ottawa: CMHC, 1981), pp. 4-10.
2. *Economic Review* (Ottawa: Department of Finance, April 1981).
3. The dollar value for outstanding mortgages does not include financing from the noninstitutional sector, such as that by vendors, relatives or by business financing. It is conservatively estimated that these would bring the figure for all outstanding mortgages to $150 billion, and for residential mortgages to well over $100 billion presently.
4. For example, the so-called Dennis and Fish Report on low-income housing caused a great stir in the early 1970's for its criticism of government inaction. Similarly, the dramatic housing price rise from 1971-75 led to the creation of the "Federal-Provincial Task Force on the Supply and Price of Serviced Residential Land" and to the creation or expansion of such programmes as the Assisted Home Ownership Program and the Assisted Rental Program.
5. The plight of the poor has been documented by many authors. See for example: *Programs in Search of a Policy: Low Income Housing in Canada*, M. Dennis and S. Fish (Toronto: Hakkert, 1972); *Housing the Urban Poor*, A. P. Solomon (Boston: Joint Centre for Urban Studies, M.I.T., 1974); *Public Housing: The Politics of Poverty*, L. Freeman (New York: Holt, Rinehart and Winston, 1969).
6. An excellent source of information on the social issues related to housing is *Man and His Urban Environment: A Sociological Approach*, W. Michelson (Don Mills: Addison-Wesley, 1976).
7. The view that housing determines social behaviour is exposed in a number of works such as: "Families in Flats," D. Fanning, *British Medical Journal*, Vol. 18 (1967): 382-86. The alternative view that housing is not central to, but perhaps merely peripherally relevant to poor social conditions can be found in *The Housing Environment and Family Life*, Daniel Wilner, et al. (Baltimore: Johns Hopkins University Press, 1962).
8. This point has been stressed in *Housing: It's Your Move*, Vol. I (Vancouver: University of British Columbia, 1976).
9. From the Canadian Real Estate Association, details on Table 5.
10. This point is stressed and documented by L. B. Smith in *Anatomy of a Crisis* (Vancouver: Fraser Institute, 1977). Also see Tables 9 and 10 in this text.
11. An example of these unwarranted fears is provided by J. Poapst in a study for CMHC entitled *Developing the Residential Mortgage Market*, Volumes I-III, (Ottawa: CMHC, 1973).
12. It should be noted that the *high* cost of mortgages is given in terms of nominal interest rates. The real interest rates between 1973 and 1975 were extremely low. (The real interest rate is what one gets when one deducts the inflation rate from the stated mortgage interest rate.) See Table 11.
13. *Down to Earth*, vols. I and II, The Report of the Federal-Provincial Task Force on the Supply and Price of Serviced Residential Land, David Greenspan, chairman (Toronto: 1978).
14. For an economic analysis of servicing standards, and a view which supports municipal policies, see Michael A. Goldberg, "Municipal Arrogance or Economic Rationality: The Case of High Servicing Standards," *Canadian Public Policy*, VI(1): 78-88. For a look at the broader issues of land use controls, see Michael A. Goldberg and Peter J. Horwood, *Zoning: Its Costs and Relevance for the 1980's* (Vancouver: Fraser Institute, 1980). An excellent general statement on the land supply issue can be found in Larry S. Bourne, "Choose Your Villain: Five Ways to Oversimplify the Price of Housing and Urban Land," *Urban Forum*, Vol. 3, No. 1 (Spring 1977): 16-24.

15. Urban Family Expenditure, Statistics Canada, cat. 62-547, 1967-72-74.

16. "Housing Transaction Costs: A Survey of Recent Experiences in Three Canadian Cities," Michael A. Goldberg and Peter J. Horwood,in *Competition in the Real Estate Industry in Canada*, S. W. Hamilton, editor (Montreal: Montreal Institute for Research and Public Policy, forthcoming).

17. For an excellent introduction to economics and its components see: *Economics*, Fifth Canadian Edition, P. Samuelson and A. Scott (Toronto: McGraw-Hill, 1980).

18. See Table 1.

19. See Samuelson and Scott, *Economics*, Introduction.

20. See Samuelson and Scott, *Economics*, Chapter 22 (Demand). Also see John M. Quigley, "What Have We Learned about Urban Housing Markets," in P. Mieszkowski and M. Straszheim, editors, *Current Issues in Urban Economics* (Baltimore, Md.: Johns Hopkins University Press, 1980), pp. 391-429.

21. See Samuelson and Scott, *Economics*, Chapters 23 and 24(Supply).

22. See Samuelson and Scott, *Economics*, Chapters 25 and 26 (Market).

23. An in-depth discussion of the transaction process can be found in Goldberg and Horwood, *Competition in the Real Estate Industry in Canada*.

24. *Canadian Housing Statistics* (Ottawa: CMHC, 1979).

25. See Volume II of the Greenspan Report for documentation and support.

26. See "B.N.A. Act, N.H.A., C.M.H.C., M.S.U.A., etc." Michael A. Goldberg, in *Canadian Confederation at the Crossroads*, Michael Walker, editor (Vancouver: Fraser Institute, 1978), pp. 321-61. Also see John Brigham, "Judicial Transformation of Property Rights: A Comparison of the United States and Canada," a paper presented at the 1982 Annual Meeting of the American Political Science Association, Denver, Colorado, September 2-5, 1982.

27. See Dennis and Fish, *Programs in Search of a Policy*.

28. See Smith, *Anatomy of a Crisis*.

29. This is not to suggest that governments can *control* the price of housing. Much of the government's past stimulation of the housing industry has had the primary goal of improving the employment situation rather than that of altering house prices.

30. Landlords are not the only losers in the rent control game. Future tenants are also negatively affected, but they are not generally of voting age. Excellent reviews of the problems arising from rent control have been published by the Fraser Institute and are recommended for readers interested in the details of rent control policies and how they backfire. See Michael A. Walker, editor, *Rent Control: A Popular Paradox* (Vancouver: Fraser Institute, 1975); and Walter Block and Edgar Olsen, editors, *Rent Control: Myths and Realities* (Vancouver: Fraser Institute, 1981).

31. See Block and Olsen, *Rent Control*, for details and documentation. For recent evidence on zoning impacts in Vancouver see J. H. Mark and M. A. Goldberg, "Land Use Controls: The Case of Zoning in Vancouver," *Journal of the American Real Estate and Urban Economics Association* 9(4): 418-35.

32. See Goldberg, "Municipal Arrogance," for an analysis of potential savings resulting from high-quality site services through savings in long-run repairs and maintenance.

33. There is growing evidence for the claim that metropolitan areas are not going to be the focus for growth in the 1980's: The evidence, from the U.S., does not appear relevant yet in Canada but it is worth following. See Brian J. L. Berry, editor, *Urbanization and Counter-Urbanization* (Beverly Hills, California: Sage Publications, 1976). Some very recent work though does suggest that Canadians should look out for this phenomenon. See Larry S. Bourne, in G. W. Gau and M. A. Goldberg, editors, *The Future of North American Housing Markets* (Cambridge, Mass.: Ballinger Publishers, 1982.

34. See Goldberg, "B.N.A. Act," Also see *The Planning Act* (Victoria, B.C.: Queen's Printer, 1980).

35. See Endrej Skabkrskis, *Demolitions, Conversions and Abandonments*, Working Papers 1-3 (Ottawa: CMHC, 1979).

36. It should be noted that the 25% rule is likely to change as more couples have few or no children and therefore have higher percentages of their incomes to spend on housing. See Table 17. A more realistic 30% is really in effect today.

37. See *Shelter Cost to Income Ratios*, Gerd M. Doepner (Ottawa: CMHC, 1978). There is a fundamental flaw in the CMHC approach of using "normal" shelter cost in a market area in calculating affordability problems. It is implicitly assumed that if those who were paying more for their shelter tried to find cheaper dwellings they could. It is also assumed that the price of these cheaper dwellings will not be driven up.

38. See *Integrated Analysis of Housing Allowances: Synthesizing a Complex Research Program*, J. D. Heinberg (Washington: The Urban Institute, 1977). A recent doctoral dissertation looks at various subsidies in detail and concludes earmarked housing subsidies are a good compromise between direct building and unconstrained income tranfers. See Kevin Johnston, "Quantification of the Cost of Alternative Forms of Housing Market Intervention in Canada" (Ph.D. diss., University of B.C., 1982).

39. It should be noted that most housing expenditures made on behalf of the poor have not caused housing prices and rents to rise: they have acted chiefly on the supply side or by setting price limits. See Raymond J. Struyk and Marc Bendick, Jr., editors, *Housing Vouchers for the Poor: Lessons From a National Experiment* (Washington, D.C.: The Urban Institute, 1981).

40. See some of Anthony Down's recent writings for examples, specifically, "The Rising Cost of Housing and What Should Be Done about It" (Washington, D.C.: The Urban Institute, 1977).

41. See Derek Hum and H. Stevens, "The Manitoba White Paper on Tax Credit Reform: A Critique," *Canadian Taxation*, Vol. 2, No. 2: 129-34. Also see Hum and Stevens, *Is Government Home Ownership Assistance the Way to Go?* (Ottawa: Canadian Council on Social Development, 1981), pp. 148-156.

42. Johnston, "Quantification."

43. Concern for low-income households was strongly voiced by the Task Force on Canada Mortgage and Housing Corporation. Its function was to review CMHC's various roles with an eye toward "privatizing" the mortgage insurance elements of CMHC. The report argues for a strengthened social housing and income maintenance program which would not be readily achievable with CMHC's present structure. See *Report on Canada Mortgage and Housing Corporation* (Ottawa: Task Force on Canada Mortgage and Housing Corporation and CMHC, 1979), pp. 105-10.

44. See Table 81, page 69, *Canadian Housing Statistics* (Ottawa: CMHC), 1981).

45. For the details on this heated U.S. debate see: "Toward Equality of Urban Opportunity," B. Frieden, in *Urban Planning and Social Policy*, B. Frieden and R. Morris, editors (New York: Basic Books, 1968); *Why Housing Affordability Calculations are Useless — And What Can Be Done About It*, J. Weicher, (Washington: The Urban Institute, 1978); and B. Frieden and A. P. Solomon, "The Controversy Over Home Ownership Affordability," *Areuea*, Vol. 5, No. 3, pp. 355-360.

46. See Table 10. The question of the future of single-family housing was recently addressed by a conference on the subject sponsored by the Canadian Council on Social Development. See Janet McClain, editor, *Is Government Homeownership Assistance the Way to Go* (Ottawa: CCSD, 1981).

47. For details see Philip Brown's paper in Gau and Goldberg, *The Future of North American Housing Markets*.

48. The present section has dealt with the Canadian case, while Weicher, *Why Housing Affordability Calculations are Useless*, has dealt with the U.S. case.

49. Greenspan, *Down to Earth*.

50. For an elaboration of this argument see Goldberg, "B.N.A. Act," and "Municipal Arrogance."

51. It is important to understand that declining house prices have typified much of the U.S. urban "problem". It is also important to understand that Canadian cities are quite different from those in the U.S. See for example, Michael A. Goldberg, "Explanations and Their Meaning for Public Policy," *Regional Science Association Papers*, 45 (1980): 159-83.

52. There is much circumstantial evidence to support the assertion that people are spending increasingly higher percentages of their income on housing: the recent house price boom in British Columbia would not have been possible without such a change. The growing number of young professional working couples with few or no children can afford to spend higher percentages of current income because their anticipated disposable permanent income is considerably higher than their present income.

53. For the details of the symposium see Gau and Goldberg, *The Future of North American Housing Markets*. The interested reader is also directed to a stimulating collection of essays on American cities that attempts to look beyond present circumstances to peer into the future of the American city (as opposed to housing alone). As one would expect, housing issues play a prominent role in such a forward view. See Arthur P. Solomon, editor, *The Prospective City* (Cambridge, Mass.: M.I.T. Press, 1980).

# Appendix I
# A Primer on Mortgages

This appendix provides some of the technical details that relate to mortgages.

POLICY CHANGES AFFECTING MORTGAGE MARKETS IN THE PAST

Major changes in mortgages over the past decade or so include the following:

1) *Freeing the NHA Interest Rate:* Before 1969 the NHA interest rate (that is, the interest rate which applies to homes financed and insured under the provisions of the National Housing Act) was fixed by regulation. After 1969, the NHA interest rate was free to find its own level in the marketplace. This made NHA mortgages much more attractive, since their yields to investors were now in line with the yields realized from other mortgage and financial instruments. Under the pre-1969 regulations NHA yields often fell far behind the market rates, thus making NHA mortgages unattractive.[1]

2) *Change in the Canada Interest Act:* In 1969 another significant piece of Canadian legislation was passed which affected the attractiveness of mortgages as an investment. An amendment to the Canada Interest Act allowed for the adoption by the market of mortgage renewals every five years, thus allowing trust companies to match their assets (their mortgages) against their liabilities (the five-year trust certificates which provided them with their source of loanable mortgage funds). This matching has enabled trust companies to expand their mortgage loans considerably; they no longer have to worry about having long-term assets at fixed interest rates and short-term liabilities (trust certificates) at interest rates which could fluctuate significantly over the term of the mortgages. Between 1969 and 1980, Canadian trust companies experienced more than an eight-fold expansion in the value of outstanding mortgage loans, becoming easily the largest single source of mortgage credit.[2] Separating the mortgage term (the length of time for which the mortgage holds) from the amortization period (the length of time over which monthly payments are based) was a major innovation which later spread to the United States, where it became known as "The Canadian Mortgage." The better matching of assets and liabilities also appealed to other financial institutions and enabled them to allocate more funds to mortgages than they had previously been able to do.

3) *Revision to the Bank Act:* In 1967 the Bank Act was changed in order to allow banks to lend money at market-determined rates. Previously, chartered

banks were not permitted to charge more than 6% per annum on their loans; this forced them out of the mortgage market during 1960-1966 when mortgage rates rose above that figure. The effect of the 1967 Bank Act revision was profound, and mortgage loans outstanding at chartered banks increased from $840 million in 1967 to $19,105 million in 1980. Chartered banks are restricted from holding more than 10% of their assets in mortgage loans, but they are still well within that limit, having roughly 6% of their assets in mortgages as of 1979.[3]

4) *Relaxing NHA Eligibility Requirements:* A number of important changes were made to the National Housing Act in the late 1960's and early 1970's which made borrowing much easier. First, NHA financing was extended to include existing houses; it had originally been restricted to new houses. Second, the maximum loan amount available under NHA financing was raised in a series of steps which recently raised the ceilings to over $100,000. Third, amortization periods were extended to a maximum of forty years, and the loan-to-value ratio was raised to a maximum of 95% on certain types of loans, and to 75% on conventionally financed loans by registered mortgage loan companies.[4] Also, the gross debt-to-service ratio was increased from 25% to 30%, and income is now defined as including 100% of both spouses' earnings.

POTENTIAL FOR FURTHER CHANGE IN MORTGAGE LENDING: A PRIMER ON
RELEVANT MORTGAGE TERMS

In order to understand the areas in which further useful innovations may be possible in mortgage lending, it is necessary to know the various elements which comprise normal mortgage lending activities. Because each of these elements is variable, a large number of innovations is possible. The principal variables in mortgage lending include:

1) *Interest rate:* This is the contract rate of interest which is calculated semi-annually in Canada, and monthly in the United States (for example, a mortgage at 12%, compounded semi-annually, has an *effective rate* of 12.36%, whereas the same *nominal rate* of 12% compounded monthly has an effective rate of 12.68%). This is important, because whereas chartered banks and life insurance companies generally calculate mortgages semi-annually, credit unions generally calculate mortgage interest monthly. One should, therefore, compare effective rates, not nominal rates. As the compounding period is changed from once to twice or twelve times per year, the nominal rate remains unchanged but the effective rate increases. It is the effective interest rate which determines the cost to the borrower in annual interest charges.

2) *Term of the loan:* Because of the changes in the Canada Interest Act and in the NHA in 1969, mortgages are now usually granted to a maximum term of five years. Before 1969 the mortgage term was generally about twenty-five years. The term of the mortgage is the period of time over which the mortgage is

in effect. With recent fluctuations in interest rates many lenders have been encouraging mortgages of only one-, two-, or three-year terms, in order to protect themselves against dramatic fluctuations: this makes it easier for lending institutions to balance the term of the mortgage against the term of their liabilities (trust certificates, passbook and other savings, and certificates of deposit). Fluctuations in inflation and interest rates will ensure that mortgage terms continue to be short. As inflation rates decline and stabilize, one can expect to see longer-term mortgages of up to five years reappear.

3) *Amortization Period:* This is the period of time over which the mortgage principal must be fully repaid. Prior to 1969 the amortization period used to be identical with the term of the mortgage. This has changed, though, and one can now get, for instance, a five-year maximum term and forty-year amortization period. The longer the amortization period, the lower the monthly payments, because the borrower is able to repay the principal over a longer period of time. And, conversely, the shorter the amortization period, the higher the monthly payments. But the longer the amortization period is, the higher the total amount of interest that has to be paid, because the borrower will have use of the principal for a longer period of time. Appendix Table 1 below presents the effects of jointly changing interest rates and amortization periods.

4) *Loan-to-value ratio:* This is the ratio of the loan amount (the principal) to the lending value of the house being purchased. The higher the loan-to-value ratio the lower the *downpayment* needed to buy the house. But a lower downpayment means a higher monthly payment, because more money will need to be borrowed. So-called high-ratio loans are those where the amount borrowed is greater than 75% of the house's purchase price. Normally, a high-ratio loan calls for a higher interest rate (usually applied as an insurance fee), because the lender is exposed to a greater risk of losing some of the principal (for instance, if the borrower defaults and is unable to meet the monthly mortgage payments). Also, the higher the ratio the higher the monthly payments, and the greater is the monthly burden on the household, which also raises the risk of non-repayment.

5) *Gross debt-service ratio:* This is the ratio of the monthly payments (that is, the principal and interest) to the borrower's monthly *gross income* (that is, income before deducting income taxes). The higher the gross debt-service ratio the greater the risk to the lender, because there is a higher probability that the household will have difficulty making its monthly payments. Gross debt-service ratios are usually about 25%: mortgage lenders generally will not lend when the ratio exceeds 30%. The combination of higher loan-to-value and gross debt-service ratios proved excessively burdensome for many Canadian households during the past several years, when already stretched household budgets had to accommodate record high levels of mortgage interest as their mortgages expired, and they had to renew at these high rates. To make matters worse, house prices also fell (precipitously in some areas like British Columbia) leaving households

with higher monthly payments on renewal for a house that had declined in value. In short, easier credit terms placed many households at risk as rates rose and mortgages had to be renewed, an issue we will discuss shortly.

6) *Prepayment terms and conditions:* It is estimated that the average mortgage in Canada is terminated after seven years, either because the house is sold or because the borrower pays off of the mortgage prior to its termination. Sometimes it is necessary to prepay a mortgage before it is due to expire, which can prove to be financially detrimental to the mortgage lender, because someone could pay off a mortgage at 16% interest at a time at which the mortgage interest rate is 12% or 13%: this would mean that the lender would have to re-invest the funds at a significantly lower rate. Moreover, since lenders match their assets and liabilities, the money for the original 16% mortgage may have been obtained by issuing a five-year trust certificate paying 14%. If the 16% mortgage is paid off after two years and rates fall to 12%, the lender will lose money because the lender still has three years to pay off the trust certificate at 14%, but can now only get 12% return on the mortgage. However, the lender is generally protected against such risk as a result of prepayment penalties which may require three or six months interest as a penalty if a mortgage is repaid before its term is up. Credit unions have generally allowed prepayment of mortgages but have charged correspondingly higher mortgage rates in order to protect themselves against loss. The recent trend has been to provide the consumer with a range of prepayment possibilities with corresponding differences in mortgage interest rates. In most cases, the greater the prepayment flexibility, the greater the cost of the mortgage. Lenders have generally pushed the risk of changes in interest rates (called *interest-rate risk*) back on borrowers both through prepayment penalties and through shortening the term of mortgages, requiring more frequent renewals and making it easier for lenders to match assets (shorter term mortgages) and liabilities (mainly deposits). Also, if mortgage rates increase, then prepayment can work to the lender's advantage, since he can relend the repaid money at higher rates.

7) *Mortgage Insurance:* The great innovation in mortgage activity under the National Housing Act came in 1954 with the movement away from direct lending to consumers by Central Mortgage and Housing Corporation, and toward insuring loans made by approved private lenders such as life insurance companies, chartered banks, credit unions and trust companies. By insuring the mortgage loan, CMHC protects the lender against loss, thus greatly reducing the risk associated with mortgage lending. Following CMHC's lead, private mortgage insurers sprang up to insure mortgages on houses which were not eligible for CMHC insurance, such as those on existing housing and mortgages which exceeded NHA maximum loan amounts. The cost of mortgage insurance is usually between ⅞% and 1½% of the value of the loan payable at the time the loan is taken out.

8) *Other fees:* In addition to the interest rate, the mortgage insurance fees and the other fees discussed above, there are a number of other costs that are usually associated with a mortgage. These include fees for the professional services required to provide the lender with the information needed to issue a mortgage, such as fees for appraisers, for land surveyors, and for lawyers or notaries. In some instances, especially when mortgage money is in short supply, lenders will also charge a *bonus*, or so-called *front end load*, as compensation for finding the required mortgage funds. Many mortgage brokers earn a 1% to 1½% fee for lining up mortgage funds and for making the necessary arrangements for a mortgage loan. The careful consumer should be aware of all of these fees and have them itemized before contracting a mortgage, because they all contribute to the effective rate being charged for the mortgage loan.

THE FUTURE OF MORTGAGE LENDING

There is a large variety of alternative mortgage designs which have come to the fore to replace or complement the traditional mortgage which usually required a 25% downpayment, had a five-year term, and had a twenty-five-year amortization period. The most obvious possible alternatives are ones that have already been tried: for instance, a greater variety in the term of the mortgage, a wide choice in the amortization period, variations in interest rates (which depend on the loan-to-value ratio of the mortgage, the term, and the prepayment options), prepayment provisions, and a choice as to having the mortgage insured privately or by the government.[5] It is now possible for the interested consumer to have a much greater choice as to the term of a mortgage than was possible even three or four years ago. As mortgage money has become more abundant, and as regulations have been relaxed, the increased competition among mortgage lenders has naturally led to there being innovations and changes in lending practices. There is another factor which needs to be examined here in some detail, namely the effect of inflation on mortgage lending practices and on the standard mortgage instrument.

*Mortgage Lending, Inflation, and the "Tilt" Problem*

During the 1930's, the fully amortized mortgage came into being as a result of a series of bad experiences with the earlier unamortized mortgage. Earlier mortgages collected interest only during the term of the mortgage (like a bond), with the borrower being expected to set aside the principal so that it could be repaid upon expiration of the mortgage loan in one "balloon" payment. During the depression many people were unable to save enough money to repay the principal. In addition, properties declined in value, and there was little incentive for homeowners to struggle to meet the balloon payment. Defaults and foreclosures were widespread. The inability to pay property taxes added further to many default and foreclosure rates. These problems led to the development of the present standard mortgage instrument: each month the borrower pays to the lender a set amount consisting of interest and a certain proportion of the principal. This monthly sum, called a *blended payment*, virtually assures the lender that the borrower will have fully repaid the principal by the time the mortgage expires. The standard blended payment mortgage has virtually eliminated the former balloon payment mortgage for residential lending. Property taxes are usually collected by the lender for the same reason, that is, in order to prevent the local governments from seizing the property because the local property taxes have not been paid.

The fully amortized mortgage has reduced the risk involved in mortgage lending by reducing the number of defaults and foreclosures to the point at which they represent today less than 1% of the loans outstanding. But these benefits to the lender have only been achieved by increasing the monthly costs to the borrower: the borrower must now pay both interest and part of the principal each month. During inflationary times, such as those we have been experiencing recently, in which both house prices and incomes rise, high monthly mortgage payments can act as a deterrent to prospective house buyers. The burden on the purchasers, particularly on young families and first-time purchasers without equity in a house, can be great indeed.[6] In order to understand fully the range of recent innovations in mortgage lending, we have to understand the nature of the "tilt" problem associated with high levels of inflation and of mortgage interest rates.

*The Tilt Problem:*[7] Under periods of high and volatile rates of inflation there will be high and volatile rates of interest. High rates of interest cause a "tilting" of interest payments in *real* terms (net of inflation) toward the present. The standard mortgage has level payments, which under high inflation rates leads to a cheapening of the dollar over time so that the borrower is paying back the lender in cheaper and cheaper dollars as time passes. Another way of saying the same thing is that the real cost declines over time as inflation erodes the value of future payments. Thus, payments tend to be higher in real terms in the immediate future and diminish in real terms over time.

The tilt problem is best illustrated by an example. Appendix Table 1 shows how an inflation rate of 10% adds to the annual payments of a mortgage from an initial level of $3,490 (assuming zero inflation and therefore a 5% real rate of interest and a 5% *nominal* rate (including inflation at 0%) up to $7,685 per year. The example assumes furthermore that borrower income rises at the inflation rate plus 2%. It can be seen that the 10% inflation rate "tilts" real payments forward in time. Whereas initially the "annual mortgage payment to income ratio" was 13.96%, in a 10% inflationary world this rises to 30.74%, placing the household in a severe cash-flow squeeze initially. However, over time rising incomes reduce this burden to a mere 2.03% in year 25, compared with a burden of 8.70% in the absence of inflation.[8] Thus, inflation poses no long-run problem to the household but it does place the household in a short-run cash-flow problem. As we will see, alternative mortgage designs are intended to overcome this tilting characteristic of the standard level-payment mortgage under high rates of interest by having artificially lower initial-year payments which rise over time with the ability of the household to absorb such increases.

**APPENDIX TABLE 1**

**COMPARISON OF MORTGAGE PAYMENTS AND PAYMENT-TO-INCOME RATIOS UNDER ZERO AND 10% INFLATION UNDER LEVEL PAYMENT MORTGAGES (LPMs)**

(Calculations based upon a $50,000 mortgage, amortized over 25 years, assuming a 5% real rate of interest,* and initial borrower income of $25,000, assumed to increase at the rate of inflation plus 2%.)

| | Year | Annual Payment | Borrower Income | Annual Mortgage Payment to Income Ratio |
|---|---|---|---|---|
| *Zero Inflation:* | | | | |
| 5% Nominal Interest | 1 | 3,490 | 25,000 | 13.96 |
| 5% Real Interest | 5 | 3,490 | 27,061 | 12.90 |
| | 10 | 3,490 | 29,877 | 11.68 |
| | 15 | 3,490 | 32,987 | 10.58 |
| | 20 | 3,490 | 36,420 | 9.58 |
| | 25 | 3,490 | 40,211 | 8.70 |
| *10% Inflation:* | | | | |
| 15% Nominal Interest | 1 | 7,685 | 25,000 | 30.74 |
| 5% Real Interest | 5 | 7,685 | 39,338 | 19.54 |
| | 10 | 7,685 | 69,327 | 11.09 |
| | 15 | 7,685 | 122,178 | 6.29 |
| | 20 | 7,685 | 215,319 | 3.57 |
| | 25 | 7,685 | 379,466 | 2.03 |

* This example assumes that the expected rate of inflation equals the actual rate, and that the nominal rate of interest is the sum of the real rate of interest and the expected rate of inflation.

*Interest-rate Risk:* Interest-rate risk is the risk that interest rates will change in such a way as to adversely affect the borrower or lender. For example, we noted previously that lenders run the risk under prepayment options of having to take a significant cut in their interest returns should interest rates drop and borrowers prepay mortgages to take advantage of falling interest rates. In such circumstances lenders were faced with the prospect of having to continue to pay depositors at older and higher rates and then relend the repaid mortgage funds at lower current rates, thus incurring a loss. Conversely, borrowers who face mortgage renewals during periods of high and/or rising interest rates run the risk of having to significantly increase their expenditures on mortgage interest. For instance, under the assumptions of Table 1 we can see that a borrower who originally took out a mortgage in stable times when there was no inflation, yet who had to renew it five years later when it came due at 15% instead of its initial 5% mortgage rate, would find that the mortgage interest payment would more than double in the early years of the mortgage. Such a household would find itself facing potentially serious cash-flow problems.

In both cases, that of the lender and that of the borrower, the problem arose because neither was able to forecast interest rates effectively. Moreover, as the twenty-five to thirty-year term mortgage has been replaced by the five-year rollover mortgage, interest-rate risk has been thrown onto the borrower by the lender. This is so because the lender can match deposit interest rates against mortgage interest rates to ensure that a suitable spread or profit exists. However, the household has no way to make an analogous offset, so that if interest rates rose sharply at the time of a mortgage renewal, the household would have no choice but to pay the new higher rates. This transfer of interest-rate risk to the borrower has no doubt helped to make mortgages more abundant by making them more attractive to lenders, but it has had the undesirable social consequence of transferring the risk to households which may not be able to absorb it adequately.

## Some Commonly Proposed and Used Alternative Mortgage Designs

In view of the foregoing discussion, we can divide the discussion of alternative mortgage designs into those that deal with the tilt problem of the borrower, and those that deal with the interest rate risk faced both by borrowers and lenders.

*New Mortgage Designs to Overcome the Tilt Problem:* A wide range of alternatives has been proposed. We will focus below on three of the most commonly proposed: the graduated-payment mortgage (GPM); the price-level-adjusted mortgage (PLAM); and the shared-appreciation mortgage (SAM).

The *Graduated-Payment Mortgage* (GPM) is designed so that payments start well below the level dictated by prevailing levels of interest. Monthly payments that increase steadily over the life of the mortage in keeping with some prespecified graduation scheme so that the borrower eventually can pay back not only all of the principal but also the accumulated differences between the early payments under the GPM and those that would have been in effect under the standard level-payment mortgage (LPM). Appendix Table 2 sets out a comparison of the LPM payments and those under a GPM. An inflation rate of 10% is assumed with a 15% *nominal* interest rate (which equals as in Appendix Table 1 a 5% *real* rate of interest net of the inflation rate). Furthermore, the example assumes that household income is rising at the inflation rate plus 2% (in other words, household income is growing at a *real* rate, net of inflation, of 2% per year). We see that compared with the LPM the initial payments under the GPM

## APPENDIX TABLE 2
## COMPARISON OF MORTGAGE PAYMENTS AND PAYMENT-TO-INCOME RATIOS UNDER A LEVEL-PAYMENT MORTGAGE (LPM) AND GRADUATED-PAYMENT MORTGAGE (GPM)

(Calculations based upon a $50,000 mortgage, amortized over 25 years, assuming a 5% real rate of interest, a 10% inflation rate, and a 15% nominal mortgage rate; and initial borrower income of $25,000, assumed to increase at the rate of inflation of the previous year plus 2%).

| Year | Beginning Principal | Interest Amount | | Inflation Component* | Annual Payment | Ending Principal | Annual Mortgage Payment to Income Ratio (Current Dollars) |
|---|---|---|---|---|---|---|---|
| | | Real Component | | | | | |
| **Level-Payment Mortgage (LPM):** | | | | | | | |
| 1 | $50,000 | $ 7,465 | | $ 5,000 | $ 7,685 | $49,800 | 30.74 |
| 2 | 49,800 | 7,435 | | 5,400 | 7,685 | 49,550 | 27.45 |
| 3 | 49,550 | 7,385 | | 5,826 | 7,685 | 49,250 | 24.51 |
| 4 | 49,250 | 7,335 | | 6,275 | 7,685 | 48,900 | 21.88 |
| 5 | 48,900 | 7,285 | | 6,748 | 7,685 | 48,500 | 19.54 |
| 10 | 46,300 | 6,885 | | 9,364 | 7,685 | 45,500 | 11.09 |
| 15 | 40,900 | 6,085 | | 11,957 | 7,685 | 39,300 | 6.29 |
| 20 | 29,800 | 4,335 | | 12,406 | 7,685 | 26,450 | 3.57 |
| 25 | 6,900 | 785 | | 2,076 | 7,685 | 0 | 2.03 |
| **Graduated-Payment Mortgage (GPM):** | | | | | | | |
| 1 | $ 50,000 | $ 2,500 | | $ 5,000 | $ 3,490 | $ 54,010 | 13.96 |
| 2 | 54,010 | 2,700 | | 5,400 | 3,850 | 58,260 | 13.75 |
| 3 | 58,260 | 2,913 | | 5,826 | 4,247 | 62,752 | 13.54 |
| 4 | 62,752 | 3,138 | | 6,275 | 4,687 | 67,478 | 13.34 |
| 5 | 67,478 | 3,374 | | 6,748 | 5,173 | 72,427 | 13.15 |
| 10 | 93,636 | 4,682 | | 9,364 | 8,483 | 99,198 | 12.24 |
| 15 | 119,570 | 5,979 | | 11,957 | 14,119 | 123,387 | 11.56 |
| 20 | 124,059 | 6,203 | | 12,406 | 24,406 | 118,228 | 11.35 |
| 25 | 41,513 | 1,038 | | 2,076 | 42,076 | 0 | 11.21 |

NOTE: If the initial payment were based on the amount necessary to amortize a 25-year mortgage at a 3% interest rate (5% real rate minus 2% real increase in income), the annual mortgage payment to income ratio would remain constant over the 25-year term.

*Inflation component based on the actual rate equalling the expected rate of 10%.

constitute only 13.96% of household income versus 30.74% for the LPM. However, by year 25 the LPM burden on the household falls to only 2.03%, whereas that for the GPM has declined to only 11.21%. Similarly, where under the LPM annual mortgage payments are constant over the life of the mortage at $7,685, under the GPM they start low at only $3,490 but rise to $42,551 in the final year. Finally, under the LPM the mortage principal declines continually over the life of the mortgage, slowly at first, then more rapidly later on. In contrast the GPM shows principal rising steadily (reflecting the accumulated underpayments in the early years of the GPM), until in the last five years of the GPM the entire balance of $118,228 in year 20 must be completely repaid by year 25.

Thus, the GPM has the desired property of starting low and rising over time. However, it also subjects the household to significant uncertainty, since the ratio of payments to income remains almost constant under the assumption of a 2% real rate of income growth for the household. Should household income fail to grow at this rate, then the household can face financial difficulties. There is evidence that households do not like to face such potential financial hazards and that despite the pain of the initial payments of the LPM many households would prefer the pain coupled with the declining debt burden over time.[10]

The *Price-Level-Adjusted Mortgage* (PLAM) is the second frequently touted vehicle for overcoming the tilt problem. It has many characteristics in common with the GPM. Its principal difference from the GPM is that where the GPM rises based on some estimate of future inflation, the PLAM is adjusted each year based on the actual inflation rate of the previous year, so that the schedule of payments cannot be set in advance the way it could be under the GPM but rather must await each year's inflation rate before being adjusted. Appendix Table 3 compares the characteristics of the PLAM and the GPM, assuming that initial inflation is 10%, the initial mortgage rate in nominal terms is 15%, household income again increases at 2% per year in real terms, and that actual inflation is 10% in years 1 and 2, 15% in years 3 through 5, 3% in years 6 to 8.[11] Under both variants the borrower faces lower initial payments than would have prevailed under the LPM. However, under the GPM the burden of these payments can fluctuate markedly if inflation rates vary, whereas under the PLAM variant and the assumption of a 2% real rate of growth in household income, the debt burden falls continuously, if much more slowly than under the LPM. As with the GPM, the PLAM does impose a burden on the household which is relatively constant over time. Moreover, as with the GPM should household incomes fail to keep pace with inflation then the household does face the possibility of significant financial stress in future years, stress which the LPM does not impose in future years because its burden in real terms declines so rapidly (see Appendix Table 1).[12]

# APPENDIX TABLE 3
## COMPARISON OF MORTGAGE PAYMENTS AND PAYMENT-TO-INCOME RATIOS UNDER A GRADUATED-PAYMENT MORTGAGE (GPM) AND PRICE-LEVEL-ADJUSTED MORTGAGE (PLAM) WITH VARIABLE INFLATION

(Calculations based upon a $50,000 mortgage, amortized over 25 years, assuming a 5% real rate of interest, an expected inflation rate of 10% when the mortgages are contracted, an actual inflation rate of 10% for years 1 and 2, 15% for years 3 to 5 and 3% for years 6 to 8, and an initial nominal mortgage rate of 15%. Borrower income is initially $25,000 and assumed to increase at the rate of inflation of the previous year plus 2%.)

| Year | Inflation Rate | Beginning Principal | Interest Amount Real Component | Interest Amount Inflation Component | Annual Payment | Ending Principal | Borrower Income | Annual Mortgage Payment-to-Income Ratio (Current Dollars) |
|---|---|---|---|---|---|---|---|---|
| **Price-Level-Adjusted Mortgage (PLAM):** | | | | | | | | |
| 1 | 10 | $50,000 | $2,500 | $5,000 | $3,490 | $54,010 | $25,000 | 13.96% |
| 2 | 10 | 54,010 | 2,700 | 5,400 | 3,850 | 58,260 | 28,000 | 13.75 |
| 3 | 15 | 58,260 | 2,915 | 8,739 | 4,247 | 65,667 | 31,360 | 13.54 |
| 4 | 15 | 65,667 | 3,283 | 9,849 | 4,905 | 73,894 | 36,691 | 13.37 |
| 5 | 15 | 73,894 | 3,695 | 11,084 | 5,665 | 83,008 | 42,929 | 13.20 |
| 6 | 3 | 83,008 | 4,150 | 2,490 | 6,546 | 83,102 | 50,227 | 13.03 |
| 7 | 3 | 83,102 | 4,155 | 2,493 | 6,756 | 83,210 | 52,738 | 12.81 |
| 8 | 3 | 83,210 | 4,161 | 2,496 | 6,993 | 82,884 | 55,375 | 12.63 |
| 9 | 3 | 82,884 | 4,144 | 2,487 | 7,221 | 82,294 | 58,144 | 12.41 |
| **Graduated-Payment Mortgage (GPM):** | | | | | | | | |
| 1 | 10 | $50,000 | $2,500 | $5,000 | $3,490 | $54,010 | $25,000 | 13.96% |
| 2 | 10 | 54,010 | 2,700 | 5,400 | 3,850 | 58,260 | 28,000 | 13.75 |
| 3 | 15 | 58,260 | 2,913 | 5,826 | 4,247 | 62,752 | 31,360 | 13.54 |
| 4 | 15 | 62,752 | 3,138 | 6,275 | 4,687 | 67,478 | 36,691 | 12.77 |
| 5 | 15 | 67,478 | 3,374 | 6,748 | 5,173 | 72,427 | 42,929 | 12.05 |
| 6 | 3 | 72,427 | 3,621 | 7,243 | 5,712 | 77,579 | 50,227 | 11.37 |
| 7 | 3 | 77,579 | 3,879 | 7,758 | 6,307 | 82,909 | 52,738 | 11.96 |
| 8 | 3 | 82,909 | 4,145 | 8,290 | 6,967 | 88,378 | 55,375 | 12.58 |
| 9 | 3 | 88,378 | 4,419 | 8,838 | 7,699 | 93,636 | 58,144 | 13.24 |

NOTE: PLAM mortgage payment-to-income ratio approximately equals GPM ratio when actual inflation equals expected inflation.

The *Shared Appreciation Mortgage* (SAM) is the final variant we look at here. The SAM seeks to provide lower initial monthly payments through sharing the appreciation in the value of the house with the lender. In return for some of this increase in equity value of the house, the lender provides a lower mortgage interest rate. Appendix Table 4 sets out the breakeven points for lenders.[13] This table shows the discount in the interest rate down the left-hand column, while across the top of the table appear the various levels of equity participation (sharing of capital gain) available to the lender. The entries in the table show the required rate of growth in capital (that is, the appreciation in house value) for the lender to break even and exactly make up for the discount. The example assumes a 15% mortgage rate in effect plus 80% loan-to-value ratio, five-year mortgage term, and a twenty-five-year amortization period. The table shows that for the lender to give a 25% discount in the mortgage (that is to cut the rate to 11.25% from 15%), assuming that the homeowner will only give up a 25% interest in the capital gain, then the house must appreciate by 12.7% per year for the lender to make back the value of the discount. It can be seen that for higher discounts the borrower must either be willing to give up larger portions of equity or else the lender must be able to count on higher rates of appreciation.

**APPENDIX TABLE 4**

**BREAK EVEN ANNUAL GROWTH RATES: SAM EXAMPLE**

| Interest Rate Discount* | Equity Participation | | | | |
|---|---|---|---|---|---|
| | 10% | 20% | 25% | 33% | 40% |
| 10% | 12.7% | 7.1% | 5.8% | 4.5% | 3.8% |
| 20 | 21.4 | 12.7 | 10.6 | 8.3 | 7.1 |
| 25 | 25.0 | 15.2 | 12.7 | 10.1 | 8.6 |
| 33 | 30.2 | 18.8 | 15.9 | 12.7 | 11.0 |
| 40 | 33.7 | 21.4 | 18.2 | 14.7 | 12.7 |

\* Mortgage with 15% market interest rate (compounded semi-annually), 80% loan-to value ratio, 5 year term, 30 year amortization period.

Summing up the foregoing alternatives, it is clear that each involves trade-offs for the borrower. In the case of the GPM and the PLAM, the borrower must willingly accept added risk that incomes will keep pace with growing mortgage payments. In the SAM the trade-off is direct and involves trading off capital gains for lower interest. Under all three variants, and any other similar attempts to overcome the tilt, lending institutions must also be able to create new deposits to match these innovative mortgages. Since financial institutions want to match the characteristics of their assets (mortgages in this case) with those of their liabilities (deposits of various forms), if a new mortgage design is to be marketed, so must a corresponding new deposit vehicle. Thus, to match the GPM there would have to be a graduated-payment deposit (GPD) instrument of some kind. Similarly, the PLAM would necessitate some sort of price-level- adjusted deposit (PLAD). Finally, the SAM would require a deposit backed in part by the appreciation of the houses financed under SAM's. Experience has shown that such innovative deposits are attractive to the public,[14] but marketing such innovations is always risky, and financial institutions have been reluctant to venture very far afield here. There is also a taxation problem since these new deposit forms would need special tax treatment to make them attractive. Principally, they would require that their increasing values would only be taxed upon realization of the increase through the sale or conclusion of the term of the instrument and that taxes would not be levied on the annual accrual of value. Despite these technical difficulties, which are all surmountable should the public strongly demand such innovative mortgages and deposits, these innovations have much to commend them. There is evidence, as noted, that the public is reluctant to make the trade-offs required for the new mortgages, though the new deposits would appear to be very attractive, but financial institution conservatism and tax treatment have slowed the issuing of such innovative deposits. The only widely implemented scheme in Canada to date has been the graduated-payment mortgage which came about initially under the terms of the Assisted Home Ownership Program (AHOP), to which we briefly turn as an example of some of the difficulties that attend alternative mortgage designs which are aimed initially at making housing more accessible.

THE ASSISTED HOME OWNERSHIP PROGRAM: ANOTHER APPROACH TO MORTGAGE FINANCE UNDER INFLATION

We can now assess the Assisted Home Ownership Program (AHOP) and its recent successor, the Graduated-Payment Mortgage (GPM) programme. AHOP was a variant of the graduated-payment mortgage, wherein AHOP purchasers were guaranteed low initial monthly payments and subsidized mortgage interest rates for the first five years of their AHOP mortgage. The subsidy was then added to the principal and had to be repaid gradually. With a forty-year amortization period, principal repayments were very modest in the first five years, which, coupled with subsidized mortgage interest rates, enabled households to purchase considerably more housing than they would have been able to under a twenty-five-year amortization period with full market interest rates.

But the cost of AHOP proved to be excessive: the grant provisions were difficult to forecast and were politically difficult to cancel. In addition, AHOP coincided closely in time with the creation of the Anti-Inflation Board, which put a major damper on wage increases, making it difficult for households to meet the rising payments. It also coincided with the peaking of housing prices, so that many households found themselves in possession of a housing unit which was not increasing in value, with incomes that were not increasing at their expected pace, and with monthly payments that were due to increase. Lenders' fears were substantiated by the dramatic increase which occurred in defaults. Many borrowers just walked away from their AHOP units, motivated apparently by rising costs of maintaining a non-increasing asset (the housing unit) on a non-increasing or only modestly increasing income, a circumstance not anticipated by policymakers at the outset. The burden on household incomes rose, and because there were no increases in the value of the housing unit there was little incentive to maintain mortgage payments (particularly since some households had invested as little as $500 down in cash with forty-year amortization periods).

In response to the growing cost of AHOP subsidies and the rising number of defaults and foreclosures, AHOP has been discontinued (although it continues on units already built under the scheme).[15] Its place has been taken by the graduated-payment mortgage programme, which operates in the same way as the one set out in Appendix Table 3. The advantages of the GPM are that it not only allows borrowers to make relatively low initial payments, but it also relieves the government of having to subsidize mortgages for unknown periods and unknown amounts. With the full insurance of the GPM's, the risk to the lender is kept to a minimum. Thus, both the borrowers' and lenders' interests are protected, with CMHC absorbing some of the costs of protection through the GPM mortgage insurance programme.

*Innovations to Overcome Interest-Rate Risk:* We earlier explored the principal innovation here, and that was the shortening of the mortgage term from twenty-five or even forty years down to five years, which began in 1969 with the changes in the Canada Interest Act and corresponding changes in NHA lending practices. As discussed previously, the five-year term allowed lenders to issue five-year deposits and thus match the terms of their assets (the five-year mortgage) with that of their liabilities (the five-year deposit). While this did relieve the lender of interest-rate risk it unfortunately placed the risk squarely on the shoulders of the borrower.

The five-year rollover mortgage has evolved during the past several years to three-, two-, one- and even half-year rollover periods. The ultimate mortgage design in this vein is obviously a mortgage that has interest rates varying continuously over its term as other interest rates (usually the prime rate charged to the very best private borrowers like large corporations) vary. This is the *Variable Rate Mortgage* (VRM), which provides borrowers with somewhat lower rates (perhaps ½ to ¾% lower) in exchange for the borrower absorbing all of the interest-rate risk. The VRM is therefore the logical extension of the idea set in motion in 1969 with the introduction of the five-year rollover mortgage.

Unfortunately, the evolution of the borrower as the absorber of interest-rate risk has not been very desirable. During the periods of rapidly rising and high interest rates that prevailed during the 1980-82 period in particular, households that had to renew their mortgages often faced staggering increases in mortgage rates. At the worst period, in the summer of 1981, households were renewing mortgages which had been in the 10-11% range at interest rates in excess of 22%.

Clearly, this was unacceptable, and a better method of handling interest-rate risk needs to be found than merely pushing it onto the borrower. Fortunately, there is the possibility of using other financial markets where interest-rate risk is routinely traded by speculators to "lay off" this risk onto those who seek to profit from it.[16] The Chicago Board of Trade already has several markets in interest-rate futures where speculators willingly absorb interest-rate risk in the expectation that they will guess correctly about the future course of interest rates and profit handsomely from it.

The Toronto Stock Exchange provides similar vehicles. The key here is that these existing financial markets can be used to transfer risk from those who do not want to bear it (lenders and households in the present mortgage market context) to those who seek to profit from bearing these risks. The existence of these financial markets, of suitable financial instruments, and of interest-risk bearing speculators opens up the possibility of developing a mortgage renewal insurance scheme whereby for nominal insurance fees paid at the outset by the borrower, the household is protected against large adverse movements in interest rates. The insuror merely lays off this risk in the appropriate financial market. Preliminary work done for the Canada Mortgage and Housing Corporation shows that premiums of 1% on a five-year mortgage will protect the household against any adverse movement.[17] The possiblity of such mortgage renewal insurance is perhaps the most exciting of all of the innovations discussed here, since it is one that both lenders and borrowers profit from and at very modest costs once the scheme is launched. While not a mortgage design *per se*, mortgage renewal insurance does hold the promise of removing from borrowers the enormous interest rate risks that they have had to bear in progressively greater amounts as mortgage terms have shortened.

CONCLUSIONS

New mortgage designs have been sought to overcome the tilt problem and the bearing of interest-rate risk. Unfortunately, as mortgage instruments have evolved to shorter and shorter terms interest-rate risk has been lessened for lenders but maximized for borrower households. Mortgage renewal insurance can remove the burden of interest-rate risk from households and place it on speculators who are willing to bear it. Therefore, it would appear that we can solve both the tilt problem and the interest-rate risk problem by combining some of the tilt designs with mortgage renewal insurance. More importantly, for those households who prefer to grapple with high initial payments under the LPM, the potential existence of mortgage renewal insurance protects them against adverse movements in interest rates, thus insuring that their debt burden will continue to decline over the life of the LPM without fear of dramatic increases in monthly payments such as those experienced during the 1980-82 period by renewing households.

# Notes to Appendix I

1. L. B. Smith, *Anatomy of a Crisis*, makes this point strongly.
2. *C.M.H.C. Annual Housing Statistics*, (Ottawa: CMHC, 1979), p. 64. They grew from $3,264 million in 1969 to $26,814 million in 1980.
3. Again, see Smith, *Anatomy of a Crisis* for further discussion on this point.
4. See *C.M.H.C. Annual Housing Statistics* for various years for summaries of changes in the National Housing Act.
5. A great deal has been written on so-called *alternative mortgage instruments* to which the interested reader is directed. See: *New Mortgage Designs for Stable Housing in an Inflationary Environment*, F. Modigliani and D. Lessard, editors (Boston: Federal Reserve Bank of Boston, 1975); and *Housing Affordability and Mortgage Terms in an Inflationary Environment*, J. P. Herzog (Burnaby: Simon Fraser University, 1978); George W. Gau, "An Examination of Alternatives to the Rollover Mortgage," (Ottawa: CMHC, 1981), mimeographed. In addition to the rather technical pieces, the *Financial Post* (Toronto) runs articles periodically explaining things in simpler terms.
6. This is precisely what has happened to many AHOP borrowers. See "The Housing Dilemma: Who Pays and How Much," Mark Ricketts, Vancouver: Fraser Institute, unpublished.
7. For an excellent discussion of the tilt problem, see J. L. Carr and L. B. Smith, "Inflation, Uncertainty and Future Mortgage Instruments," in G. W. Gau and M. A. Goldberg, editors, *The Future of North American Housing Markets* (Cambridge, Mass.: Ballinger Publishers, 1982), pp. 203-231.
8. The example in Apendix Table 1 is taken from Carr and Smith, "Inflation," Table 10-2, p. 211.
9. Appendix Table 2 is taken from Carr and Smith, "Inflation," Table 10-2, p. 211.
10. This finding came out rather strongly in survey work carried out in the United States in the mid-1970's. See Kent W. Colton *et al.*, "The National Borrower Study" Cambridge, Mass.: The Joint Center for Urban Studies of M.I.T. and Harvard University, mimeographed, 1978.
11. Taken from Carr and Smith, "Inflation," Table 10-3, p. 220.
12. This is a very real problem facing the PLAM and the GPM. See Michael A. Goldberg, "Price Level Adjusted Mortgages: The Concept, Extant Experience, Evaluation Criteria and Some Interim Conclusions about its Utility in Canada," a paper presented to a CMHC Symposium on "Mortgage Instruments for the 1980's" held in Ottawa, Ontario, January 13-15, 1982.
13. The table is taken from George W. Gau, "An Examination of Alternatives," p. 46.
14. See Goldberg, "Price Level Adjusted Mortgages," pp. 13-15.
15. See Ricketts, "The Housing Problem," for a detailed discussion of AHOP and its problems.
16. A successful financial innovation has been the development of futures markets in mortgages allowing yet another means for dealing with uncertainty and interest risk. See George W. Gau and Michael A. Goldberg, "Interest Rate Risk and Residential Mortgages: Efficient Allocation of Risk through Financial Futures Markets," mimeographed, (Vancouver, B.C.: Faculty of Commerce, University of British Columbia, 1982).
17. For detail on the mortgage insurance idea and a complete discussion of interest rate risk, see: George W. Gau and Dennis R. Capozza, "Mortgage Rate Insurance: Overview, Risk Management, and Pricing," a report done for Canada Mortgage and Housing Corporation (Ottawa, CMHC), July 1982.

# Appendix II
# Annotated Bibliography

*A. BOOKS*

Aaron, Henry J. *Shelter and Subsidies. Who Benefits from Federal Housing Policies?* Washington, D.C: The Brookings Institution, 1972.
Aaron examines the current Federal Housing Policies in the United States, with particular reference to the Housing and Urban Development Act of 1968. It is an in-depth study which is probably of more interest to the specialist than to the general reader.

All Sector National Housing Conference. *Housing in Canada: A Continuing Challenge.* Don Mills, Ontario: The Canadian Real Estate Association, 1982.
The members of this conference discuss a wide range of issues related to housing, including government aid in housing for the disadvantaged and the elderly; the implications of fiscal and monetary policies of the federal government; co-operative housing; advantages of rental housing; and rent control. Also deals with the role of developers, energy and design efficiency of houses, and housing adequacy.

Beid, R. M., and Slack, N. E. *Residential Property Tax Relief in Ontario.* Toronto: University of Toronto Press, 1978.
This book looks at the role, incidence, and effectiveness of the property tax system in Ontario. It concludes that property tax may not be as regressive as the traditional view has assumed, and that property taxes might not be much different in the absence of relief measures.

Bellush, Jewel, and Hausknecht, Murray, eds. *Urban Renewal: People, Politics and Planning.* Garden City, New York: Anchor Books, Doubleday and Company, 1967.
This collection of essays deals with the problem of poverty and urban renewal, constitutional issues and the political processes involved in urban renewal, the problems of relocation, and the progress of renewal. It also deals with some new ideas and innovations in this area. It provides a good overview of these problems as they occur in the United States.

Bourne, Larry S., and Hitchcock, John R., ed. *Urban Housing Markets, Recent Directions in Research and Policy.* Proceedings of a Conference held at the

University of Toronto, October 27-28, 1977. Toronto: University of Toronto Press, 1978.
The delegates and contributors to this conference made up an interdisciplinary forum: they come from different academic disciplines, from the private sector, and from all three levels of government. The papers include discussions of the following: alternate concepts and definitions of urban housing markets; the diversity of local housing markets, and the gaps between research and policy formulation; the recent land and housing price boom; the aggregate housing supply and the dynamics of price changes; filtering; developer behaviour; and the social implications of housing policies. It includes an edited transcript of the plenary discussion.

Clayton, Frank. *Search for Shelter: Economics of Housing.* Toronto: Canadian Federation for Economic Education, 1981.

Crowley, Ronald W., and Gertler, Leonard O. *Changing Canadian Cities: The Next 25 Years.* Toronto: McClelland & Stewart, 1977.
Diversified examination of Canadian cities, including chapters on demographic perspectives; urban patterns and environment; the human condition in the cities with notes on the city as a moral issue, and the city in literature; and ideas on policies and strategies for the future.

Cullingworth, J. B. *Canadian Housing Policy Research: Some Initial Impressions.* Toronto: University of Toronto Press, 1980.

——————. *Essays on Housing Policy: The British Scene.* London: George Allen and Unwin, 1979.
The set of essays focuses on the "practical and political difficulties of devising measures which meet policy objectives, and the conflicts which arise in pursuing them." Several issues are discussed in light of the "institutional, historical and financial framework within which housing policy is formulated and operated."

Economics Department, U.S. League of Savings Associations. *Homeownership: Coping With Inflation.* Chicago: Economics Department, U.S. League of Savings Association, 1980.
This study deals with how inflation has altered and affected the nature of homeownership. It considers first-time and repeat buyers, and buyers by city and region. It concludes with a summary of the implications of these findings for housing policy.

Dennis, Michael, and Fish, Susan. *Programs in Search of a Policy: Low Income Housing in Canada.* Toronto: Hakkert, 1972.

This report was "commissioned to provide background material for revisions of the National Housing Act in 1972 and for a possible rewriting of legislation in 1973." It is critical of all past and present housing policies and recommends that there be a guaranteed annual income, with a shelter allowance instituted as an interim measure. It is both thoughtful and comprehensive, and is of of value to anyone who wishes to gain a general understanding of housing problems in Canada.

Fallis, George. *Housing Programs and Income Distribution in Ontario.* Toronto: University of Toronto Press, 1980.
This book deals with the effects of housing rental and ownership programmes, including the residual lending programme, the Home Ownership Made Easy plan, and AHOP, as well as provisions of the income tax laws dealing with housing. Comparisons are made between ownership and rental costs as they affect incomes.

Frazer, Debra. *Credit, A Mortgage for Life: A Review of Consumer Debt and Credit in Canada and the Impact of Increasing Shelter Costs on the Nature of Debt.* Ottawa: Canadian Council on Social Development, 1981.

Frieden, Bernard J., and Morris, Robert, ed. *Urban Planning and Social Policy.* New York: Basic Books, 1968.
This comprehensive collection of essays, which relates both to urban planning and to social policy, aims to create a better understanding of the problems facing American cities today.

Gans, Herbert J. *People and Plans.* New York: Basic Books, 1968.
This thoughtful and well-written exploration of urban problems in the United States emphasizes the problems of poverty and race. It favours the elimination of poverty as the best way to begin solving America's current urban problems.

Gau, George W., and Michael A. Goldberg, ed. *The Future of North American Housing Markets.* Cambridge, Mass.: Ballinger Publishers, 1982.
These conference papers explore demand, supply, mortgage financing, and housing policy issues that are likely to affect housing into the next century. Papers dealing with common problems in the U.S. and Canada are paired, allowing useful comparisons to be made between the future housing markets in the two countries. While generalty of an academic nature these papers are accessible to interested readers.

Genstar Homes. *Observations on Housing and Land Development.* Montreal: The Company, 1978.

Goldberg, Michael A., ed. *Recent Perspectives in Urban Land Economics: Essays in Honour of Richard U. Ratcliffe and Paul F. Wendt*. Vancouver: Urban Land Economics Division, Faculty of Commerce and Business Administration, University of British Columbia, 1976.

This collection of seventeen papers by nineteen authors deals with the economic issues relating to urban land, housing, Canadian and American mortgage markets, real estate and education, and finance and valuation.

Grigsby, William G., and Rosenburg, Louis. *Urban Housing Policy*. New York: APS Publications, 1975.

With specific reference to the city of Baltimore, an analysis is given of housing and the poor in the U.S. The conclusions include the suggestion that because individual cities are so different, national programmes cannot solve all the housing problems; more local programmes are needed. The text is readable but contains some quite technical discussions.

Grigsby, William G; White, Sammis B.; Levine, Daniel U.; Kelly, Regina M.; Perelman, Marsha Reines; Claflen, George L. *Re-thinking Housing and Community Development Policy*. Philadelphia: The University of Pennsylvania, Department of City and Regional Planning, 1977.

This book presents an examination of contemporary housing problems and policies in the United States. The emphasis is on the dimensions of the problem, the connection between housing problems and community development and the question of policy at all levels of government. Readable, topical, and critical of current legislation in the housing field and of American urban policy in general.

Grimes, Orville F., Jr. *Housing for Low Income Urban Families*. Economics and Policy in the Developing World. Baltimore: The World Bank for The Johns Hopkins University Press, 1976.

This is an introduction to, and overview of, current housing problems all over the world. The major emphasis is on the problem of housing for the poor. It avoids sentimentalization and the rhetoric which often accompanies this topic and includes a statistical Appendix with twenty-two tables.

Hayek, F. A.; Friedman, Milton; Stigler, George J.; de Jouvenel, Bertrand; Paish, F. W.; Pennance, F. G.; Olsen, E. O.: Rydenfelt, Sven; Walker, M. A. *Rent Control: A Popular Paradox. Evidence on the Economic Effects of Rent Control*. Vancouver: The Fraser Institute, 1975.

This collection of essays by different authors on a number of aspects of rent control includes examples of rent control experimentation in various countries. The essays are all based on the thesis that rent controls should be abandoned. The book is extremely readable, for the most part, but one-sided.

Heung, Raymond. *The Do's and Don'ts of Housing Policy: The Case of British Columbia*. Vancouver: The Fraser Institute, 1976.
This volume explores the conduct of housing policy in B.C. with particular reference to rent control and public provision of housing by the Province of British Columbia. The study criticizes the bases for such policies and suggests instead that consideration be given to a system of housing allowances directly to needy households, which would be economically more efficient than rent controls and production subsidies.

Kesselman, Jonathan R. *Self-Financing Policies for Mortgage Interest, Relief in Inflationary Periods*. Vancouver: University of British Columbia, Department of Economics, 1978.

Lorimer, James, and Ross, Evelyn. *The City Book. The Politics and Planning of Canada's Cities*. Toronto: James Lorimer and Company, 1976.
This is a "from the roots up" collection of essays which were popular in the '60's, but which are now hard to find. It includes discussions of land ownership, citizen and city politics in various Canadian urban centres, the role of experts in policy making and implementation, critical evaluations of particular architects and planners and of the Canadian planning profession. It also includes case studies of three urban development projects, and a section on policy issues and analysis.

McClain, Janet, ed. *Is Government Homeownership Assistance The Way To Go?* Ottawa: Canadian Council on Social Development, 1981.
Proceedings of a symposium on homeownership assistance held in Calgary in the fall of 1981. Deals with various issues, such as the role of federal and provincial governments in housing assistance, the effects of homeownership assistance programmes, housing supply strategies, and the reaction of the lending community to alternate mortgage instruments. Concludes that government intervention should be limited to special cases, such as aiding first-time buyers, elderly homeowners, and rural homeowners.

Markusen, J. R., and Scheffman, D. T. *Speculation and Monopoly in Urban Development: Analytical Foundations with Evidence for Toronto*. Toronto: Published for the Ontario Economic Council by University of Toronto Press, 1977.
This is a presentation of a "theoretical analysis of the land development process, the change in land prices, and the effects of speculation, monopoly elements and public policy on land developments," with specific references to the Toronto land market. It is quite technical, and mainly of interest to specialists.

Michelson, William. *Man and His Urban Environment. A Sociological Approach*. Reading, Mass.: Addison-Wesley, 1976.

This sociological overview of modern urban problems includes those occasioned by lifestyles, age, class, values and various pathologies. It emphasizes the connection in any given study between the researcher's perspective and the conclusions, and advocates a more interdisciplinary approach to the planning of urban environments.

Modigliani Franco, and Lessard, Donald, eds. *New Mortgage Designs for Stable Housing in an Inflationary Environment*. Proceedings of a Conference held at Cambridge, Massachusetts, January, 1975, sponsored by The Federal Reserve Bank of Boston, U.S. Department of Housing and Urban Development, and the U.S. Federal Home Loan Bank Board. Boston: Federal Reserve Bank of Boston, 1975.

The forward of this book states that "continuing developments in both the monetary and housing fronts bear out the importance of finding ways to alleviate the impact of inflation on housing." This is a collection of papers examining various mortgage instruments used all over the world, and some exploration into alternatives.

Poapst, J. V. *Developing the Residential Mortgage Market*. Volumes 1, 2, 3. A Report Prepared for Central Mortgage and Housing Corporation, 1973.

These three volumes were prepared for the Special Project Team on New Financing Mechanisms and Institutions which was formed by CMHC in 1970 in order to explore means for increasing the access of private investors to housing finance. Three suggested innovations in the residential mortgage market are examined here: a residential mortgage market, mortgage investment companies, and variable term mortgages.

Ricketts, Mark. "Subsidies in Search of a Solution," Chapter 4 of an unpublished manuscript on Canadian Housing policy; Vancouver.

This is an in-depth examination and evaluation of the Assisted Home Ownership Programme (AHOP), which concludes that the built-in defects of the programme render it ultimately ineffective, at best, or an addition to the general housing problem, at worst. It is thoughtful, thorough, well written, and of interest to the specialist and lay person alike.

Smith, Lawrence B. *Anatomy of a Crisis. Canadian Housing Policy in the Seventies*. Vancouver: The Fraser Institute, 1977.

This monograph is written for the general educated public and is easy to read. It examines the Federal Housing Policy from 1935 to the present, and also comments on provincial programmes in Ontario. Smith is critical of the shift that housing policy underwent during the '70's.

_____. *The Postwar Canadian Housing and Residential Mortgage Markets and the Role of Government*. Toronto: University of Toronto Press, 1974.
This is an examination of the Canadian housing mortgage markets from a technical and academic perspective. This specialist's book includes tables, figures and graphs.

Smith, Lawrence B., and Walker, Michael, ed. *Public Property, The Habitat Debate Continued*. Vancouver: The Fraser Institute, 1977.
This compendium of articles deals with various suggestions for controlling urban development and also with the implications of those suggestions. The issues of concern here arose from the Habitat Conference which was held May 31 - June 11, 1976, in Vancouver. Some of the subjects include the price of land; government intervention; demand and supply; monopoly; the urban land market; and public landownership.

Solomon, Arthur, P. *Housing the Urban Poor. A Critical Evaluation of Federal Housing Policy*. Cambridge, Mass.: The MIT Press, 1974.
Contemporary problems associated with housing the U.S. urban poor are dealt with here. Particular attention is paid to various alternate strategies for housing the poor. Solomon also sets forth suggestions for a new national housing policy.

_____, ed. *The Prospective City: Economic, Population, Energy and Environ-Developments*. Cambridge, Mass.: The MIT Press, 1980.
Essays by some of the foremost American researchers on urban issues. The volume is divided into five major sections: "City and Suburbs — Past, Present and Future"; "The Intrametropolitan Location of People and Jobs"; "Prospects for Renewing Our Central Cities"; "Transforming Our Post-Industrial Suburbs"; and "Shaping the Metropolis — The Role of Public Policy."

Struyk, Raymond J., and Bendick, Marc, Jr., eds. *Housing Vouchers for the Poor: Lessons from a National Experiment*. Washington, D.C.: The Urban Institute 1981.
This volume explores the effectiveness of the $160 million U.S. Experimental Housing Allowance Program (EHAP). The discussion ranges from the structure of the programme to its impacts on households, neighbourhoods, and the administrative institutions charged with implementing and carrying out the experiments. EHAP has enormously expanded our knowledge of housing market operations in general and housing assistance programmes specifically.

Tucillo, John A., and Villani, Kevin E., editors. *House Prices and Inflation*. Washington, D.C.: The Urban Institute, 1981.
This collection of essays results from a conference sponsored by the U.S.

Department of Housing and Urban Development (HUD) to look into rising house prices and housing affordability. While finding that there was no general affordability problem, it was agreed that inflation and special tax treatment tend to make homeownership attractive, thus increasing demand and raising prices, and that the measurement of house price increases is poor at best and unduly influences the Consumer Price Index.

Urban Land Economics Division, Faculty of Commerce and Business Administration, University of British Columbia. *Housing: It's Your Move*. Volume I and II.
An examination of the current housing problems in British Columbia. Volume I, written for the general reader, deals with the issues. Volume II is a collection of technical reports which are likely to be of primary interest to the specialist.

Weicher, John C. *Urban Renewal. National Program for Local Problems*. Washington, D.C.: American Enterprise Institute for Public Policy Research, 1972.
Accessible to the layperson, this book includes discussions of the legislative development of urban renewal, of the way in which a typical urban development project is carried out, of the economic efficiency of urban renewal, of the effect of urban renewal on various groups of citizens, and of residential and nonresidential renewal programmes.

Weicher, John C., Villani, Kevin E. and Roistacher, Elizabeth A., eds. *Rental Housing: Is There a Crisis?* Washington, D.C.: The Urban Institute, 1981.
This collection results from a HUD conference held to explore the nature of the decline in rental housing construction and the increasing conversion of many rental units to condominium tenure. Primary suggestions to improve the rental stock related to changing subsidies which favour homeownership and discouraging rent controls at the local level.

## B. ARTICLES, MONOGRAPHS AND REPORTS

Achour, Dominique. "Evolution of Housing Policy." *Urban Forum* 4, no. 3: 18.

Arnott, Richard, with the assistance of Nigel Johnston. *Rent Control Options for Decontrol in Ontario*. Toronto: Ontario Economic Council, Policy Study Series, 1981.
This monograph explores the various options open to the Province of Ontario to decontrol rents which were controlled in December 1975. After analysing rent

control in Ontario and the large literature on rent control from other cities and jurisdictions, the study moves on to suggest a decontrol strategy for Ontario. Essentially, the strategy builds on the present system but over a five-year period sets out a mechanism for allowing larger rent increases until in year five rents should be at market at which time rent control should be abandoned.

Blumenfeld, Hans. *On Prices of Residential Lots and Houses: A Critical Evaluation of the Data and Conclusions of the "Greenspan Report".* Toronto: Dept. of Urban and Regional Planning and Design, 1980.

Bourne, Larry S. "Choose Your Villain — Five Ways to Oversimplify the Price of Housing and Urban Land." *Urban Forum* 3, no. 1: 16-24.

Canadian Mortgage and Housing Corporation. *Background Document on Social Housing.* Ottawa: CMHC, 1981.
Prepared for the All Sector Housing Conference, this paper presents some options for resolving social housing problems. Four types of housing aid, all of which are used in Canada, are discussed, and their advantages and disadvantages are brought out. Options discussed are: support and stimulation of housing production, general income redistribution, housing allowances, and direct provisions of housing through social housing programmes.

_____. *A Medium-Density Housing Study.* Study conducted by the Architecture and Planning Staff of the Professional Standards and Technology Sector of CMHC. Ottawa: CMHC, 1977.

Clayton, Frank A., and Lampert, Greg. "Homebuilders Suffer High Interest Rates." *Canadian Business Review* 7 (Summer 1980): 7-9.

Collins, Diana. "A View from the Other Side — Citizens Participate in Planning Urban Housing." *Urban Forum* 3, No. 5: 14.
Looks at rising citizen participation in planning neighbourhoods, focusing on the problems and benefits of participation in achieving social goals. Concludes that participation is beneficial, but that it is encumbent upon both citizens and administrators to support policies that strike a balance between community and local interests.

Doepner, Gerd M. "Shelter Cost to Income Ratios: Affordability Problems and Housing Need in Canada's CMAS." (Draft 1). Ottawa: Central Mortgage and Housing Corporation, October 27, 1978.
Presented here is the Canadian input to a joint study on shelter-to- income ratios, undertaken by the U.S. Department of Housing and Urban Development (HUD)

and CMHC. It includes a descriptive analysis of all households affected by higher than average shelter-to-income ratios, and also a housing needs analysis which focuses on a normative approach to the problem and provides a priority statement for housing policy purposes.

*Down to Earth*, 2 vols. Report of the Federal-Provincial Task Force on the Supply and Price of Serviced Residential Land, April, 1978.
This report, prepared for the Canadian government and the governments of eight provinces and of the Northwest Territories, examines the reasons why land and housing prices rose so dramatically during the early 1970's. Volume 1 is limited to "findings and conclusions, and avoids recommendations," and is accessible to the layperson.

Eldred, Gary, and Zerbst, Robert H. "Improving Multiple Regression Valuation Models Using Location and Housing Quality Variables." Reprinted from *Assessors Journal* 12, no. 1, by Urban Land Economics, Faculty of Commerce and Business Administration, University of British Columbia, Vancouver.
This is a discussion of techniques for identifying the factors which affect house prices, with the emphasis on location (neighbourhood) factors. It is typical of a large body of literature which approaches house prices by breaking it into various components such as location, size of lot, number of rooms, or the existence or nonexistence of a fireplace.

Frazer, Debra. *Who Benefits from Tax Shelters?: A Background Paper on the Development and Use of Tax Deferral and Tax Exemption Measures for Housing and Residential Building in Canada*. Ottawa: Canadian Council on Social Development, 1979.

Frieden, Bernard J., and Solomon, Arthur P., "The Controversy over Homeownership Affordability." *AREUEA Journal* 5, no. 3: 355-360.
This paper argues strongly for the possible emergence of a housing affordability crisis. It is at considerable odds with the Weicher papers described here.

Frieser, George. "Housing Market Squeeze: The Preservation of the Canadian Economic System, Based on Private Enterprise, Will Enable Canadians to Remain Amongst the Best Housed People in the World." *Canadian Business Review* 7 (winter 1980): 28-30.

George, Peter M. "The Housing Issue in the Greater Vancouver Regional District." Planning Department, GVRD, Vancouver, May 4, 1973.
These are notes toward an elucidation of housing needs, both physical and social, in the Vancouver area. They arose from the GVRD's concern to define

and explore the characteristics which constitute a "liveable region" that would manifest itself in the Vancouver Regional District.

Heinberg, John D. "Integrated Analysis of Housing Allowances: Synthesizing of a Complex Research Program." The Urban Institute, Washington, D.C., prepared for presentation at the Ninetieth Annual Meeting of the American Economic Association on December 30,1977.
Findings are presented here about the housing allowance concept. The conclusions are based on the U.S. Experimental Housing Allowance Program.

Herzog, John P. "Housing Affordability and Mortgage Terms in an Inflationary Environment." Department of Economics and Commerce, Simon Fraser University, Burnaby, B.C., 1978.
This is a fairly technical review of various mortgage instruments and their ability to make housing more affordable.

"Housing Indicators." Program and Market Requirements Division, National Office, Central Mortgage and Housing Corporation, May, 1977.
This volume comprises twenty-two pages of graphs and tables concerning various aspects of housing in Canada, gleaned mostly from Statistics Canada and CMHC surveys.

"Housing in the Seventies." Report of the National Housing Policy Review. U.S. Department of Housing and Urban Development, Washington, 1974.
This commissioned report formed the basis for the housing policy recommendations included in President Nixon's message to the American Congress, September 1973. It deals with the history of Federal intervention in the housing market, housing programmes, production, technology and finance. It is both detailed and comprehensive.

"Housing Requirements Model: Projections to 2000." Program and Market Requirements Division, Central Mortgage and Housing Corporation, March, 1978.
Contained here are the technical details and findings of the project that inspired this paper, "Projecting Long-Term Housing Requirements and Assessing Current Housing Needs."

"The Implementation of a Housing Policy to Achieve Federal Priorities for 1978–79". Central Mortgage and Housing Corporation; Ministry of State for Urban Affairs, March, 1978.
A brief, succinct, survey of the recent changes in the federal housing policy, and of the considerations which led to these changes. It includes a look at low-

income housing policy, assisted housing policy, the Residential Rehabilitation Assistance Program, and federal aid for community services.

"Interest Amortization Tables: 5% to 25% by Increments of ¼%." Toronto: McGraw-Hill Ryerson Limited, 1971.

Kain, John F. "Housing Policy Evaluation, Research and Experimentation in the U.S." Department of City and Regional Planning, Harvard University. Paper prepared for the Conference of German and American Scientists, Heidelberg, 1977.
This technical overview of recent American housing programme evaluation efforts, social experiments, and research calls for more federal support for research on housing markets.

Kennedy, Stephen D. "Evaluation of In-Kind Transfer Programs: Some Implications from the Preliminary Analysis of the Housing Allowance Demand Experiment." Cambridge, Mass.: Abt Associates. Prepared for presentation at the Ninetieth Annual Meeting of the American Economic Association on December 30, 1977.
This is an evaluation of a large-scale, multi-million-dollar experiment done to assess the impact of housing allowances, and in particular, to assess how in-kind transfer affects demand.

Kesselman, J.R. "Mortgage Policies for Financial Relief in Inflationary Periods." *Canadian Public Policy*, Volume VII, Number 1, Winter 1981.

Lowry, Ira S. "An Overview of the Housing Assistance Supply Experiment." The Rand Corporation, Santa Monica, California, September, 1977.
This cautious examination and evaluation of the U.S. Housing Assistance Supply Experiment advocates further observation and further time for more accurate observation.

McLain, Janet. "Social Housing in Canada: A Review of Recent Developments" (federal and local housing policies). *Perception* 2(July-August 1979): 17-20.

"Projecting Long-term Housing Requirements and Assessing Current Housing Needs: The Canadian Experience". Monograph prepared for the Seventh Session of the working party on Housing Economics, Commission for Europe Committee on Housing, Building and Planning, Geneva, 24-28 April 1978. Ottawa: Ministry of State for Urban Affairs, Information Resource Service, 1978.

Proudfoot, Stuart B. "The Politics of Approval Regulating Land Use in the Urban Fringe." *Canadian Public Policy* 7, no. 2: 284.
Discusses the longer approval process of land use decision-making on the basis of technical, political, and market factors. Policies of intensive public scrutiny of land use changes and the encouragement of community participation in the making of land use decisions are defended on public interest grounds.

Quann, Dorothy. *Racial Discrimination in Housing: A Discussion Paper on the Type of Prejudices and the Recent Incidence of Racial Discrimination in Rental and Ownership Housing Across Canada.* Ottawa: Canadian Council on Social Development, 1979.

"The Rental Market: Recent Trends in Vacancy Rates and Rent Increases." Program and Market Requirements Division, CMHC, December, 1978.
This paper mainly consists of charts and graphs which illustrate the connection between vacancy rates and rent increases in Canada during the 1970's. The text is brief, succinct, and easily understood.

"Report of the Federal Task Force on Housing and Urban Development." Ottawa, 1969.
Commissioned by the Federal Government, this report outlines the housing situation in Canada and proposes a number of recommendations. It is thoughtful, informative, unusually well written, and accessible to anyone concerned with housing issues.

Report 1 of the Task Force on "Shelter and Incomes." Policy and Research Coordination, Central Mortgage and Housing Corporation, March, 1976.
This report was prepared by CMHC for the consideration of the president and vice-president of CMHC; it is an examination of shelter and incomes in Canada which aims to improve the effectiveness of CMHC's present and future programmes.

Appendices to Report 1 of the Task Force on "Shelter and Incomes." Policy and Research Coordination, Central Mortgage and Housing Corporation, March, 1976.
Written for the Cabinet and the management of CMHC, this paper includes recommendations on the adjustment of rent and income requirements, alternative ways to define the population eligible for subsidies, recommendations for revisions to income-related subsidies and programme eligibility criteria, and recommendations concerning policy options for future government decisions relating to shelter assistance.

Silver, Irving R. "Housing and the Poor." Ottawa: Ministry of State for Urban Affairs, November, 1971.
Discusses the problems, concepts and solutions surrounding low-income housing from an economist's perspective, and suggests that because low-income housing is part of the more general problem of the poor, it cannot be solved in isolation.

Smith, Lawrence B. "Canadian Housing Policy in the Seventies." *Land Economics* 57, no.3: 338-52.

_____. "Housing Assistance: A Re-evaluation." *Canadian Public Policy* 7, no. 3: 454.
Re-evaluates the appropriateness of housing assistance programmes in Canada, maintaining that, in today's economy, it is more appropriate for less housing assistance than in the past.

_____. "Research Monograph No. 2: Housing in Canada: Market Structure and Policy Performance." Central Mortgage and Housing Corporation, Ottawa , 1971.
This examination of some of the forces operating in the housing market includes a discussion of the history of the Canadian housing, an examination of the primary supply and demand forces, a statistical analysis, and an analysis of housing policy. It is mainly technical and is probably of most interest to the academic and the specialist.

Steele, Marion Louise. *The Demand for Housing in Canada*. Ottawa: Statistics Canada, 1979 (Census Analytical Study) Document no. 99-763E cn.

Streich, Patricia. "Housing Policy and Welfare Shelter Assistance." Report for Task Force on Shelter and Incomes, Central Mortgage and Housing Corporation, September, 1976.
This brief examination of the housing plight of Canada's welfare recipients looks at policy and makes suggestions for change. It is clearly written and to the point.

_____. "Rural and Remote Housing in Saskatchewan." Background Report No. 3, The Shelter and Incomes Task Force, CMHC, August, 1976.
This rather gossipy report on the housing problems and policies in Northern Saskatchewan is useful and refreshing because it exposes the tangles and embarrassments which have resulted from certain housing policies.

*Towards a Strategy for Land Reform in Canada.* Statement prepared for the Board of Governors of the Canadian Council on Social Development by the Housing Committee. Ottawa: Canadian Council on Social Development, 1978.

Weicher, John C. "The Affordability of New Homes." *Areuea Journal* 5: 209-226. Center for Urban Policy Research, Rutgers University.
Argues that the rising prices of new homes are not a genuine problem, because incomes are increasing proportionately, and that the extent to which new homes *are* more difficult to buy is attributable to rising mortgage interest rates (which are caused by the general price inflation). Also argues that first-time buyers are in a more difficult position than current owners when it comes to buying a house, and that conventional rules of thumb are not very useful guides to the actual behaviour of buyers.

_____. "New Home Affordability, Equity, and Housing Market Behavior." *Areuea Journal* 6, no. 4: 395-416. Center for Urban Policy Research, Rutgers University.
This technical analysis of affordability in the United States argues that equity is an important, although often overlooked, factor. It also points out that so far equity has been difficult to compute.

Willson, Katherine. *Housing Rehabilitation in Canada: A Review of Policy Goals and Program Design.* Toronto: Centre for Urban and Community Studies, University of Toronto, 1980.
Focuses on the Residential Rehabilitation Assistance Program (RRAP) in relation to the development of housing policy, CMHC loan development programmes, social housing policy, and the development of the Neighbourhood Improvement Program. Concludes by summarizing the program implications of different policy goals concerned with housing rehabilitation.

**AVERAGE FAMILY EXPENDITURE BY FAMILY INCOME (IN $ PER YEAR)**

| | | All Classes, | Under $4000 | $4000-$4999 | $5000-$5999 | $6000-$6999 | $7000-$7999 | $8000-$8999 |
|---|---|---|---|---|---|---|---|---|
| A. Food | 1967 | 1522.0 | | | | | | |
| | 72 | 1844.2 | 858.9 | 1111.6 | 1315.1 | 1492.3 | 1512.5 | 1694.1 |
| | 74 | 2412.3 | 1028.0 | 1340.7 | 1532.9 | 1574.7 | 1649.9 | 1846.4 |
| | 76 | 2869.4 | 973.5 | 1329.6 | 1661.9 | 1741.5 | | 1854.9 |
| | 78 | 3344.7 | [ | 1380.0 | | ] [ | 1939.7 | ] [ |
| B. Shelter | 1967 | 1273.0 | | | | | | |
| | 72 | 1743.2 | 966.1 | 1130.7 | 1298.8 | 1368.3 | 1413.6 | 1540.6 |
| | 74 | 2101.2 | 1070.8 | 1276.5 | 1394.8 | 1399.7 | 1513.9 | 1669.8 |
| | 76 | 2809.6 | 1173.5 | 1580.5 | 1663.8 | 1859.3 | | 2067.5 |
| | 78 | 3429.8 | [ | 1647.6 | | ] [ | 2134.1 | ] [ |
| 1) Rental | 1967 | 502.4 | | | | | | |
| | 72 | 759.1 | 652.0 | 815.3 | 807.9 | 817.8 | 855.3 | 855.4 |
| | 74 | 769.0 | 719.7 | 829.6 | 852.7 | 953.8 | 1002.2 | 991.0 |
| | 76 | 1012.8 | 833.0 | 1041.9 | 1051.8 | 1104.7 | | 1430.0 |
| | 78 | 1191.4 | [ | 1078.9 | | ] [ | 1417.3 | ] [ |
| 2) Owner Property Tax | 1967 | 180.1 | | | | | | |
| | 72 | 229.0 | 85.0 | 82.5 | 126.7 | 95.1 | 124.4 | 175.4 |
| | 74 | 272.0 | 85.8 | 129.9 | 129.9 | 90.9 | 104.3 | 135.8 |
| | 76 | 322.9 | 81.2 | 129.7 | 111.2 | 167.5 | | 128.1 |
| | 78 | | [ | | | ] [ | | ] [ |
| 3) Owner Repairs | 1967 | 80.5 | | | | | | |
| | 72 | 114.8 | 41.8 | 30.2 | 61.8 | 40.7 | 50.7 | 79.0 |
| | 74 | 183.7 | 52.3 | 67.0 | 80.0 | 73.3 | 60.6 | 92.8 |
| | 76 | 214.4 | 32.0 | 61.3 | 93.0 | 133.5 | | 79.0 |
| 4) Owner Mortgage Interest | 1967 | 198.6 | | | | | | |
| | 72 | 282.3 | 24.9 | 27.3 | 66.3 | 78.2 | 104.5 | 171.4 |
| | 74 | 406.9 | 29.7 | 26.9 | 53.8 | 41.3 | 75.4 | 141.7 |
| | 76 | 546.0 | 17.8 | 31.0 | 23.1 | 44.1 | | 64.4 |
| | 78 | — | — | — | — | — | | — |
| 5) Fuel Light & Water | 1967 | 230.0 | | | | | | |
| | 72 | 264.4 | 145.5 | 146.1 | 189.5 | 221.7 | 239.9 | 265.5 |
| | 74 | 300.5 | 160.0 | 204.9 | 224.4 | 208.2 | 246.1 | 254.4 |
| | 76 | 438.0 | 165.7 | 238.5 | 295.7 | 295.9 | | 249.6 |
| | 78 | 540.1 | [ | 287.8 | | ] [ | 3596 | ] [ |
| 6) Household Operations | 1967 | 318.8 | | | | | | |
| | 72 | 403.8 | 163.6 | 227.7 | 275.2 | 284.5 | 303.6 | 345.7 |
| | 74 | 526.6 | 194.9 | 270.5 | 301.5 | 342.1 | 384.9 | 452.2 |
| | 76 | 697.1 | 217.5 | 296.2 | 352.0 | 408.3 | | 469.1 |
| | 78 | 814.6 | [ | 322.1 | | ] [ | 434.9 | ] [ |
| 7) Furniture & Floor Coverings | 1967 | 135.2 | | | | | | |
| | 72 | 225.9 | 45.3 | 61.1 | 106.1 | 104.1 | 96.7 | 161.4 |
| | 74 | 338.5 | 62.7 | 85.2 | 113.3 | 136.6 | 150.5 | 207.9 |
| | 76 | 373.4 | 26.4 | 55.3 | 94.0 | 154.9 | | 190.7 |
| | 78 | — | — | — | — | — | — | — |
| 8) Appliances & China etc | 1967 | 145.5 | | | | | | |
| | 72 | 176.3 | 41.9 | 65.1 | 86.6 | 95.8 | 116.9 | 157.6 |
| | 74 | 251.9 | 49.7 | 93.0 | 98.3 | 124.1 | 149.2 | 200.0 |
| | 76 | 306.8 | 50.3 | 70.2 | 88.3 | 123.5 | | 148.6 |
| | 78 | — | — | — | — | — | — | — |

| $9000-$9999 | $10,000-$11,999 | $12,000-$14,999 | $15,000-$19,999 | $20,000-$24,999 | $25,000 and over | $25,000-$29,999 | $30,000-$34,999 | $35,000 and over |
|---|---|---|---|---|---|---|---|---|
| 1720.8 | 1930.9 | 2155.6 | 2467.3 | 2855.4 | 3450.1 | | | |
| 1982.2 | 2171.7 | 2468.6 | 2817.9 | 3159.6 | 3853.4 | | | |
| | 2242.6 | 2475.7 | 2958.9 | 3400.2 | | 3726.4 | 4141.8 | 4971.9 |
| 2241.0 | ] | [ | 6105.2] | [3695.0] | [4025.6 | ] | [4361.6] | [5407.1] |
| 1770.6 | 1744.0 | 1969.4 | 2205.9 | 2586.8 | 3339.9 | | | |
| 1775.3 | 1864.8 | 2102.0 | 2397.6 | 2664.1 | 3407.5 | | | |
| | 2153.9 | 2378.5 | 2819.7 | 3306.1 | | 3553.7 | 3969.7 | 4786.3 |
| 2409.1 | ] | [ | 5989.9] | [3664.7] | [4197.5 | ] | [4528.1] | [5431.7] |
| 967.2 | 804.6 | 720.8 | 691.5 | 574.5 | 571.6 | | | |
| 1036.1 | 977.5 | 801.6 | 715.8 | 592.1 | 412.9 | | | |
| | 1252.8 | 1345.2 | 1077.3 | 934.8 | | 765.2 | 697.2 | 512.6 |
| 1546.2 | ] | [ | 3001.1] | [1155.8] | [965.2 | ] | [825.4] | [659.6] |
| 168.6 | 218.7 | 291.2 | 353.6 | 481.4 | 638.4 | | | |
| 145.5 | 181.8 | 273.9 | 3323.3 | 410.7 | 605.4 | | | |
| | 203.6 | 184.5 | 307.8 | 401.2 | | 488.5 | 562.7 | 770.0 |
| | ] | [ ] | [ ] | [ ] | [ | ] | [ ] | [ ] |
| 90.7 | 117.5 | 136.2 | 171.2 | 197.9 | 491.0 | | | |
| 71.8 | 106.0 | 187.8 | 243.8 | 277.3 | 605.4 | | | |
| | 103.9 | 107.9 | 200.6 | 301.5 | | 364.4 | 320.1 | 472.6 |
| 199.6 | 300.9 | 408.6 | 490.6 | 713.2 | 491.0 | | | |
| 207.1 | 233.0 | 382.9 | 584.0 | 741.3 | 408.9 | | | |
| | 124.8 | 324.8 | 535.4 | 853.1 | | 926.0 | 1256.6 | 1425.0 |
| — | — | — | — | — | — | | | |
| 271.4 | 316.4 | 335.9 | 407.9 | 459.2 | | | | |
| 275.7 | 342.2 | 369.7 | 425.6 | 582.4 | | | | |
| | 341.3 | 340.4 | 444.4 | 515.2 | | 577.6 | 637.4 | 788.2 |
| 352.8 | ] | [ | 862.9 | ] | [580.5] | [647.1 | ] | [755.6] | [918.9] |
| 324.0 | 402.1 | 466.8 | 545.0 | 681.5 | 1117.6 | | | |
| 460.2 | 530.6 | 578.4 | 675.5 | 1000.2 | | | | |
| | 537.8 | 624.2 | 668.2 | 811.6 | | 890.2 | 978.2 | 1425.9 |
| 537.2 | ] | [ | 1440.1 | ] | [856.5] | [1000.3 | ] | [1080.7] | [1398.0] |
| 181.6 | 245.2 | 284.2 | 895.8 | 419.7 | 660.2 | | | |
| 311.2 | 314.0 | 311.3 | 401.4 | 505.4 | 716.7 | | | |
| | 256.7 | 299.9 | 361.9 | 426.6 | | 533.2 | 601.8 | 950.3 |
| — | — | — | — | — | — | | | |
| 157.3 | 200.3 | 232.3 | 264.4 | 324.3 | 369.0 | | | |
| 208.3 | 211.2 | 266.2 | 303.3 | 358.8 | 463.3 | | | |
| | 204.5 | 249.5 | 311.7 | 363.7 | | 426.8 | 535.4 | 694.3 |
| — | — | — | — | — | — | | — | — | — |

APPENDIX III (Continued)
## AVERAGE FAMILY EXPENDITURE BY FAMILY INCOME (IN $ PER YEAR)

| | | All Classes, | Under $4000 | $4000-$4999 | $5000-$5999 | $6000-$6999 | $7000-$7999 | $8000-$8999 |
|---|---|---|---|---|---|---|---|---|
| 9) Miscel- | 1967 | 100.1 | | | | | | |
| laneous | 72 | 115.6 | 17.9 | 34.8 | 50.3 | 71.8 | 86.6 | 100.2 |
| | 74 | 152.0 | 19.9 | 26.9 | 57.7 | 43.0 | 64.3 | 76.6 |
| | 76 | — | — | — | — | — | — | — |
| | 78 | — | — | — | — | — | — | — |
| 10) Services | 1967 | 41.2 | | | | | | |
| | 72 | 51.7 | 22.1 | 18.9 | 24.4 | 24.4 | 28.8 | 34.2 |
| | 74 | 72.5 | 21.9 | 31.1 | 39.0 | 23.8 | 35.3 | 41.7 |
| | 76 | — | — | — | — | — | — | — |
| | 78 | — | — | — | — | — | — | — |
| C. Clothing | 1967 | 664.0 | | | | | | |
| | 72 | 784.9 | 177.7 | 324.2 | 426.4 | 442.8 | 536.4 | 619.3 |
| | 74 | 993.4 | 199.0 | 303.7 | 421.9 | 495.5 | 569.2 | 595.3 |
| | 76 | 1253.7 | 187.7 | 277.6 | 414.7 | 525.7 | 624.0 | |
| | 78 | 1396.5 | [ | 276.3 | | ] [ | 502.3 | ] [ |
| D. Transpor- | 1967 | 938.0 | | | | | | |
| tation & | 72 | 1295.5 | 237.4 | 485.7 | 496.8 | 690.2 | 850.7 | 1144.8 |
| Travel | 74 | 1712.0 | 217.2 | 395.2 | 576.7 | 593.1 | 881.5 | 1185.4 |
| | 76 | 2198.3 | 133.0 | 433.7 | 393.0 | 696.0 | | 1233.9 |
| | 78 | 2334.8 | [294.1 | | | ] [ | 728.4 | ] [ |
| E. Medical | 1967 | 268.0 | | | | | | |
| Care | 72 | 279.7 | 86.8 | 138.3 | 180.8 | 185.3 | 238.4 | 256.3 |
| | 74 | 297.6 | 87.2 | 138.4 | 155.1 | 200.6 | 204.9 | 231.4 |
| | 76 | 350.5 | 65.4 | 147.8 | 146.4 | 160.7 | | 245.9 |
| | 78 | 391.2 | [ | 105.3 | | ] [ | 171.2 | ] [ |
| F. Recreation, | 1967 | 406.0 | | | | | | |
| Reading & | 72 | 556.6 | 145.2 | 345.5 | 272.6 | 314.3 | 387.1 | 435.7 |
| Education | 74 | 724.4 | 160.3 | 244.5 | 318.3 | 427.3 | 481.7 | 491.6 |
| | 76 | 916.9 | 172.7 | 260.7 | 307.9 | 417.5 | | 504.9 |
| | 78 | 1251.8 | [ | 345.8 | | ] [ | 469.6 | ] [ |
| G. Personal | 1967 | 187.0 | | | | | | |
| Care | 72 | 204.0 | 75.1 | 108.3 | 138.6 | 169.3 | 178.5 | 194.3 |
| | 74 | 239.7 | 76.0 | 114.2 | 138.3 | 142.6 | 179.4 | 161.7 |
| | 76 | 280.1 | 70.0 | 111.7 | 139.9 | 143.4 | | 191.0 |
| | 78 | 336.4 | [ | 113.9 | | ] [ | 175.2 | ] [ |
| H. Tobacco & | 1967 | 321.0 | | | | | | |
| Alcohol | 72 | 414.0 | 118.9 | 284.8 | 276.9 | 370.3 | 352.1 | 398.4 |
| | 74 | 478.3 | 149.1 | 219.2 | 287.4 | 276.2 | 326.4 | 368.9 |
| | 76 | 585.0 | 137.7 | 194.2 | 245.2 | 324.8 | | 418.1 |
| | 78 | 641.9 | [ | 198.6 | | ] [ | 327.2 | ] [ |
| I. Other | 1967 | 106,0 | | | | | | |
| | 72 | 191.7 | 46.6 | 61.3 | 164.9 | 144.1 | 127.7 | 187.0 |
| | 74 | 242.3 | 49.5 | 132.4 | 131.3 | 104.4 | 150.2 | 179.5 |
| | 76 | 388.2 | 43.6 | 114.5 | 142.7 | 127.0 | | 181.4 |
| | 78 | 6412.2 | [ | 564.7 | | ] [ | 957.3 | ] [ |
| J. Total | 1967 | 6830.0 | | | | | | |
| Current | 72 | 8190.7 | 2966.6 | 4368.6 | 5071.8 | 5692.2 | 6168.6 | 7275.9 |
| Expenditure | 74 | 10467.0 | 3365.2 | 4639.6 | 5499.5 | 6797.7 | 7552.4 | 8359.5 |
| | 76 | 13204.4 | 4907.5 | 5701.0 | 6748.6 | | 8209.3 | |
| | 78 | 20326.9 | [ | 5248.4 | | ] [ | 7839.9 | ] [ |

Source: Statistics Canada, *Urban Family Expenditure*, Catalogue 62-547 and 62-550 V.2 Major Urban Centres. Statistics Canada, *Family Expenditure in Canada*, Catalogue 62-550.

| $9000-$9999 | $10,000-$11,999 | $12,000-$14,999 | $15,000-$19,999 | $20,000-$24,999 | $25,000 and over | $25,000-$29,999 | $30,000-$34,999 | $35,000 and over |
|---|---|---|---|---|---|---|---|---|
| 103.2 | 127.9 | 197.3 | 278.7 | 384.5 | | | | |
| 76.6 | 109.3 | 131.6 | 161.3 | 243.6 | 440.6 | | | |
| — | — | — | — | — | — | — | — | — |
| — | — | — | — | — | — | — | — | — |
| 45.7 | 41.8 | 57.3 | 1 92.4 | 1 90.8 | 159.2 | | | |
| 57.3 | 53.2 | 70.5 | 1 87.7 | 1 96.8 | 161.2 | | | |
| — | — | — | — | — | — | — | — | — |
| — | — | — | — | — | — | — | — | — |
| 723.5 | 768.5 | 983.1 | 1213.0 | 1623.3 | 1873.2 | | | |
| 691.2 | 833.7 | 937.9 | 1187.2 | 1558.1 | 2028.9 | | | |
| 861.6 | 951.6 | 1175.1 | 1546.3 | | 1755.7 | 2076.9 | 3091.8 | |
| 677.8 | ] [ | 2152.0 | ] | [1415.4] | [ 1830.4 | ] | [1934.5] | [2946.4] |
| 1056.6 | 1490.7 | 1639.4 | 2104.2 | 2556.2 | 2666.5 | | | |
| 1286.2 | 1445.2 | 1763.1 | 2091.7 | 2716.0 | 3422.7 | | | |
| | 1258.4 | 1797.9 | 2281.9 | 2730.7 | | 3140.0 | 4254.0 | 4850.3 |
| 1125.4 | ] [ | 4047.4 | ] | [2662.7] | [3108.6] | | [3286.7] | [4546.9] |
| 248.4 | 292.5 | 340.2 | 395.4 | 464.3 | 627.0 | | | |
| 275.9 | 290.7 | 352.8 | 413.9 | 516.9 | | | | |
| | 283.4 | 316.2 | 345.8 | 426.4 | | 475.7 | 503.9 | 671.0 |
| 246.3 | ] [ | 1049.3 | ] | [420.7] | [ 489.0] | | [ 529.2] | [680.1] |
| 518.8 | 530.1 | 674.1 | 835.5 | 1129.1 | 1417.6 | | | |
| 591.5 | 686.0 | 842.9 | 1038.8 | 1594.8 | | | | |
| | 669.3 | 709.4 | 805.3 | 1089.5 | | 1371.5 | 1546.3 | 474.7 |
| 614.2 | ] [ | 1868.1 | ] | [1332.3] | [ 1696.2 | ] | [1765.2] | [2676.9] |
| 196.9 | 236.8 | 305.1 | 356.8 | 387.4 | | | | |
| 201.2 | 211.8 | 242.2 | 276.0 | 329.6 | 425.6 | | | |
| | 222.7 | 246.9 | 267.4 | 323.3 | | 382.6 | 414.7 | 565.1 |
| 214.5 | ] [ | 587.4 | ] | [351.9] | [ 417.6 | ] | [ 467.3] | [590.8] |
| 383.9 | 438.1 | 480.1 | 566.5 | 653.8 | 838.7 | | | |
| 403.3 | 439.1 | 488.4 | 560.3 | 602.4 | 856.6 | | | |
| | 536.3 | 581.0 | 740.7 | | | 763.7 | 772.7 | 1040.3 |
| 409.2 | ] [ | 1191.2 | ] | [707.0] | [ 817.0 | ] | [ 811.2] | [1051.9] |
| 166.7 | 237.3 | 234.1 | 256.2 | 288.6 | 416.2 | | | |
| 231.0 | 278.3 | 308.4 | 355.8 | 465.1 | 560.5 | | | |
| | 282.1 | 245.2 | 398.2 | 483.4 | | 591.3 | 580.5 | 859.6 |
| 2103.3 | ] [ | 9727.3 | ] | [6613.9] | [ 8791.3 | ] | [10393.1] | [16254.2] |
| 7513.6 | 8590.9 | 9794.2 | 1168.12 | 14087.6 | 17346.9 | | | |
| 9171.9 | 10463.2 | 12780.3 | 14620.9 | 18977.3 | | | | |
| 9587.1 | 11005.0 | 13059.5 | 15846.1 | | 17857.1 | 20637.6 | 26636.2 | |
| 10578.6 | ] [ | 37785.9 | ] | [21721.1] | [ 26373.5 | ] | [29157.6] | [40984.0] |

(1978 figures are not broken down into the same categories and so the numbers would differ, especially category 1) Other.)

squalor. The rich were also an unlovable bunch, having derived most of their wealth from shameless exploitation of peasant labor. This forced transfer of wealth by Robin Hood and his Merry Men (an early form of welfare, it seems) was therefore justified, this argument goes, because the situation was so inequitable.

The alert reader will have already noticed that this view of unethical or even illegal behavior is close to the ancient "the ends justify the means" proposition. The purpose of this section is not to explore this particularly thorny thicket yet one more time, but it is instead to note simply that in times of economic desperation there will always be an increase in the incidence of such behaviors. The financially strapped small restaurateur, desperately staving off bankruptcy, uses the federal and state withholding funds that he has deducted from his current payroll to pay instead some particularly threatening creditors. He rationalizes his action by noting that the great state of Missouri and Uncle Sam are rich and powerful, while he is weak and helpless, and vows that he will pay them later when his cash flow improves.

One can obviously think of hundreds of such situations without much effort. We normally are less quick to judge such troubled small businessmen harshly than we are the drug lords, but there is still something about their behavior that bothers us. We shall later explore some alternatives available to the troubled restaurateur, or the contemporary Robin Hood, that may not work immediate miracles, but that are completely honest and aboveboard, and may well remove the inequity or solve the problem in the long run.

4. Some persons are moral and ethical dummies, i.e., uneducated in this area. While it is almost inconceivable that a contemporary American person could pass through both high school and college without at least *some* exposure to the great ethical theories of both the past and present, there is no doubt that the formal teaching of ethics has declined somewhat in the latter third of this century. When a 21-year-old college senior defines utilitarianism as "the belief that everything is useful," or asserts that something that is ethical "is a petroleum additive," then we might logically consider beefing up our educational efforts in this area.

In short, some people simply do not understand what ethics or standards of right and wrong they are applying when they make a decision. As we've already hinted, most people use one of two general philosophies when making decisions related to an ethical dilemma. Many businesspersons attempt to resolve a dilemma by deciding on the action which, they perceive, will result in the greatest benefit for the most people (astute readers already recognize this as the philosophy known as utilitarianism). Others, confronted by the same dilemma, may decide instead to choose the course of action which, they believe, least infringes on any one person's basic human rights. (In other words, do unto others as you would have them do unto you.) Although we will not be so judgmental as to advocate one of these philosophies as better than the other, the point we are attempting to make is that most business decision makers have not been formally educated in applying such philosophies to decision making in business.

5. Possible rewards outweigh possible punishments for unethical behavior. As the Harvard professor Douglas McGregor noted many years ago: By and large people are not dumb, they are smart.[1] They are never smarter, it seems, than when they are mentally calculating the payoffs for certain types of behaviors. Psychologist Victor Vroom labeled this sort of behavior *expectancy theory* (also known as "thinking-person's theory"), and it explains a lot of decisions that we make. In any given situation where there is a decision to make, people will make sophisticated but subjective estimates of the positive and negative consequences likely to result from any action they take, and act accordingly. These calculations, even those made by persons not having much formal education, routinely put the most powerful computers to shame.

In practical terms, if an unethical behavior is likely to lead to a reward but not to a punishment, the more likely it is that the unethical behavior will occur. While this revelation may not startle any readers, it is a useful and sensible argument in favor of many things that corporations and other organizations are already doing in the area of ethics: establishing codes of ethics to educate employees and spelling out the consequences to employees if the ethical code is violated. The office clerk is not so likely to "borrow" computer diskettes, pens, notepads, or petty cash if he or she knows that the penalty for getting caught engaging in such behavior is a reprimand, docking of pay, or suspension without pay.

6. **All's fair in love, war, and business.** Some people regard any business activity that defeats the competition and increases profits as fair. They even use warfare concepts such as "guerilla warfare," "preemptive first strikes," and "counterattacks" to justify unethical actions.[2] Given the destructive, wasteful nature of the history of warfare, this business-as-war comparison raises serious ethical concerns.

Other ethical concerns are raised when people view business as a game, like football or boxing, in which ordinary rules do not apply. What if a boxer decided it was wrong to knock out his opponent? Games have rules and referees to ensure safety and equality and to call "time-out" when the going gets rough. But in business, customers, who are not economically self-sufficient, cannot call "time-out." The position of business ethics in the game, therefore, is to make clear what rules do and should apply in business. It is also important that these rules be appropriate to the compulsory nature of participation in the "game."[3]

7. **There is powerful organizational pressure on individuals to commit unethical acts.** If there is one thing that we value more in American society than individual integrity, it is individual self-reliance. Ours is a nation that glorifies individualism, praises acts of individual courage and decisiveness, and, to a greater extent than any modern nation, encourages our young people to be themselves. Not surprisingly, this whole societal orientation has led to the development of an entrepreneurial outlook that actively contributes to the continued health of the American economy. Just when the doomsayers are encouraging us to give it up and let the Japanese or the Germans dominate the world economy, a new generation of entrepreneurs seems to spring up to develop whole new industries like computer chips and home computers or to revitalize troubled or dying industries like steel and timber.

Our pride in the power and creativity of the individual has led, at least in part, to the development of values and standards of behavior which hold that each individual is responsible for his or her actions, and that each individual bears responsibility for his or her ethical choices. As a society, we shy away from allowing any group, including government, to make these choices for us; our continued strength as a democracy is due at least in part to our continued and vigorous defense of individual rights and freedoms. We continue to be extremely suspicious of any group or individual within our society (including the president of the United States) that seems to wield too much power or seems too eager to grab more power.

Considering this proud tradition of individual liberty and responsibility, it can be downright depressing to read about incidents that clearly show that organizations and the leaders or officials of those organizations have great power over the individual. If we were to ask a group of normal adult Americans, for example, "Would you knowingly give a possibly fatal electric shock to an innocent person who had not harmed you in any way, when you were not being threatened in any way?" the universal answer would be "no." Yet the hard reality, as we shall see, is that about 60 to 65 percent of that same group *would* administer such a shock, under conditions in which their individual judgments were influenced by power.

## A Shocking Abuse of Power

In the 1960s, Yale psychologist Stanley Milgram became interested in the defense offered by many of the Nazi war criminals during the Nuremburg trials, that they carried out numerous atrocities because they were "following orders." To study some of the conditions under which individuals obey other persons they perceive to be authority figures, Milgram designed an ingenious series of experiments (which were themselves alleged to be unethical) involving simulated electric shock.[4] The subjects in the first, and most famous, of the experiments were adult males who responded to newspaper ads in New Haven, Connecticut, and who arrived at the laboratory assuming they were going to take part in a learning experiment.

Upon their arrival, they met Milgram, who was dressed in a white lab coat, and their co-subject, who was actually Milgram's confederate. After a rigged straw drawing, the naive subject always became the "teacher" and Milgram's aide the "learner." The subjects were told that the experiment was supposed to determine the effects of punishment on learning. The learner was then strapped into place out of sight of the teacher, who was placed in front of a large shock generator, which had thirty switches on it, delivering from 15 to 450 volts of shock. The 450-volt switch was labeled: "Danger – Severe Shock – XXX."

As the experiment began, the learner began to make mistakes in repeating words given him by the teacher; after each mistake the teacher was ordered to administer increasing dosages of shock. Unbeknownst to the teacher, the whole situation was, of course, a fake. At "65 volts" the learner began to grunt, at "285 volts" he screamed in pain, and after that level (following a disturbingly ambiguous thumping sound, as though a body might have hit the floor), there was silence. Before the experiments began, Milgram asked a group of psychiatrists how many subjects they thought would administer shock to the highest level – XXX. Their prediction was that only 4 percent would do it.

The results were shocking, if the reader will forgive the expression: Of the initial group of 40 subjects, 26 went all the way to the 450-volt level. Despite their protests, and obvious discomfort, when Milgram would say, "The experiment requires that we go on," or "You have no other choice; you must go on," they went on. In a later version of the experiment, one of Milgram's graduate assistants, who was dressed casually and introduced himself as a graduate student, gave the same verbal instructions in the same situation, but only 15 percent of the subjects gave shock at the highest level.

The experiments created an ethical furor because the subjects were not prepared for the level of stress they were to experience, and because they had been misled about the actual purpose of the experiment, even though this was explained to them before they left. These very serious considerations aside, the experiments dramatically illustrated how powerful the presence of an "expert" authority can be in influencing individuals to engage in acts they normally would not consider. Despite the fact that many of Milgram's subjects said that they felt the experiment was wrong, and asked for permission to stop, they nonetheless went ahead with it and followed instructions to the end.

The results of Milgram's studies are sobering for those of us who value independent ethical decision making by enlightened individuals. The power of organizational authority is great: Organizations normally have the power to hire and fire individuals. Perhaps in the light of these findings, we can be more sympathetic to Lieutenant Calley, who felt that his superiors' authority made it permissible to fire on civilians at My Lai (Vietnam); to members of the People's Temple ordered to commit suicide at Jonestown, Guyana; or to a clerk in a retail clothing shop anywhere in America ordered by the boss to label a cheap copy of a designer's dress—a knock-off—as an original designer garment.

15

# The Electrifying Power of Authority

*"I'm shocked you're telling me to do this, Dr. Milgram —
and even more shocked that I'm doing it!"*

# Why the Truth Will Win Out

Although this short discussion of forces and factors that sometimes lead to unethical decisions in business and government may discourage the more pessimistic reader, it is our firm belief that periods of moral crisis in a society as resilient and creative as ours lead precisely and promptly to periods of reform and rejuvenation. Our history is one of successful coping with problem after problem, and crisis after crisis. It is unfortunate, of course, that we regularly seem to let problems snowball into near calamity before we take action to end them.

Because the doomsayers and naysayers have to this point drawn our scorn, we must now in fairness give them their due: They often draw attention to serious problems that we might otherwise neglect in the rush of modern life. Our favorite doomsayers, we must sheepishly confess, are the vigilant members of the American press, who continue to root out corruption, expose fraud, and sound the alarm when abuses of power begin to threaten freedoms, especially their own. Do we need to reiterate that freedom of the press is a vital ingredient of a modern democracy, and that we need to fight mightily to preserve that freedom, even when it leads to wretched excess?

The continued health, and basic honesty, of our culture manifests itself again and again when an Ivan Boesky is jailed; when an Evan Mecham is indicted; or when a Jim Wright is forced to resign the House Speakership for abusing his powers. The hue and cry that follows such episodes reveals yet again the deep desire of the American people to continue to have a nation ruled by laws and not by men, and to live in a society governed by principles of justice and fairness.

This volume is a modest attempt to help the average person, particularly a North American working for a private or public organization, practice an honest and ethical lifestyle, even if this might not seem easiest. We shall explore some of the moral and ethical dilemmas that we all face, and point the way to a career and life marked by improved ethical decisions, but we shall never claim that we have a quick fix or a sure cure for all that ails us.

## References in Chapter One

1. Douglas McGregor, *The Human Side of Enterprise* (New York: McGraw-Hill, 1960).

2. Charles L. Tomkovick, "Time for a Cease-Fire with Strategic Marketing Warfare," in *Advances in Marketing*, ed. Peter J. Gordon and Bert J. Kellerman (Southern Marketing Association, 1990): 212.

3. Eric H. Berversluis, "Is There No Such Thing as Business Ethics?" *Journal of Business Ethics*, 1987, no. 6: 81-88.

4. Stanley Milgram, *Obedience to Authority* (New York: Harper and Row, 1974).

- During a period of ethical furor, such as the 1980s, doomsayers will rush out to predict the end of the world—or at least the end of civilization as we know it. We believe the actual result is the opposite: *There will be an increase in ethical sensitivity and standards* throughout the American nation.

- What is ethical and what is not is pretty well understood by the average American. An *ethical* act is something judged as proper or acceptable based on some standard of right and wrong. It is one that results in the greatest benefit for the most people, or one that does not infringe on basic human rights. Ethical acts increase everyone's *self-esteem* or self-respect.

- Honesty is an enduring ethical value because it increases *trust* and *confidence* in all of our relationships and transactions. The reason the ancient cliche, "Honesty is the best policy," refuses to go away is that it is still true. Honest!

- We should not be too quick to judge persons who cheat, because there are powerful pressures on both individuals and organizations to commit unethical acts. It is more important to understand *why* individuals and organizations sometimes cheat than to *judge* them.

- While there are many reasons why unethical acts are committed, some of the key reasons include the following:

   1. Some individuals and organizations are immature or mentally unbalanced. There are a few people who just never grow up: They want what they want and they want it now. Occasionally

psychopaths, like Adolph Hitler, achieve great power and do evil deeds; but the evil they do is in the guise of good.

2.  Some individuals are dominated by *economic needs*, or what judgmental persons usually call greed. Call up your favorite Colombian drug lord if you need a reference here.

3.  Special circumstances sometimes cause unethical or illegal behavior. Special circumstances usually means desperation. Small businesspeople on the verge of bankruptcy may skim cash or withhold payments to the IRS, for example.

4.  Some people are *uneducated* in ethical theory. One of the healthy outcomes of the 1980s has been a major increase in college, high school, and even grade school courses in ethics.

5.  *Rewards* sometimes outweigh *punishments* for unethical behavior. When people expect that they will be able to get away with it, when it is attractive, they are more likely to do it.

6.  People sometimes view business in terms of *warfare* or as a *game*. But business is not a war or a game, because people cannot call *time-out*; they must participate (buy and sell goods and services) in order to survive.

7.  Organizations sometimes put *powerful pressure* on individuals to commit unethical acts. Lieutenant William Calley and Lieutenant Colonel Oliver North ("I was just following orders") are two relatively recent examples. A bit further back in history, the Nazi war criminals used the same argument in their defense at the Nuremburg trials.

■ There are *powerful pressures* in American society that help keep us honest. One is the honesty and optimism of the American people. Another is the fact that an eternally vigilant free press makes it very difficult for those who commit unethical or illegal acts to hide it for long.

Insights & Guidelines from Chapter One

## ETHICAL CHOICE AND AN EXTRAORDINARY AMERICAN

*While ordinary Americans are routinely faced with complex and difficult choices, occasionally ordinary Americans find themselves in truly extraordinary situations. The following incident discusses a truly extraordinary career choice and its consequences. The "star" of the case may have been an ordinary man, living a rather dull life, before he made his choice, but he soon became a most extraordinary (and probably desperate!) person. As you read the case, please do your best to keep in mind the printed disclaimer that sometimes appears in high-speed, high-performance auto commercials on television where a professional driver puts a new car through its paces: "These maneuvers extremely dangerous. Do not attempt in real life." Obviously, names and places have been changed to protect the guilty.*

"DR. DAVID DOUBLEMINT:
DOUBLE YOUR PLEASURE, DOUBLE YOUR FUN!"

In 1985, Dr. David Doublemint was an assistant professor of business administration at Northern State University in College Station, Illinois. A stocky, slightly balding man, he was the envy of his colleagues because he had succeeded in negotiating a three-day-a-week teaching schedule, which left his Tuesdays and Thursdays free and his weekends unencumbered. Despite some occasional grumbling from his colleagues about his favorable schedule, he was a popular and congenial figure, well liked by both faculty members and students.

Doublemint kept office hours on the afternoons of his assigned teaching days. Other days of the week, he was never seen on the Northern State campus. This arrangement did not provoke intense curiosity because it was assumed that on these other days he was busy at home, working on the management text that he had told his colleagues he was writing. Telephone calls to his home on nonteaching days were taken by his answering machine and normally were returned within a day or two. His overall job performance was satisfactory.

Unbeknownst to his students and colleagues, Doublemint was actually leading an extraordinary double life! The days he was not available on the Northern State campus, he was elsewhere—specifically on the campus of another university, City University in nearby

Chicago, where for two days a week and numerous weekends he was also employed full time as an assistant professor of business administration. On Tuesdays, Thursdays, and weekends in the City University executive MBA program, he was known to his colleagues and students as Dr. David Doublethink.

In the role of Dr. Doublethink, he cut a slightly more dashing figure than he did in the role of Dr. Doublemint. His balding head was covered by a curly toupee, and he wore a beard and moustache. He was the envy of his colleagues because he had succeeded in negotiating a two-day a week teaching schedule, as well as performing on weekends in the MBA program. He was an affable and friendly figure, well liked by his colleagues and students, and his overall job performance was satisfactory.

He had taken the CU job after teaching two full years at Northern State. He had gone to great lengths when interviewing in Chicago to disguise his identity: He had arranged for phony transcripts in the name of David Doublethink to be mailed directly to CU, and his letters of reference were creative forgeries of the letters he had used when he interviewed at Northern. He had also obtained a fraudulent social security number, birth certificate, and driver's license. The toupee and beard completed the transformation: He was quite literally Pygmalion in the classroom!

The motives for his daring deception of two employers were financial, as nearly as is known. He apparently had two ex-wives who sued him repeatedly for various transgressions when they learned that he had taken the job at Northern State. He apparently loved the ponies as much as he loved the ladies, and dropped nearly as much money at the racetrack as he did paying off his former wives. He was truly a man on a treadmill, but he succeeded in maintaining the deception for over two years before it all began to unravel.

An honest printer turned out to be Doublemint's undoing. He had asked a small print shop in Bloomville, Illinois, to make copies of forged letters of reference when he applied for the job at City, and the printer spotted the rather crude changes that Doublemint had made in the originals. The printer agonized for a year and a half, however, before he called Campus Security at Northern State University. Doublemint was soon charged with forgery and fraud, and was rapidly fired by both his employers. ■■

# 2

## Tough Choices In A Tough World

*My name is Laura Wilson. I am currently a student at Smithe State University, majoring in management. I do house cleaning as a side job to help with the costs of school.*

*While doing laundry in the home of a client, a registered nurse, I found some medicine clearly marked with the name of the hospital where she worked. I thought maybe it was an honest mistake, but as weeks passed I began finding more and more medicine in the pockets of my client's work scrubs as I was doing laundry. This made me wonder if my client was stealing these drugs.*

*I started becoming more aware of drugs in other places around the house. I began wondering what the pills were for. Were the patients (whose names were on the bottles) getting placebos instead of medicine they needed? How was the medicine affecting her ability to work and the quality of her work?*

*After debating within myself about what I should do, I decided to anonymously call the director of nursing at the hospital where she was working and explain my concern. The director talked with my client about the situation, which angered her. After the director talked to her, the nurse put two and two together, and fired me. Although all my other clients know the nurse, and may know what happened, none of them have fired me.*[1]

The classic American western movie portrayed a simple world of right and wrong, where the good guy wore white and the bad guy wore black. The moviegoer knew the good guy was going to win in the end —despite having to hang over the cliff by his toenails with the bad guy pushing him down, or being tied to the railroad tracks with a steam-puffing locomotive approaching fast. Much of the appeal of the western was precisely that it cast moral and ethical issues in stark and simple terms: the bully rancher versus the timid farmers; the hired gunfighter versus the local sheriff. The money-paying patron could count on a positive and upbeat outcome, usually involving serious lead poisoning of the black-hatted varmint, and all in about two hours. Good had vanquished evil in yet another Saturday matinee.

The real world, alas, presents us with more complicated and painful choices, as the opening story about Laura's dilemma illustrates so poignantly. Should Laura have done anything about the apparently illicit drugs discovered in the apartment she was cleaning? It was fairly clear to her that the nurse had stolen them or falsified prescriptions, yet there might have been another explanation for their presence. Were they being stored temporarily? No, that didn't make sense. What good reason could there be for all those prescription medications in the apartment? It didn't make sense, unless they were being used to satisfy a serious drug habit.

To call the hospital was to risk losing a client, not a happy prospect for a student struggling to finance her education with a part-time business. Did she have the right to meddle in a personal matter? Would the nurse react angrily to the disclosure? Probably. Would the hospital abruptly fire the apparently drug-abusing employee, a course many organizations take as a first resort in dealing with chemically dependent employees, or would it attempt to get her help? An agonizing real-world choice had to be made: To do nothing was to guarantee living with the guilty knowledge that she was condoning illegal behavior by not reporting it. Should she just confront the nurse one on one, and clear it up that way?

And so it goes in an often messy world, with as many gray and shady areas as sunlit meadows, and with many ethical and moral decisions to be made that sometimes can't easily be avoided. The issue is sufficiently vexing, perplexing, and just plain difficult. To help lessen the perplexity and complexity of ethical decision making, it may be informative to examine the elements that contribute to such tough choices, especially in the world of work.

## Conflicts Between Personal Ethics, Organizational Relationships, and Opportunity

If you will pardon us, we would like to briefly examine some of the factors that contribute to the tough choices that seem to be inherent in business, and which, unfortunately, sometimes lead to unethical and illegal actions. Although we have attempted to tackle this wearisome task in a light-hearted vein, this little chat may be quite important in furthering our understanding of why and how people make unethical choices.

A number of social scientists and academics have provided us with a great deal of useful information, much of it based on scientific research, as to why people may choose to behave unethically at work, even people who normally behave ethically at home. They have identified three basic elements that seem to lead people to make unethical choices at work: an individual's personal moral standards, the relationships in and values of the organization in which the person works, and the opportunity to act unethically.

Personal Moral Standards  In general people learn moral values and standards of right and wrong from their families, teachers, and clergymen. These values and standards are then used to make decisions when people are confronted with tough choices throughout life. However, while moral decision making at home may be guided by an individual's religious training and the teachings of family, friends, teachers, and other significant people in his or her life, all this training does not necessarily lead an individual to make ethical decisions at work.

It has long been believed that people who demonstrate high ethical standards at home automatically apply these standards at work. And if you believe that, then we've got some ocean-front property right in the middle of Arizona that we'd like to sell you. In fact, research suggests that people change their ethical standards between home and work. One such study showed that two-thirds of the managers in a survey of about 200 marketing managers used a different set of moral decision-making standards at home than at work.[2] In a classic 1960s *Harvard Business Review* article, Albert Z. Carr pointed out that many people are good citizens in the community and act ethically at home and in church and school, but they have no problem cheating, stealing, and deceiving others at work.[3] This might well lead you to ask why different people seem to apply different standards to help them make tough choices.

Part of the answer to this question may lie in the work of social psychologist Lawrence Kohlberg, who developed a popular model that helps explain why individuals often make very different ethical choices when confronted with the same dilemma.[4] The central idea in his theory, which is now well documented and widely accepted, is that people differ widely in their degree of *moral development*. Kohlberg shows that most of us go through three basic stages of development in our moral and ethical thinking (see Table 2-1), although not all of us will reach Level III—postconventional morality—in our lifetimes.

Kohlberg uses a case entitled "The Stolen Drug" to illustrate his model, which may remind the reader of Laura Wilson's dilemma.

*A woman in Europe was near death from a rare kind of cancer. The doctors knew of only one drug that might save her, a form of radium that a druggist from the same town had recently discovered. The drug was expensive to make, but the druggist was charging ten times what it cost to produce the drug. He paid $200 for the radium, and charged $2000 for a small dose of the drug.*

*The sick woman's husband, Heinz, went to everyone he knew to borrow the money, but he could only get together about $1000, half of the cost. He told the druggist that his wife was dying and asked him to sell it cheaper, or let him pay later. But the druggist said, "No, I discovered the drug and I'm going to make money from it." Heinz became desperate and broke into the man's store to steal the drug for his wife.[5]*

While this case illustrates a choice that is not only tough, but agonizing, the responses of individuals to Heinz's choice differ widely, and can be explained in terms of the level of moral development they have reached.

## Table 2-1

## Levels of Moral Development and Examples of Moral Reasoning

| Level of Development | Major Characteristics | Examples of Moral Reasoning Regarding Theft |
|---|---|---|
| Level I Preconventional Morality | *Usually characteristic of children. Judgments of right or wrong are made in terms of avoidance of punishment or deference to authority.* | *"It's wrong to steal because if you get caught, you go to jail." "Stealing's O.K. if your dad says you can do it."* |
| Level II Conventional Morality | *Approval of others is a major determinant of judgments. There is much concern with upholding society's standards and compliance with authority.* | *"It's wrong to steal because people won't like you." "I stole it because I was following orders."* |
| Level III Postconventional Morality | *Moral and ethical choices are based on rationality. Individual conscience and free choice are the basis for judgments, with full acceptance of personal responsibility. Morality is based on personal conviction.* | *"Stealing for pure personal gain is usually indefensible, with a few exceptions." "Theft for an altruistic reason in a situation where the law is ambiguous may well be justified."* |

Adapted from Lawrence Kohlberg, "Cognitive-Development Approach to Moral Education," *The Humanist* (November-December 1972): 13-16.

Young children, who are generally at Level I—the preconventional level—judge Heinz's behavior in very concrete terms. They might respond, "It was wrong for him to take the drug because he'll get caught and be punished for stealing." At Level II—the conventional level reached by most of us—a response might be, "He was right to steal the drug, because he took a vow to protect his wife when he married her." At Level III—postconventional morality—a person might respond, "The principle of the sanctity of life coupled with the unjustness of the law that is failing to protect his wife justified Heinz's theft of the drug."

Kohlberg noted that postconventional moral development is characterized by the individual's concern with right and wrong, quite apart from self-interest, the views of others, or the views of authority figures. Ethical judgments are made increasingly from the frame of reference of the individual: His or her conscience, his or her own definition of moral principles, or his or her enlightened personal judgment become the basis of action or decision.

Thus, it appears that people evolve through several stages of moral development, changing their ethics and ethical behavior accordingly. As they pass through these different stages of moral development, how they perceive and respond to tough choices changes to reflect their moral growth. This may well explain why two people will resolve the same dilemma in different ways. Just as people at each of the three levels perceived Heinz's dilemma and judged his resolution in different ways, businesspeople at different stages of moral development perceive the tough choices that arise in the workplace differently and apply different standards to the resolution of such choices.

There is clear evidence from scholarly research, however, that individuals' personal moral development and ethical standards are not necessarily the central element that guides their decisions in the workplace.[6] Consequently, "good" people may not continue to be "good" people when they work with unethical people or in an organization that pressures them to perform and achieve company goals at any cost.

Organizational Relationships and Values People learn standards of right and wrong not only from their families, teachers, and clergymen, but also from others with whom they work. In fact, excluding time spent sleeping, most of us spend 50 percent of our lives at work, and we often come to view those we work with as a second "family." Common sense tells us, then, that the ethics of our company and of those with whom we work will strongly influence our ethical behavior on the job.

Our relationships with underlings, colleagues, and bosses may raise ethical problems, such as fulfilling obligations, honesty, and mutual agreements that lead to ethical issues. Employees may have to deal with assignments they perceive as creating ethical dilemmas. For example, a saleswoman asked by a colleague to lie to a customer on the phone about the actual delivery date of a delayed shipment of goods must decide what to do and worry about offending a long-time friend if she tells the truth. Additionally, the ethics of the organization itself may create ethical dilemmas, particularly when they conflict with an individual's personal standards.

As we've noted already, the authority of superiors can powerfully influence the ethical behavior of their subordinates. Bosses can control their employees' daily activities and directly influence their behavior by putting into practice the company's real ethical standards. The power of managers is directly related to the amount of pressure they can exert to get their employees to carry out their orders (remember the shocking results obtained in Milgram's study). A boss who wants his or her employees to lie, cheat, or steal to achieve a company goal is in a strong position to reward unethical behavior. Young employees, in particular, say they do as they're told to demonstrate loyalty in matters of judgments of morality. A single managerial action, it seems, is worth a thousand words.

Although co-workers may lack the power of supervisors, they also exert a mighty influence on individual decision making. People often look to their colleagues and peers as role models to decide how to handle ethical dilemmas or issues. For example, if a salesperson sees that his colleagues pad their expense accounts, he may feel less inhibited about padding his own expense account when the opportunity arises (more on opportunity in a minute). In this regard, guilt truly seems to love company.

Although most people fail to think of companies and industries as having values and ethics like people do, social scientists have coined the term *corporate culture* to describe the values, traditions, legends, customs, and systems of rewards and punishments of organizations. Many of us are familiar with those touching American Express commercials in which the friendly American Express associate goes above and beyond the call of duty to assist a person who has become separated from his or her wallet in a foreign land. In fact, American Express employees share dozens of such "legends" with each other, true stories in which American Express employees have done just that. Stories like these, when circulated among other employees, help spread the message that customer service is vital to the success of the company; they help employees recognize the company's values and standards. When confronted with their own tough choices, American Express employees may well recall these legends, which illustrate the company's values, and use them as guidance.

Corporate culture is not always used to such positive ends, however. When a person decides to behave unethically or even illegally, it may be that the organization's culture, as revealed in its values, traditions, pressures, and rewards, provides the incentive to stray. It has been suggested that Wall Street provided a "corporate" culture, complete with lax regulations, mind-boggling rewards (in the billions of dollars for some lucky souls), stories of huge successes, and a government tradition of looking the other way that was conducive to insider trading, stock parking, and other transgressions that were so often in the news in the 1980s. When an organization's culture encourages unethical activities, then, the company should not be so surprised to learn that one of its managers bribed an official, stole secrets from another company, or refused to hire an older employee because it may well be that the manager perceived the action as acceptable within the company based on its culture.

Opportunity  The third and final influence on ethics at work is opportunity, which, for our purposes, will be loosely defined as conditions that limit barriers or provide rewards. An employee may perceive an opportunity when he or she can act unethically and be rewarded or, at the very least, suffer no penalty. For example, an employee who receives a big raise after paying a bribe to obtain a key contract may come to view bribery not only as an acceptable activity, but as the virtual key to the kingdom within the organization.

It is likely that we will discover that opportunity was a major factor in many of the unethical activities associated with the savings and loan imbroglio of the late 1980s. Deregulation of the banking industry gave S&Ls the opportunity to engage in high-risk banking activities; inattention by government banking officials meant no one was minding the store to keep greedy hands out of the candy jar. This double whammy of opportunity was perhaps too great a temptation for some S&L managers to resist, and these weak souls began lending money to anyone who knew how to write a business plan; many borrowers were rather creative in meeting collateral requirements ("Well, gee, Mr. Loan Officer, this here 50-acre cow pasture is worth $5 million"). The result: Each and every one of us, our children, and maybe even our grand-children, are now stuck with a bill for a mere $500 billion or so to bail out failed S&Ls.

It should be clear from this short discussion that even normally ethical people can behave unethically under the right circumstances. Although each of us may feel that we are highly ethical (right up there at Kohlberg's Level III, of course), we *can* be influenced by the ethics of others and the company and industry in which we work, and by the opportunity to achieve something desirable through sometimes dubious means. When everyone else in the office takes home pens and note pads or pirates computer programs from the office computer, and no one ever gets punished for it (or caught), the decision to take home a couple of packages of Post-it™ note pads doesn't seem so bad. Further, when a person has low ethical standards to begin with, he or she may even fail to *realize* that there is something wrong with such behavior. When everyone in the organization is stuck at Kohlberg's Level I, don't be too surprised when things run amok, or company property grows little legs and runs away at night.

## A Workplace Full of *Really* Tough Choices

Many of the tough choices we face in the workplace relate to problems, situations, or controversies in which we must choose among several actions, which may be judged by others as right or wrong (whether we like it or not). These choices often develop from conflicts between an individual's personal moral standards and the strategies, policies, or values of the organization in which he or she works. It is often difficult to discern when a "promotional incentive" becomes a bribe, for example, or to recognize when an advertisement is deceptive, or to know how much puffery can go into a sales presentation, or to identify sexual harassment or racial discrimination. We need to remember that we usually are not trained in our personal, home, and family lives to deal with such tough choices, but these are real ethical issues that we must deal with (and frequently!) in the business world. It is important to note that personal ethical issues, such as abortion, sexual activity, drinking, and smoking are not the focus of our discussion here. These become business issues *only* when they influence a person's performance or endanger others. The development of "smoke-free" buildings all over the country is a recent example of a personal habit that was recognized as endangering others.

Many of the tough choices we face are decisions that will affect others both inside and outside the organization. In general, most businesses seem to be overly concerned with ethical issues that could damage their reputations. Such companies try to avoid scandals and front-page news coverage of incidents that appear to damage them or their products. Most of these tough choices can be sorted into four general categories: conflicts of interest, fairness and honesty, communications, or organizational relationships. Obviously, this list is not all-inclusive, but these categories can help foster *recognition* of ethical issues, which is the first step in learning to handle tough choices.

Conflicts of Interest  When a person is faced with the tough choice of deciding whether to advance his or her own personal interests or those of the organization, a *conflict of interest* exists. For example, in North America it is usually accepted that employees should not accept bribes, personal payments, gifts, or special favors; people who do so are often placing their own interests ahead of those of their employer, as well as those of competitors and consumers. Of course, in many other parts of the world, bribery is an acceptable way of doing business. Offering or accepting bribes in the conduct of foreign business has led to the downfall of many American managers, however. If you do in Rome what the Romans do, you may well go to jail in America.

Conflicts of interest pose an even greater issue when they are hidden from others. When Barry L. Bigwig, a real-estate developer who just happens to serve as a director of the hometown savings and loan association, obtains especially favorable financing for a project from that same S&L, he has placed his personal interests ahead of those of the S&L, as well as other customers of the S&L. As the truth inevitably comes out, customers may question why Mr. Bigwig has received such a good deal when they have not; others may question whether the deal was in the best interest of the depositors. These days, such questions are often followed by calls from Congressional investigators.

**Honesty and Fairness** The terms *honesty* and *fairness* have universal appeal, like mom and apple pie, and businesspeople are expected to follow these principles as well as all applicable laws and regulations. When businesses knowingly harm customers, clients, employees, or competitors through deception, misrepresentation, or coercion, however, they are acting in their own self-interest and violating these basic principles. More importantly, when these principles are violated, it destroys trust and makes it difficult, if not downright impossible, to conduct business.

**Communications** Some of the tough choices that arise in the workplace involve honesty in personal memos and daily conversations with others in the organization. Other issues include deception in advertising messages and lying in communications with government or regulatory organizations. In fact, lying is a major ethical issue in business today. One national poll revealed that people believe they are lied to by politicians, businesspeople, and even their best friends, among others. Once again, lying and deceptive communications create ethical issues because they destroy trust and complicate business transactions. Because lying is such a serious problem, the subject will be given a full-bore treatment in Chapter 3.

**Organizational Relationships** Tough choices in organizational relationships concern how people in the organization relate to customers, suppliers, employees, co-workers, and others. Some of these choices include whether to disclose confidential information obtained from others (like the boss's secretary), how to meet obligations and responsibilities, how to avoid unduly pressuring others and possibly encouraging them to behave unethically, and whether to take someone else's work and present it as one's own without providing credit or compensation (what we used to call plagiarism in college). How often is a strategic plan or report simply copied, with a quick change of name, and passed on as original work?

35

Although the previous discussion may have been a bit tedious and academic, we feel it is important that you know that we're talking about the tough choices and ethical issues businesspeople often face; we're *not* making judgments about what activities are ethical or unethical. Few of us always make the best decision, but the more informed we are, and especially the more quickly we recognize an ethical issue, the more likely we are to have an opportunity to resolve it successfully and ethically.

## Using Intuition as a Guide for Making Tough Choices

Many of us rely at times on "gut feelings" in making choices. We sometimes buy a product impulsively because it "feels right," or we buy a lottery ticket because we "get a hunch" that we will win the giant lotto prize. We just know that we are making the right decision. Psychologists have a word for such feelings: They call them *intuition*. Those of us who are familiar with intuition, or accustomed to using it, know that it can often be marvelously and uncannily accurate, but that it can also be hilariously and dangerously inaccurate.

Why is it, firstly, that intuition can sometimes be so accurate? Perhaps the most simple and straightforward answer that can be given here is that each of us has two brains, or at least two brain hemispheres or halves that are known to possess markedly different yet complementary functions.[7] Our left brain is our computer: It helps us make logical decisions, it reasons, and it functions in a highly conscious way. Most of us are pretty clearly aware of our left brain and how it functions.

The right brain, on the other hand, is our emotional and creative self. It tends to function without our conscious awareness, but it is busy processing information nonetheless. It is actively involved in governing our emotions, and is directly responsible for helping us make some of the illogical but necessary leaps in thinking that are essential to the creative process. It is responsible for many of the so-called gut feelings we have, but it is also where we deal with some of our irrational feelings such as guilt, that generalized (and often inaccurate) feeling that we have done a bad thing.

Enough about the fact that we have two rather separate brains, as exciting as that is, and on to the fact that right-brain processes used by intelligent and sane adults are often very useful and accurate guideposts.

For instance, Laura Wilson, the young student at the beginning of this chapter, immediately felt that the presence of numerous prescription drugs in the nurse's apartment was wrong. What we will now call an "ethical gut twinge" is a feeling that a choice we are making is wrong, and it is a feeling that incorporates a lot of information that our right brain has been actively, if unconsciously, processing for us.

When a decision feels wrong, the ethical gut twinge is a warning and a guidepost. If we pay attention to it, and use it as a signal to sit down and think things through, it may save us a peck of trouble in the long run. Our own counsel may be all we need in some of these situations, but as intelligent adults we may also need to take the time to talk to good and trusted friends. Centuries ago the English poet John Donne observed that no man is an island in and unto himself. That ancient observation has proven prophetic when it comes to making complex ethical choices in a world that seems filled with gray areas.

A note or two on why intuition or gut feeling is sometimes wrong. If an immature person, such as a small child, is responding to gut feelings—and is by definition functioning at Level I or Level II on Kohlberg's moral development scale—the feeling will simply reflect fear of punishment or conventional disapproval. Many "nice guy" managers are fixated at one of these levels, as are many of the problem employees they have to deal with. The result is almost always aggravation or worsening of the problem behavior.[8]

People who are emotionally disturbed may also have inappropriate or inaccurate gut feelings. While emotional disturbance is a complex and much-misunderstood phenomenon, it almost always has two characteristics: (1) The individual's perceptions are seriously distorted, and (2) there are very strong feelings of guilt and inadequacy, and, often, a pattern of extremely low self-esteem. Such persons often simply are not able to make accurate judgments that withstand the scrutiny of others, and may have seriously distorted perceptions of right and wrong. Our system of criminal justice recognizes this fact by allowing seriously disturbed persons to plead not guilty to major crimes by reason of insanity.

The majority of us, particularly those in managerial positions, could probably learn to trust our feelings *more*, however, and not less. In a somewhat frivolous mood one night, one of the authors, after a long day of working on this manuscript, penned a few lines in the spirit of comic relief that somehow still seem valid several months later:

# Choices Are Sometimes Tough

*If the choice is a tough one*
*And you're a little uptight,*
*If the answer ain't easy,*
*And you're feeling some fright,*
*If your guts say it's wrong,*
*Well, they're probably right!*

Our readers will probably agree with us that it would be useless to continue this chapter after such a daring exploitation of poetic license, for which we accept full responsibility.*

---

* The left-brained reader will rapidly detect a shameless right-brained excuse to slip some bad poetry into this otherwise left-brained paragraph. Some readers will regard this entire passage as just plain lame-brained. To each his own, we say.

1. Based on a student's personal communication to the authors, April 30, 1990. Names and places have been changed to protect both the innocent and the guilty.

2. John Fraedrich, "Philosophy Type Interaction in the Ethical Decision Making Process of Retailers," (Ph.D. diss., Texas A&M University, 1988).

3. Albert Z. Carr, "Is Business Bluffing Ethical?" *Harvard Business Review* (January-February 1968): 143-153

4. Lawrence Kohlberg, "The Cognitive-Developmental Approach to Socialization," in *Handbook of Socialization Theory and Research*, ed. D.A. Goslin (Chicago: Rand McNally, 1969).

5. Adapted from Lawrence Kohlberg, "The Development of Children's Orientations Toward a Moral Order: I. Sequence in the Development of Moral Thought," *Vita Humana,* 1963, no. 6: 18-19.

6. O.C. Ferrell and Larry Gresham, "A Contingency Framework for Understanding Ethical Decision Making in Marketing," *Journal of Marketing* 49 (Summer 1985): 87-95.

7. For an excellent discussion of the separate functions of the so-called split brain, see Robert Ornstein, *The Psychology of Consciousness* (San Francisco: W.H. Freeman, 1975).

8. For an excellent discussion of "nice-guy" managers and problem employees, and how to deal with both, you may wish to consult Gareth Gardiner, *Tough-Minded Management of Problem Employees: Don't Be a Gutless Nice Guy!* (Springfield, IL: Smith Collins, 1990).

■ Unlike the classic western movie, where right and wrong were simply and clearly defined (good guys wore white; bad guys wore black), and where right always triumphed, real-world ethical issues are much more *complex* and *messy*. Even when we feel we are doing something right, painful consequences sometimes follow.

■ People may be motivated to behave unethically because their personal moral standards are inadequate for the task. Social psychologist Lawrence Kohlberg developed a popular model that helps explain why individuals often make very different ethical choices in the same dilemma. He has shown that many of us achieve different degrees of *moral development.*

1.  At Level I, the *preconventional stage,* young or immature persons make very *concrete* ethical decisions based on fear of *punishment* or anticipated *rewards.*

2.  At Level II, the *conventional stage* reached by most of us, *society's* standards influence us most heavily.

3.  At Level III, the *postconventional stage,* individual conscience is most important in making ethical decisions. The individual takes *full responsibility* for his or her actions.

■ Personal morals and standards do not always translate into ethical behavior at work because people are also influenced by unethical others in their organization or by the values of the organization itself (the organization's *corporate culture*), or they may have the opportunity to take advantage of a situation for personal gain.

■ Most tough choices people are faced with in the workplace fall into four categories: conflict of interest, honesty and fairness, communications, or organizational relationships.

■ *Gut feelings* are sometimes a useful guide to ethical choice, because the *right brain*, or creative/emotional side of the brain, is involved in such feelings. What we call *intuition* is a right-brain function and can be very accurate. Gut feelings may also be inaccurate, however. Persons who are immature or *disturbed* may have very inappropriate gut feelings. Many of us, however, could learn to *trust our feelings more*.

Insights & Guidelines from Chapter Two

## ETHICAL CHOICE AND
## THE RETAIL FOOD INDUSTRY

*Any good grocery-store manager should pros-
ecute a suspected shoplifter, right? Wait a
minute, it's not always quite that simple, as the
following incident may demonstrate. The choice
faced by a store manager was suddenly made very tough indeed when the
alleged shoplifter turned out to be the wife of a senior company executive. For
those of you who enjoy making quick and highly critical moral judgments about
the behavior of others, this incident will give you ample opportunity to do
exactly that. As we sometimes do, we have cast a cloak of anonymity over the
case to protect the guilty, but the words are those of a former manager in the
grocery industry.*

### "FOUL PLAY AT THE FLORAL DISPLAY"

The floral department manager of a local outlet of a large national
supermarket chain returned from her lunch hour one day to find that,
oddly, most (but not all) of the flowers had been removed from one of
the silk flower arrangements on display. The sight of the few remaining
flowers in what had been a full display, and their scattered appearance,
led the manager to make immediate inquiries into what had happened.

A clerk from a nearby area mentioned that a woman had been
asking about the various flower arrangements, and that she had been in
the floral department during lunch hour. He added that she was the
only customer he had seen in the floral department for some time. He
recognized the woman as the wife of the highest-ranking district
manager for the company at that time.

The department manager then asked the cashiers whether any
floral arrangements had been purchased during the last hour. Sure
enough, only one had been, by the district manager's wife. The cashier
remembered that the full, beautiful arrangement seemed priced aw-
fully low, but she had not become suspicious because the customer *was*
the district manager's wife. At this time, the purchase itself was verified
by receipt tapes and departmental sales readings. The amount of
money the woman had paid was for a much smaller display of natural
flowers.

Although everyone was still in a state of disbelief, a case against the woman was rapidly building. The florist now brought the matter to the store manager's attention, even though the evidence was largely circumstantial. After the manager had been given a detailed account of what had occurred, he stated simply that justice would best be served if the people involved kept quiet and dropped the matter.

This was the real-life decision. Regardless of what management and ethics textbooks state should happen, this is what *did* happen. Of course, tales of this importance aren't often kept quiet, and the story made its inevitable progression through the store rumor mill.

The store employees soon developed a poor attitude over the justice handed out. Some suggested that if the woman had been a regular store employee, she would have been fired; if she had been a regular customer, she would have been prosecuted. But because she was the boss's wife, the situation was ignored and everyone looked the other way. The employees felt betrayed and saw the political implications as unjust.

The evidence, albeit circumstantial, was there, however, and the choice not to make accusations based on that evidence, as well as the possible career implications the alternative might carry, must have been tough. But it is a tough world, and employees have feelings, too. The manager probably made the only sensible decision he was capable of in his position. Because the evidence was circumstantial, it probably would have been pretty risky for him to accuse the woman of shoplifting. His mistake, however, may have been in not having the confidence to explain his decision to those involved. This simple act could have prevented the attitude problems, and earned him respect in the future. Good management principles would dictate involving the employees closest to the situation in the decision, or at least explaining the action taken on such a tough ethical matter. ■■

your company stinks, and your spouse is stupid." Such an abrupt, tactless, and massive dose of honesty is likely to lead to immediate unemployment. Two timeless maxims apply here: (1) Silence is (sometimes) golden, and (2) discretion is the better part of valor. Far better to risk something like, "You know, Chief, I would like to talk with you sometime about some of the problems our company is having, and some of my ideas for dealing with them." A useful survival rule, if you are contemplating an outburst of honesty that might prove risky, is to run it by one or two of your colleagues for their appraisal before you run in and bounce it off the boss.

## The *Political* Versus the *Competent* Organization

Although it doesn't necessarily have to, the word *political* has a bad reputation in our society. To millions of Americans it all too often means sneaking, conniving, hypocritical, and dishonest. To be political means to be shameless, to be a public liar, and to do business in the dead of night behind closed doors.

While the word *political* can also have many positive connotations (willing to compromise, to negotiate, and to save face), we are using the term to refer to organizations based on dishonesty and manipulation. Political organizations may be both public or private: Neither sector has a monopoly on virtue or honesty. Political organizations are distinguished by the fact that they are willing to do just about anything to succeed in the short run, and by the fact that in the long run, they do *not* succeed (unless they change their ways).

The classic example of the political organization is, coincidentally, the patronage political office, where all jobs are secured as the direct result of some favorable connection with the duly elected officeholder. It is not *what* you know, it is *who* you know that matters. If the head of the organization fails to win re-election, all job holders go down the proverbial tube together. While pale-faced arguments are sometimes made to justify the system ("The fear of losing their jobs will keep them honest," or "Every four years we're going to get new blood"), the almost inevitable outcome is an organization where everyone focuses on the need to survive, and where getting the job done may or may not be important to survival.

Lest you think that public organizations are getting a bad rap here, many private organizations also fit the description. Rather than focus on the failings of such companies, however, it may be much more positive and useful to identify some of the characteristics of companies that are *conspicuously* competent. This is just what Tom Peters and Robert Waterman did in their best-selling 1982 book, *In Search of Excellence*, in which they described some of the guiding principles of American's truly excellent companies—firms like Merck, Liz Claiborne, 3M, Wal-Mart, IBM, McDonald's, and Johnson & Johnson.[4]

Almost without exception, these firms are driven by high standards and carefully chosen values. They are customer oriented: They realize that to succeed they must stay in close touch with customers and strive to please. IBM, for example, attempts to answer all customer complaints within 24 hours, and it measures internal and external customer satisfaction on a monthly basis to ensure that it stays close to its customers. These companies realize that productivity results from people, and they treat their employees with trust, respect, and dignity—and implement their suggestions.

Peters and Waterman suggest that America's excellent companies are frequently "loose-tight" in terms of their organization; that is, they are tightly controlled by their values, but they are very loosely organized. They give their employees plenty of room to be creative, entrepreneurial, and competent. Often their CEOs have a strong commitment to the highest ethical standards and values, as was the case with Thomas Watson, Sr., founder of IBM. While that proud company is widely recognized for its excellence in the computer industry, it is less well known that since the early 1950s, IBM has made a major commitment to hiring members of minority groups. Long before affirmative action was a recognized term, IBM already recognized the importance of maintaining a work force representative of all members of society and valued the contributions of its minority employees.

One of the things that really stands out about the excellent companies cited by Peters and Waterman is that they focus on people: customers and employees, not products, reports and memos, or equipment. In general, they have found ways of reducing destructive competitiveness among employees, often because they have alternatives to promotion (profit sharing, praise and recognition, participation in management and decision making, intrapreneurship programs—where creative employees are given free time to work on their own idea —and job enrichment) as a means of rewarding employees. America's excellent companies recognize that having highly motivated employees working together as a team to get the job done is a sure road to success, a lesson that the Japanese have long since learned.

## As Usual, the Japanese Do It Differently

Although the American culture has many virtues, including a high degree of creativity and resiliency, one of its failings is that it is very egocentric and slow to learn from the experience of other nations. Fortunately, in the last 20 years we have decided that we have much to gain by carefully studying how the Japanese practice management.

With regard to the training and promotion of managers, the Japanese have a concept that would also make sense in a great many American organizations. Newly hired Japanese managers are not encouraged to expect a promotion for at least ten, and up to fifteen, years. During the interim, the trainee is rotated from department to department at two- to three-year intervals, until he (and lately, she) becomes familiar with all of the major functions of the organization. At the end of a decade or so of this sort of cross-functional experience, a *group* of managers is typically promoted together, quite literally as a management team. The notion of a "fast track," with energetic rivals competing vigorously for a few available promotional slots, is simply foreign to the Japanese mind.

This emphasis on developing a wide variety of skills, along with the great value the Japanese place on teamwork and group loyalty, obviously pays off in terms of developing competence and reducing destructive rivalries. While the Japanese may compete destructively in other areas of their society (the tremendous competition among Japanese youth for admission to prestigious universities comes to mind), their emphasis on cooperation and competence in the workplace is a dynamic principal in their great economic success.

89

## ESOPs: The New Wave in American Business

In recent years, many American employees have begun acting like they own the place, for the very good reason that more and more of them do. Employee stock ownership plans, or ESOPs, are rapidly coming of age in America. Close to 10,000 American firms now offer ESOPs in one form or another, and in about 1,500 of those firms, employees own a majority of the stock.[5] ESOPs have become popular partly because they receive highly favorable tax treatment, but also because they have been very successful, on balance.

ESOPs have come into their own as a way of saving companies that would otherwise face bankruptcy, often because of aging and inefficient physical plants. Old lumber and steel mills are familiar examples. In most of these cases, when employees become owners, they rapidly find ways of increasing productivity, even though they often must vote to take short-term wage or salary cuts while they are getting the business back on its feet again.

ESOPs work because when employees become owners, they must all work together to re-energize and resurrect the firm. A very high premium is thus placed on competence and creativity. Morale reaches new heights as highly motivated employees work hard to turn around their company. The reward for doing so, of course, is that each employee-owner participates directly in the company's new prosperity through the increased value of his or her stock. Not surprisingly, most employee-owned organizations are highly democratic, and manipulative political games have minimal value. *Merit* and *hard work* are what truly matter; the practitioner of M & M theory is a misfit in such organizations.

While long-range predictions are always risky, it seems likely that ESOPs will continue to increase in both size and number, and may well become the dominant American organizational form in the twenty-first century. If this development should in fact occur, it will be a healthy one indeed, representing as it will yet another move toward competency based organizations, and a move away from manipulative and politically based ones.

## Ethical Leadership

The ability of managers to guide and direct others toward achievement of goals significantly affects the quality of the decisions made in an organization. Because managers have the power to motivate and reward others and enforce organizational policies, they provide a strong influence on ethical decisions. M & M theory simply will not work in any organization that has a strong leader who engenders respect and provides a standard of ethical conduct among its members. For example, when workers see that lying, cheating, and stealing will not earn them a promotion or any other badge of success, then most will cease these activities. When they see that massaging the boss and maligning co-workers are not acceptable techniques for getting ahead in the organization, these activities too will cease. When the boss acknowledges and responds to ethical problems, everyone gets the message as to what actions are acceptable for resolving an ethical issue. Positive reinforcement for ethical behavior usually encourages that behavior; negative reinforcement for unethical actions discourages it. If we may repeat one of our favorite ethical maxims, a single managerial action may be worth a million words!

One company found a novel way to get its employees to become more honest by occasionally offering a reward to employees who publicly confessed to major mistakes. The objective of this unconventional policy was to provide an opportunity for employees to learn from each others' mistakes and to take responsibility and "fess up" without fear of being fired. The salesperson who admitted he lost an account by offering a small gift to a purchasing agent (the customer's company had a policy of turning down any vendor who offered a bribe) received a $250 award for his honesty in admitting the mistake. At the same time, of course, the company hopes that other salespeople will learn from this mistake that the giving of gifts to obtain business is not acceptable.

Good leaders let it be known that the way to earn rewards (promotions, raises, and the like) is not through massaging the boss or maligning co-workers, but rather through achieving company goals in an ethical manner. Strong leadership develops cohesiveness within the organization, and helps employees gain loyalty, support, and trust from a compassionate leader. Without strong ethical leadership, massaging and maligning behavior may be rampant, especially if it is inadvertently rewarded by the organization's culture. Strong leadership comes from the ability to guide others toward achievement of goals while controlling rewards and punishments that encourage ethical behavior.

Ethical leadership has been a hallmark of America's excellent companies, as we noted earlier in our discussion of IBM and its founder, Thomas Watson, Sr. Branch Rickey of the Brooklyn (now Los Angeles) Dodgers broke the color line in major league baseball more than 40 years ago, when racism was a fact of life in our national pastime; the Dodger organization is still recognized for its excellence many years after Rickey's death. Thomas Watson, Sr., and Branch Rickey may now be gone physically, but their spirit lives on as a vital and continuing part of the corporate cultures they left behind.

## References in Chapter Five

1. David C. McClelland, *The Achievement Society (Princeton*, NJ: Van Nostrand, 1975).

2. William M. Carley, "Secrets War: GE Presses Campaign to Halt Rivals' Misuse of Turbine-Parts Data," *The Wall Street Journal*, August 16, 1988, p. A10.

3. Andy Paztor and Rick Wartzman, "The Clique: How a Spy for Boeing and His Pals Gleaned Data on Defense Plans," *The Wall Street Journal*, January 15, 1990, pp. A1, A6.

4. Much of the material in this section has been adapted from Thomas J. Peters and Robert H. Waterman, Jr., *In Search of Excellence* (New York: Harper & Row, 1982).

5. Frederick Ungeheuer, "They Own the Place," *Time*, February 6, 1989, pp. 50-51.

■ A *cherished American belief* is that hard work, being nice, and being a good team player are what it takes to get ahead and to become *successful*. The *reality*, however, is sometimes different.

■ In the traditional *hierarchical* organization, where several different employees often compete for the same promotion, the thing to do to get ahead often seems to be to *massage* your boss and *malign* your neighbor. In simple language, this means flattering your boss so you look good, and doing what you can to make your co-workers look bad.

■ The person who uses such *manipulative* behaviors to get ahead in the great American rat race will always feel *dishonest*, and will suffer from feelings of low *self-esteem*.

■ While there is no magic formula for getting away from manipulative behaviors, refreshing doses of *honesty* are to be recommended. In a situation where you might normally *cover your butt* and *blame your neighbor*, try being *honest*. The *risk* you take may well pay off in feelings of increased pride and integrity. Please don't try a huge, *foolish* dose of honesty all at once, however.

■ In organizations that are *political*, people get ahead by being manipulative. Merit often doesn't matter: *Who* you know is more important than *what* you know. In *competent* organizations, traditional American values are at work: Hard work, high standards, and cooperative behavior are what matter.

■ America's *excellent* companies are almost without exception competent and value good relationships with *people* (customers and employees, both) rather than with policies and procedures.

94

- The *Japanese* have a lesson or two to teach us about competency. Japanese managers don't expect rapid promotions, become competent in several different areas of the company, and are rewarded for being good *team players.*

- ESOPs (employee-owned businesses) may well be the *new wave* in American business in the twenty-first century. In ESOPs, all employees typically work hard together because if they do, and the company is profitable, *everyone wins.* ESOPs already have a very strong track record.

- M & M theory will not work in an organization that has a strong leader who creates respect and provides a living standard of ethical conduct. Good leaders let it be known that the way to earn promotions, raises, and other such rewards is not through massaging the boss or maligning co-workers, but rather through achieving company goals in an ethical manner.

## ETHICAL CHOICE AND
## THE BABY FOOD INDUSTRY

*Those of use who are loving parents, despite our bad days, would be horrified if we thought we were buying a commercially prepared food product for our beloved infants that turned out to be* something other than what it was advertised to be, and possibly even dangerous. We tend, as American consumers, to accept that the baby foods we find on our grocers' shelves are pure and safe. Most are, to be sure, but every now and again a case comes along that shakes our confidence.

*The incident that follows not only demonstrates the need for personal and government vigilance in maintaining product safety, but also deals with the extreme reluctance of the executives bearing direct personal responsibility for the production and sale of fraudulent, and potentially unsafe, products to admit their guilt.*

### "BEECH-NUT APPLE JUICE: NOT QUITE THE REAL THING!"*

Baby-food giant Gerber dominates the infant food market, but the Beech-Nut Nutrition Corporation has historically held second place. Beech-Nut has traditionally enjoyed a reputation for the quality and purity of its foods, including its apple juice, which was labeled and promoted as 100 percent fruit juice. There is no doubt whatsoever that this is what it once was, but in the 1970s things began to run amok at Beech-Nut after the company was sold to a group headed by entrepreneur Frank Nicholas.

---

* Information for this case was taken from Alix M. Freedman, "Nestlé Seeks to Sell Beechnut, Dogged by Scandal of Bogus Apple Juice," *The Wall Street Journal*, July 6, 1989, p. B1; Chris Welles, "What Led Beech-Nut Down the Road to Disgrace," *Business Week*, February 22, 1988, pp. 124-128; and Betty Wong, "Conviction of Nestlé Unit's Ex-President Is Overturned on Appeal in Juice Case," *The Wall Street Journal*, March 31, 1989, p. B5.

Nicholas displayed the dark side of the entrepreneurial spirit all too fully. His buy out of Beech-Nut was one of the first of the so-called leveraged buy outs involving large sums of borrowed money, and he soon ran the company into major financial difficulties. By 1977 Beech-Nut was in such desperate straits that it jumped at a chance to buy apple-juice concentrate from a supplier named Interjuice Trading Corporation at about 20 percent below the market price. This was a major opportunity to save money, because apple concentrate was used in products accounting for 30 percent of Beech-Nut's sales.

Too good to be true, you say, such a good deal. Chemists in the research and development department at Beech-Nut were equally suspicious of the low cost of the apple-juice concentrate, particularly in view of rampant rumors of adulteration in the industry, and they immediately began to run tests on it. While the tests were not precise enough to be conclusive, the results indicated to the Beech-Nut chemists that the Interjuice concentrate was probably made of beet sugar, apple flavor, caramel color, and corn syrup; not a shot of apple juice in the whole damned thing! By this time, Beech-Nut had been purchased by Nestlé S.A., and was under tremendous pressure from Nestlé to improve its still precarious financial position.

After two Beech-Nut employees visited the Interjuice apple concentrate supplier, and were not allowed into the concentrate-processing facility, suspicions about the concentrate were magnified. Jerome LiCari was director of research and development for Beech-Nut, and in August 1981 he sent a memorandum to Operations Head John F. Lavery, and later to President Neils L. Hoyvald, expressing his concerns about the purity of the apple-juice concentrate. The two executives not only took no action in response to LiCari's memorandum, Lavery even threatened to fire LiCari, who soon resigned.

In 1982 a private investigator hired by the Processed Apples Institute, Inc., a trade association, told Beech-Nut that its apple concentrate was a phony—a chemical concoction, based on new and accurate test information. He asked the company to join a lawsuit against the concentrate producers, but Beech-Nut refused. Had the company joined the lawsuit, it might well have nipped the case in the bud and gotten off with a fine. Its stonewalling led directly to its downfall, however.

The case unraveled over a four-year period, and in 1986, a 470-count indictment was returned against Beech-Nut and its two top executives. Both Neils Hoyvald and John Lavery pleaded not guilty and denied any wrongdoing, but were nonetheless convicted of almost 800 counts of violating the Food and Drug Act in 1988. In March 1989, however, a federal appeals court overturned most of the convictions because the case had not been tried in the area in which the crimes occurred. As of this writing, it is scheduled for retrial at an unspecified time in the future. Beech-Nut itself has since been sold to Ralston Purina. ■■

# 6

## Tough-Minded
## Management
## Of Ethical Problems

In a business and professional world filled with tough managerial choices, numerous ethical conflicts, all-too-frequent temptations, and constant organizational pressures, it is never *too* surprising when things go awry in the workplace (the Pentagate scandal and the $500-billion savings and loan industry fiasco come immediately to mind). The really surprising thing, though, is the number of companies that have continued to be ethical, even during the decade of the 1980s, which has been increasingly characterized as a decade of greed gone wild. Even in an era of permissiveness and rampant self-interest, managers who are genuinely concerned and have an enlightened concept of their own interest have usually made choices that will stand them in good stead during the remainder of this century, which has begun as a decade of heightened social and environmental awareness. Because personal moral standards, organizational pressures (pressures due to an organization's values and the power of co-workers and managers), and opportunity so strongly influence the ethics of businesspeople, management techniques for effectively resolving ethical conflicts are essential. One such technique, which we believe has great value for resolving ethical issues, is the concept of tough-minded management.

## Tough-Minded Management[1]

Tough-minded management is an approach for helping managers deal effectively with problem employees and problems in general. To understand and apply tough-minded management to ethical problems in the workplace, let's take a close look at the notion of tough-minded management by first looking at its opposite numbers: nice-guy and tough-guy management.

"Nice-Guy Management" A whole generation of American managers has arisen who are so "nice" that they let problem employees (those who are not performing satisfactorily for any reason) get away with murder because they don't have the intestinal fortitude to deal directly, face to face, and promptly with such persons. These "nice-guy managers" are typically pleasant middle-class American men and women who are afraid of conflict and of the possibility of being disliked by their employees.

The direct result of this fear is managerial avoidance: unwillingness to face up to problems, often accompanied by physical avoidance of the problem employee—practices which unwittingly make problems worse. When a manager avoids dealing with the problem of an employee who is cooking the firm's books (perhaps to boost his or her own bonus), cheating a client, sexually harassing other employees, or creating some other problem, the manager sends a message to that employee that such behavior is O.K., and even that anything goes in this particular work environment. Another message the employee receives is that the manager is totally gutless; the resulting lack of respect from *all* employees leads to chaos in the work environment. Everyone begins to take advantage of the manager who cannot face up to problems. Like any neurotic person, the nice-guy manager unconsciously brings about the very thing he or she fears most, which in this case means not only being disliked but *hated* by employees.

The avoidance of, or aversion to, dealing with problems is usually accompanied by a serious lack of managerial *honesty*. The manager lies to himself or herself, by pretending that the problem does not exist ("It's just a temporary problem, and it'll go away"); by making up all kinds of excuses for not taking action ("This guy's a compulsive thief, and since I'm not a psychologist, I can't help him"); and by lying to superiors and subordinates ("I'm going to wait for a week or two, and if things don't get better, then by golly I'm going to do something"). The whole avoidance pattern is accompanied by a form of mental judo that is designed to protect the gutless nice-guy manager from the unpleasant truth: He or she is responsible for making problems worse by failing to take action, and the *real* problem is the gutlessness of the manager.

One of the most unpleasant and destructive outcomes of a long period of gutless management, or nice-guy avoidance, is that the employee is lulled into a false sense of security by the manager's inaction, while the manager begins to develop an intense hatred for the employee. It matters not that the hatred felt by the manager for the employee is simply a projection of the manager's self-hatred. The manager's anger grows until, one day, it is expressed in an "I hate your guts" flip-flop: The manager calls the employee in, and, in a voice shaking with rage, advises the startled nonperformer that he or she is fired, effective immediately. A classic, so-called lose-lose confrontation ensues, which often leads to fisticuffs or other forms of violence: The gutless nice guy has again brought about the very thing he or she fears. In contemporary American management, we seem to have an over-abundance of nice guys (see Table 6-1).

"Tough-Guy Management" On the other side of the coin, some managers use "tough-guy" tactics, not just in moments of rage, but as a continuing management style or philosophy. Tough-guy management is the historical or traditional American style, as was exemplified by the exploitative tactics of the robber barons in the early days of laissez-faire capitalism, where employees were cogs in the wheel and nothing more. In dealing with problem employees, contemporary tough-guy managers make immediate use of all the authority available to them, and promptly use punitive measures to deal with any employee who has transgressed, whatever the problem or underlying circumstances behind the problem.

Tough-guy management gets results in the short run because fear is a powerful motivator, but in the long run the tough-guy manager also creates chaos, as alienated employees quit or find ways to get even with a manager they hate. Fear is ineffective as a long-term motivator, as any parent will tell you, because it tends to dissipate or disappear after repeated threats or punishments, and because the child rapidly and skillfully learns to avoid the punitive parent. Employees are every bit as creative and cunning as children when they learn to cope with, and

# Table 6-1

## The Continuum of Managerial Authority and Social/Ethical Effectiveness

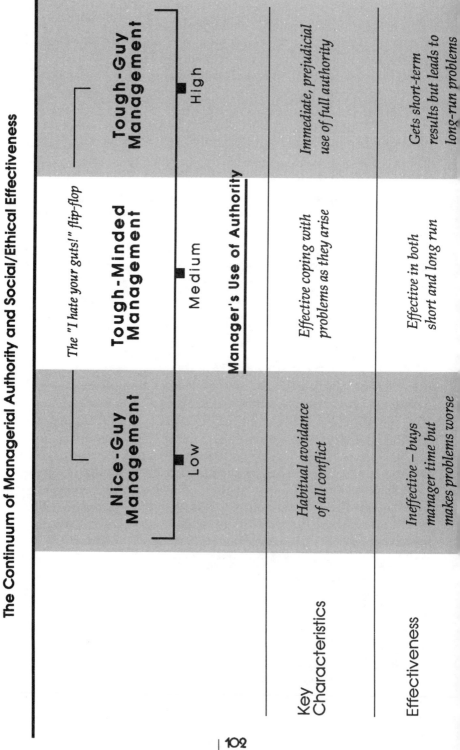

| | Nice-Guy Management | Tough-Minded Management | Tough-Guy Management |
|---|---|---|---|
| | The "I hate your guts!" flip-flop | | |
| | Low | Medium | High |
| | **Manager's Use of Authority** | | |
| Key Characteristics | Habitual avoidance of all conflict | Effective coping with problems as they arise | Immediate, prejudicial use of full authority |
| Effectiveness | Ineffective – buys manager time but makes problems worse | Effective in both short and long run | Gets short-term results but leads to long-run problems |

| | Neville Chamberlain / Millions of modern Americans | Harry S. Truman / Winston Churchill / Lee Iacocca | Adolph Hitler / Saddam Hussein |
|---|---|---|---|
| **Historical Practitioners** | Neville Chamberlain Millions of modern Americans | Harry S. Truman Winston Churchill Lee Iacocca | Adolph Hitler Saddam Hussein |
| **Psychological Characteristics** | Employees walk all over management, which loses all respect. Manager lives in personal hell. | Management is liked AND respected | Management gets some respect in short-run, but is hated in long-run |
| **Level of Moral Development** | Level II – conform, and be pleasant | Level III – individual conscience guides problem solving | Level I – avoid punishment, or use punishment |
| **Ethical Strategies** | Deny responsibility for problems. Appease critics. | Take responsibility for problems and solve them. Anticipate and prevent problems. | Deny responsibility for problems. Aggressively attack critics. |

103

Adapted from Gareth S. Gardiner, *Tough-Minded Management of Problem Employees: Don't Be a Gutless Nice Guy!* (Springfield, IL: Smith Collins, 1990).

then get even with, the punitive tough-guy manager. Moreover, fearful, angry employees may resort to dubious activities in their efforts to preserve their jobs and income while they attempt to get even with their cruel bosses.

"Tough-Minded Management" Tough-minded management, as it was first described by management consultant Joe Batten, lies between the nice-guy and the tough-guy extremes.[2] The "tough-minded manager" is first and foremost an honest realist: He or she realizes that, with a few exceptions, problems will not go away, and indeed will normally get worse if they are not dealt with quickly and effectively. He does not play let's-pretend-what-a-nice-world-it-is games, and does not lie to himself about the problem and what needs to be done about it. The tough-minded manager cares about her employees and their problems, and her ethical concern is heightened by the knowledge that a problem employee whose problem behaviors worsen will become destructive both to himself or herself and to others in the organization.

Tough-Minded Management in Action The concept of tough-minded management also includes a practical and effective five-step method for dealing with a problem employee.

1. Meet face to face with the employee, and treat the employee courteously and as an adult.
2. State the problem objectively, in terms of job performance, and without accusations or moralizing.
3. Listen to the employee talk about the problem in a supportive and open-minded way.
4. Suggest or demand a promise of action from the employee that will solve the problem, if the employee does not suggest one.
5. Be prepared to follow up, and document the case where necessary.

The immediate psychological result that managers experience when they follow these tough-minded problem-solving steps is an increase in self-esteem, and an increased willingness to tackle future problems in an honest, open way. The immediate managerial result is an improvement in the behavior of the problem employee. It is our contention that if a tough-minded manager is willing to simply state the problem to the employee in an objective way in a face-to-face meeting (as opposed to sending the person a memo or letter), the problem will be well on its way to resolution over 80 percent of the time, because the employee will be motivated to do something about it.

Gutless nice-guy appeasement (for example, buying off corporate raiders with "green mail") simply leads to more debt that can sink a company and leave its workers jobless. Gutless lying to creditors about the "check being in the mail" simply enrages creditors, and encourages them to sue. Of course, tough-minded employees, when confronted with a problem boss, can take the same series of steps that a manager must in dealing with a problem employee. Tough-minded problem solving is much more than a mere managerial style, it is a philosophy of life, a philosophy marked by willingness to take risks, by personal honesty and integrity, and by a far-sighted understanding of the actions that must be taken in dealing with any conflict or problem, including ethical ones.

There is probably no single reason why effective managers learn to apply tough-minded principles in situations where a problem must be solved, or a tough managerial choice made. However, there are at least two powerful dynamics that lead many of us to move away from ineffective nice-guy or tough-guy strategies and toward more effective and tough-minded ones: the need to have a high level of self-esteem, and the intellectual awareness that dealing with problems effectively and objectively is a necessary managerial value if one is to be successful.

## Applying Tough-Minded Management to Business Ethics

We believe that tough-minded management is an effective way to cope with ethical problems as they arise. Following the five problem-solving steps of this approach can help managers exert ethical leadership, and gain respect, loyalty, and cooperation from employees in the process. Tough-minded management is but one approach for resolving ethical problems in the workplace, however. It does not identify ethical issues and problems for us, nor does it tell us what the proper ethical solutions to these problems might be. But then, we have promised several times in this book not to tell you what is right or wrong, ethical or unethical. Understanding the principles of tough-minded management does arm you with a practical technique for dealing with problems once you have determined what you want to accomplish and what ethical standards to apply. You or your organization must determine what ethical standards will be your guiding force.

Both nice-guy management and tough-guy management have proven ineffective as approaches to fostering ethical behavior in an organization. In fact, tough-guy approaches are often used both *consciously* and *unconsciously* to encourage subordinates to engage in unethical behavior. In a classic (fictional) example, John B. Tough, the head of the advertising department in a consumer-goods firm and a long-time practitioner of the tough-guy school of management, tells Judy, a new employee in the department, "I want the competition's sales figures on area stores within 48 hours." Judy, who of course wants to make a good impression on her new boss, asks innocently, "How do I get our competitor's sales figures, sir?" The tough-guy manager asserts, "It doesn't matter how you get them, as long as they're on my desk in 48 hours." Still unsure of how to proceed with this ambiguous assignment, Judy questions some of her co-workers, who suggest that she use any means necessary to avoid the dreaded wrath of their boss. They share with her the story of the consequences her hapless predecessor faced when he failed a similar assignment: fired, with no severance pay! The message becomes clear: Judy must resort to some deceptive means to infiltrate the competitor's organization and retrieve the sales figures or suffer the consequences. As this scenario illustrates, employees motivated by fear may resort to unethical actions to avoid punishment: The need to reduce fear is so powerful that it overwhelms every other consideration.

On the other side of the coin, nice-guy managers generally fail to provide any ethical leadership or direction to employees at all. It is so temptingly easy to avoid dealing with the fact that Ima Swindler is padding her expense account or Harvey Hawker is using unethical or possibly even illegal techniques in securing sales. It is easy to justify inaction by saying, "Well, she is successful and has good sales," or, "Who am I to question whether he is right or wrong in his approach?" There are many excuses and many good intentions used to explain why a manager does not take action when it is obvious that unfair, deceptive, or manipulative approaches are being used to achieve goals.

In a consulting project, we confronted a national sales manager with the fact that some salespeople in her organization were offering customers bribes in order to obtain sales. The sales manager responded, "Don't tell me any more about this. I don't want to know about it." Such a nice-guy reaction is typical of many managers who know about improper behavior but refuse to deal with it, usually in the hope that it will just go away. The problem usually does not go away, however. It generally gets worse. Eventually a crisis develops, and the manager must now resort to lies: "I didn't know anything about it. I had a great deal of trust in my employees, and I am surprised that they did the things that they did." The road to ruin sometimes seems to be paved with *both* good intentions and lies.

The tough-minded manager, as you may have surmised by now, neither encourages unethical behavior nor avoids dealing with it. He or she tries to eliminate opportunities for unethical activities by confronting the problem head on. This manager meets with the employee face to face, treating the employee courteously. The problem is stated objectively (for example, "I've noticed that your expense accounts are 25 percent higher than allowed by company policy"), without accusations or judgments. The manager *listens* supportively to the employee talk about the problem (perhaps, for example, the current policy has failed to take into account inflation, or there is some other legitimate problem that warrants investigation), and then asks what the employee intends to do about the problem. The manager later follows up to ensure that the problem has indeed been taken care of.

When an employee has been confronted directly with an ethical problem, that person becomes aware that he or she is under the watchful eyes of the supervisor, and that the behavior will not be tolerated. He or she knows that further action will be taken if the problem is not resolved and what that action will be. This is the bottom line of tough-minded management. It effectively removes the opportunity for unethical behavior by spelling out exactly what the consequences will be.

## The Tough-Minded Manager and Ethics

The very essence of tough-minded management is a constructive outlook accompanied by a willingness to tackle problems wherever they may be found, and the recognition that avoidance of tough choices will only lead to tougher choices in the long run. Because the tough-minded manager is a highly intelligent and realistic human being, he or she consistently recognizes and usually follows seven key ethical values that lead to more effective management. He or she:

1. Accepts that risks must often be taken, and that conflict is inevitable, in making tough choices;
2. Understands that short-run losses may be inevitable and unavoidable to achieve long-run success;
3. Believes that the best approach to business is integrity, especially in the long run;
4. Is aware that ethical problems may arise in the workplace, and of how ethical decisions are usually made in the workplace;
5. Has reached a level of moral development where economic self-interest is not paramount, and where personal ethical values are important;
6. Has learned that trust is the glue that holds business relationships together;
7. Believes strongly that maintaining self-esteem and self-respect outweighs material gain.

These statements of values represent our opinions in a book where we promised not to moralize. Anyone should feel free to question them, of course, but we believe many businesspersons are guided by them. They are known and followed by many successful managers in the business world. In contemporary America, there are some heartwarming examples of tough-minded managers and their organizations taking effective and ethical action when confronted with tough real-world choices.

# Lee Iacocca and the Chrysler Corporation[3]

In recent years, Lee Iacocca has become something of an American hero, and for good reason: He exemplifies tough-minded management in action. Taking over a nearly bankrupt Chrysler Corporation in 1978, Lee Iacocca engineered a dramatic turnaround. He sold off the profitable tank division to raise cash. He secured a $1 billion federally guaranteed loan. He persuaded a reluctant UAW to accept major wage concessions, largely by going to the union, opening the books, and levelling with its leadership about Chrysler's desperate situation. He also made a strategic decision to make Chrysler smaller, closing several unprofitable plants and discontinuing Chrysler's slow-selling line of luxury cars. He focused the company instead on its compact and subcompact lines, which were selling much more briskly. The net result was that the company began turning the financial corner by 1983, albeit at two-thirds its former size.

By now Iacocca was an American legend. He accepted the conflict that results from plant closings and wage rollbacks. His straight, blunt, and honest speaking style had great appeal to Americans, accustomed as they were to anonymous and invisible chief executive officers of major corporations. As is the case with any new hero, however, he was closely examined to see if he had feet of clay. His response to the odometer-disconnection scandal that overtook Chrysler in the summer of 1987 seemed to indicate that, although he is subject to the same human failings as the rest of us, his feet were solidly on the ground.

In his book, *Talking Straight*, Iacocca described at length how he felt when he learned of the fact that some Chrysler executives in the St. Louis area had been driving new Chrysler vehicles with their odometers disconnected, and that the cars were later sold as new (some had even had minor accidents and were repaired before being put on sale).

> *So we proceeded. On the day that we ran our ads (taking responsibility for the odometer disconnections, and announcing compensation would be paid to affected consumers), I called a press conference in Detroit to offer a personal apology. I told everyone that test-driving with the odometers disconnected was plain "dumb." Selling cars that had been damaged, I added, "went beyond dumb all the way to stupid." I said it was unforgivable and it wouldn't happen again.*

*It was clear right away that the public liked our response. Three days later, the same people who did the first customer survey went back and asked the identical group how many had heard about our reaction. The number was 53 percent. When they were asked if they approved of our response, 67 percent said they did (55 percent in the original survey disapproved of the odometer disconnections). The survey people were astounded at how fast this flip-flop took place simply because I'd stood up and declared, "I screwed up."*[4]

Perhaps the unaccustomed spectacle of the CEO of a major corporation taking personal responsibility for a "screw-up" was enough in itself to change public opinion, but whatever the cause, Chrysler made a rapid recovery from the odometer-disconnection fiasco, and to this date it has not happened again.

What *did* happen in the early 1990s was that Chrysler suffered a serious economic downturn, which most industry analysts attribute to its attempt to diversify into the aerospace and defense businesses. Some of Iacocca's former admirers became his critics, accusing him of not minding the store. Among other charges they leveled at him was the accusation that he had spent far too much time on the Statue of Liberty restoration and on the numerous media appearances that are demanded of a folk hero. In characteristic fashion, Iacocca confessed to *The Wall Street Journal* that he had indeed made mistakes that were to blame for many of his company's woes. "I'm confessing my sins here," he said, but he also promised to make a major effort to get the company back on track.[5] Whatever the eventual outcome, his willingness to admit his mistakes (without blaming anyone else) reminds us of the tough-minded saying, "When the going gets tough, the tough get going."

## Johnson & Johnson and Tylenol Tampering[6]

During an interview, William May, director of the Program in Business Ethics at the University of Southern California, posed an interesting question: Should business go beyond minimal legal requirements when an ethical issue is involved? Noting that the law often defines the moral minimum required, his answer to his own question is a resounding "yes," and is backed by numerous examples of why ethical behavior is good business. The most interesting example is that of Johnson & Johnson and Tylenol tampering.

In the fall of 1983, several innocent American consumers died after they consumed extra-strength Tylenol capsules that had been laced with cyanide by a homicidal maniac. A major national scare rapidly developed. Because it was not possible to protect Tylenol capsules from a disturbed person bent on this kind of mayhem, and because a culprit was not apprehended, Americans were terrified that they might inadvertently purchase a capsule product that would kill them. James Burke, the CEO of Johnson & Johnson, and his senior executives were faced with an agonizing choice: Should they continue to sell the possibly deadly Tylenol capsules or withdraw the product from the marketplace?

As Professor May notes, "The financial wizards on Wall Street advised J & J not to recall Tylenol. They thought they'd lose market share."[7] When Burke and his executive team decided to withdraw the product, however, Johnson & Johnson continued to prosper, aided by the confidence of the consumer in the integrity of the company. And today, the re-introduced Tylenol, albeit not in capsule form, continues to be a best-selling pain reliever.

## The Concepts of Enlightened Self-Interest and Proactive Behavior

These two examples of tough-minded management in action illustrate a point that mature and honest companies and individuals all understand: It is in their own best interest, particularly in the long run, to be ethical and honest. Companies like Chrysler and Johnson & Johnson have long since learned that going beyond the law and practicing ethical behavior pays off for them in terms of customer trust and their ultimate profitability. This is the concept of *enlightened self-interest*.

In some cases the lesson was learned painfully. In *Talking Straight*, Lee Iacocca noted Ford's disastrous handling of safety problems with its Pinto subcompact early in the 1970s (the little cars tended to catch on fire when they were rear-ended), where Ford minimized the problem by publishing a cost-analysis table showing that the cost in human lives resulting from an unsafe gas tank was "lower" than the cost of redesigning the tank, which would have cost about $11 per car. The resulting public outcry against Ford, which led directly to a business downturn, taught Iacocca, then a young marketing manager at Ford, a lesson that served him well when the odometer-disconnection problem arose.[8]

Whatever the precise cause or reason, organizations tend to be ethically smart or stupid; that is, they have reached lower or higher levels of ethical and moral maturity, in the same way that individuals have. Tough-minded managers have often become tough minded because they have discovered in the course of a lifetime that being gutless nice guys and lying and covering up mistakes just doesn't cut it. Avoidance makes problems worse, and leads to more avoidance and to a loss of respect by and for the individual manager and the organization.

Many business principles textbooks cite a number of "strategies" for dealing with ethical problems. The strategies fall along a continuum, and the alert reader will notice a virtually direct increase in intelligence, tough-mindedness, and moral maturity from one strategy to the next.

In the *reaction* strategy, the business often avoids or denies a problem until the public finds out about it, thus generating all sorts of public ill will. Audi's handling of the sudden acceleration problem with its 5000 model is a good case in point. In the *defense* strategy, the business minimizes the problem, or even lies about it, and tries to avoid additional obligations. It often engages in legal maneuvering, seeks the support of trade groups that support its way of doing business, and lobbies to avoid government action and regulation. Most of the major tobacco marketers, for example, have used defense strategies to keep the government from banning all tobacco advertising. Most defense strategies, however, ultimately fail. In the *accommodation* strategy, the company accepts responsibility for its actions, but doesn't necessarily do anything effective to change its behavior or solve the problem. Exxon has been the target of bitter accusations about its ineffectiveness in clearing up the *Exxon Valdez* spill. Despite running national full-page newspaper ads proclaiming responsibility for the mess and vowing to clean it up, most independent authorities, and the public in general, were highly critical of Exxon's actual effectiveness.

Finally, there is the *proactive* strategy. Companies that are genuinely enlightened are proactive: They acknowledge and respond honestly to problems and voluntarily take actions that are socially responsible to solve the problem before they are pressured to do so.

Johnson & Johnson's actions in the face of the Tylenol-poisoning incident are illustrative of this strategy. Proactive companies are wise and mature enough to recognize that ethical and socially responsible behavior may cost them money or profits in the short run, but in the long run they will come out all right.

In a society that sometimes seems hopelessly addicted to the quick fix and the sugar-coated pill (or in the view of many psychologists, to delusional thinking), proactive companies are adults in a world of children. They enjoy the respect that any good citizen does, but they also enjoy one of the most rewarding psychic payoffs of ethical and socially responsible behavior: They respect themselves as individuals, they respect the society they live in, and they often have tremendous organizational pride. America needs more such managers, and more such companies, and it is the view of these authors that in the twenty-first century it shall have more of both.

There is also a clear relationship, of course, between the types of strategies employed by management in dealing with ethical problems, the continuum of managerial authority, and Kohlberg's moral development levels, diagrammed in Table 6-1. Tough-guy managers brook no dissent: They operate at Level I, in Lawrence Kohlberg's model of moral development, judging right and wrong in terms of avoidance of punishment and deference to authority. When a problem occurs for which they or their organization seems responsible, they not only *deny* any responsibility for the problem, they often vigorously attack their critics. They are oriented toward avoiding punishment, or dispensing it, if possible. Saddam Hussein, the territory- and oil-hungry leader of Iraq, in his invasion of Kuwait and aggressions against other Arab nations, has shown himself to be a practitioner of the tough-guy approach to management. His threats of military action and chemical warfare against anyone who disagrees with his views remind one of the threats of the schoolyard bully when he hasn't gotten his way.

Nice-guy managers are also motivated to avoid dealing with ethical problems. They are functioning at Level II in Kohlberg's model, in which approval of others and compliance with authority are important. They will avoid the problem if they can, but they will also be concerned with possible social disapproval if the problem cannot be avoided through procrastination or denial. Their major concern in dealing with the problem will be to *appease* their critics, and they may often resort to a public-relations campaign to convince the public they have resolved the problem. This activity may come at the expense of taking real and effective action to deal with the problem itself. The reactions of major oil companies to rapidly rising gas prices at the pump after the Iraqi invasion of Kuwait—which included running ads in major publications proclaiming their public-mindedness—are a good recent example.

Tough-minded managers know that problems will not go away if they are not dealt with effectively, so they deal with them effectively. They have reached Level III on Kohlberg's moral-development scale, and their conscience is their main compass in finding their direction when a problem occurs. The compass almost always points them toward a *proactive* and responsible course when a problem must be dealt with—a problem that could not reasonably be anticipated. If they sense that a problem may be developing, they tend to take action to *prevent* it. Often, however, tough-minded managers are called in only after a problem has already mushroomed into a crisis, as was Lee Iacocca when Chrysler was on the verge of bankruptcy.

## A Tough-Minded Philosophy of Ethics

Employees may be motivated to behave unethically because their own personal moral standards are inconsistent with the task to be accomplished, or they have been unduly influenced by others in their organization or by the values of the organization itself, or they may simply have the opportunity to take advantage of a situation for personal gain. Whatever the reasons behind an employee's behavior, however, and whatever he or she may believe about the rightness or wrongness of the action, it is always the responsibility of tough-minded managers to enforce the ethical standards of an organization. The most effective form of enforcement that has yet been invented, of course, is *prevention* of the problem in the first place. The ethical philosophy of the proactive tough-minded manager will always be marked by that old saying, "An ounce of prevention is worth a pound of cure." Tough-minded managers are also aware of an old management joke that reminds us, when we're up to our necks in alligators, it's hard to remember that our mission is to drain the swamp.

1. This section has been adapted from Gareth S. Gardiner, *Tough-Minded Management of Problem Employees : Don't Be a Gutless Nice Guy!* (Springfield, IL: Smith Collins, 1990).

2. Joe Batten, *Tough-Minded Management* (New York: American Management Association, 1963); Joe Batten, *Tough-Minded Leadership* (New York: American Management Association, 1989).

3. Many of the facts in this section were adapted from Lee Iacocca, with Sonny Kleinfield, *Talking Straight* (New York: Bantam books, 1988).

4. Ibid, p. 128

5. Paul Ingrassia and Bradley A. Stertz, "With Chrysler Ailing, Lee Iacocca Concedes Mistakes in Managing," *The Wall Street Journal,* Sept. 17, 1990, p. A1.

6. Many of the facts in this section were adapted from William May, "Good Ethics is Good Business," *New Management* (Spring 1987): 58.

7. Ibid.

8. Iacocca.

■ Many American managers, unfortunately, are *gutless nice guys.* They hate conflict, avoid dealing with problems, and let employees get away with murder. To face themselves, they spend a lot of time lying to themselves about their gutless avoidance behaviors.

■ Some nice-guy managers become so *enraged* when people continue to take advantage of them that they try *tough-guy* tactics: They resort to authoritarian management methods that fail.

■ *Tough-minded* managers recognize that problems will not go away if neglected, and they take *effective steps* to deal with problems. They sit down face to face with problem employees and get effective results.

■ Tough-minded management gets *results* in both the short run and long run with problem employees, and with all sorts of ethical problems. Tough-minded managers have a *far-sighted* philosophy of life marked by a determination to maintain personal *integrity.*

■ Tough-minded managers consistently make socially responsible and ethical decisions when they are faced with a problem. Lee Iacocca's handling of the Chrysler odometer-disconnection scandal, and Johnson & Johnson's management of the Tylenol-poisoning incidents are good examples.

■ The concept of *enlightened self-interest* is one that mature organizations all understand: that it is in an organization's best interest, particularly in the long run, to be *ethical* and *honest.*

■ Mature organizations are typically *proactive*. When faced with an ethical problem, they take *responsible* action to solve the problem before they are pressured to do so. Less mature companies use defensive strategies that usually just get them into more trouble.

## ETHICAL CHOICE AND
## A PUBLICLY REGULATED UTILITY

*Publicly regulated utility companies are usually in the news when one of two things happens: (1) A nuclear power plant produces an "event" (a euphemism for the unexpected release of radiation), or is attacked by a consumer group for being dangerous and/or expensive, or (2) the utility makes an appearance before a state utility commission, requesting a rate increase, where it normally encounters consumer groups protesting the requested rate hike. Not surprisingly, many utilities have become highly defensive when such events occur. Safety and expense issues in the utility industry will undoubtedly continue to make claims on the public's attention throughout the 1990s.*

*Whatever the merits of these issues, and they are certainly complex, every now and then a utility case comes along that is a little different.*

## "CILCO BLOWS 'EM UP GOOD!"*

Reruns of the SCTV comedy series are still seen on television stations throughout North America. In one of the well-known SCTV skits, Canadian funny man John Candy plays the role of a talk-show host who first interviews his guests, and then ". . . blows 'em up good!" As the hapless guest disappears in a cloud of smoke, and while shreds of clothing blow all about, Candy cheerfully discusses the fate of his next guest. We can assure you that the skit regularly cracks up children in the five-to-seven-year age bracket, and that while adults sometimes look at it askance, they often laugh, too.

Recently, Springfield, Illinois, was treated to its own episode of the SCTV skit by CILCO (the Central Illinois Light Company), a publicly

---

* Information for this case was taken from Judy Miller, "CILCO Takes Responsibility for Blast that Blew up House," Springfield, IL *State Journal-Register*, November 3, 1989, p. 13; Judy Miller, "'It's a Miracle' Two Survived Blast," Springfield, IL *State Journal-Register*, November 2, 1989, pp.1-2; Bernie Schoenburg, "CILCO Faces ICC Fines from '89 Home Blast," Springfield, IL *State Journal-Register*, September 27, 1990, p. 12.

regulated utility that supplies both natural gas and power to consumers in central Illinois. On Wednesday, November 1, 1989, a three-man CILCO crew arrived at the house of Buraldine Daykin, aged 78, and her mother, Ruth Crumly, aged 97, to connect their gas service to a newly installed main line. Alas, the two elderly women were not notified of this fact; and, worse, their gas meter was inadvertently left on.

When Ms. Daykin went into the basement of the house and turned on a light, the house blew up! "I pulled the chain on the light and everything just exploded," Ms. Daykin said. She had gone into the basement to investigate an odor of gas. Fragments of glass, mortar, and wood flew into surrounding yards and the street. Damage to the house was estimated at about $70,000. Ms. Daykin ran screaming into the yard as fire spread quickly through the house, and one of the CILCO workers ran into the house and rescued Ms. Crumly. Ms. Daykin's hands and hair were burned, and Ms. Crumly was badly frightened. The house was literally blown off its foundations, and onlookers were amazed that the two women survived the blast.

Because the meter to the house had not been turned off, gas was being pumped into the house at about 40 pounds of pressure; normal residential gas pressure is about one pound. The house had quite literally filled up with the gas fumes. When Ms. Daykin turned on the basement light, it ignited the fumes, resulting in the horrendous explosion that might easily have killed the two women. Dramatic pictures were shown of the two on local television stations, and both made statements that they felt fortunate to be alive.

CILCO immediately took full and complete responsibility for the accident. The next day the company made a formal statement that its work crew had "goofed," and accepted full responsibility for the explosion. "The customer's gas meter was inadvertently left on by a CILCO crew, allowing a higher-than-normal volume of gas to flow into the customer's home," said the statement. "Once the crew became aware of the situation, the servicemen attempted to evacuate the home, but the explosion occurred before the occupants could be removed from the house," it continued.

"To the best of our knowledge, it was miscommunication" among the three-member crew that caused the accident, said Ray Dexheimer, CILCO's general manager in Springfield. In all subsequent statements made to the media, both Dexheimer and other company officials continued to accept responsibility for the matter, and stressed that a fair settlement would be negotiated with the two women and their attorney. Both women were immediately offered temporary housing by the company.

Ah, the power and the pain of honesty! In late September of 1990, the Illinois Commerce Commission (ICC) announced that it would begin proceedings against CILCO, alleging that its workmen had been negligent in the matter, and ordered it to show why civil penalties should not be assessed. CILCO continued to accept responsibility for the accident. "I would imagine that we'll continue to cooperate with them," said CILCO spokesman Tom Flanagan. He also noted that a new house for Ms. Daykin was under construction, and that CILCO was working with her insurance company on paying for the house. ■■

# 7

## Tough-Minded Choices And Managerial Survival

### Ethics Without the Sermon

Some years ago, Laura Nash, a Harvard Business School professor, wrote an article entitled "Ethics Without the Sermon," in which she remarked that many academics are seriously out of touch with the day-to-day ethical decisions faced by working businesspeople and are inclined to be too theoretical. None of this will surprise our readers, we are sure. In fine academic language, she assures us, "Like some Triassic reptile, the theoretical view of ethics lumbers along in the far past of Sunday School and Philosophy I, while the reality of practical business concerns is constantly measuring a wide range of competing claims on time and resources against the unrelenting and objective market-place."[1] Businesspeople, it would seem, have some tough choices to make, and on a daily basis, and this is as about as close as Nash comes to preaching a sermon.

What she *does* do in this article is to list twelve questions that can be used to examine the ethics of virtually any business decision (see Table 7-1). They are remarkable because they are so basic and thoughtful. When she asks, for example, "Are you confident that your position will be as valid over a long period of time as it seems now?" she is simply asking us to examine the *consequences* of our intended course of action, particularly in the long run. She is not preaching to us about *what* we should do in an ethical situation, only asking us to do our best to think things through.[2]

## The Ideas of Sir Adrian Cadbury

Sir Adrian Cadbury, chairman of Cadbury Schweppes PLC, takes up similar themes in his article, "Ethical Managers Make Their Own Rules," which gives a pretty good indication of its contents. Cadbury begins by recounting a story involving his grandfather, who in 1900 owned and ran the second-largest chocolate company in Britain. The elder Cadbury confronted an ethical dilemma in true tough-minded fashion after receiving an order from Queen Victoria to send a decorative tin with a bar of chocolate inside to all her soldiers serving in South Africa. The ethical dilemma faced by Cadbury's grandfather was that while the order meant additional work for his factory, he was deeply and publicly opposed to the Anglo-Boer War raging in South Africa at the time. He resolved the dilemma by accepting the order, but filling it at cost, therefore making no profit out of the transaction. Cadbury notes that his grandfather ". . . made no profit out of what he saw as an unjust war, his employees benefited from the additional work, [and] the soldiers received their royal present . . . ."[3]

The story is instructive, however, more because it illustrates several of Cadbury's themes: (1) The least ethical thing a person can do is to shelve or avoid making a painful decision, (2) when a decision is ethical, it will withstand public scrutiny, (3) companies and managers must be judged by their actions and not their "pious statements of intent," and (4) in modern times there has been a regrettable tendency to reduce complex ethical arguments to simple black and white alternatives. This last development, Cadbury believes, has largely been the result of special interest groups that single-mindedly pursue their particular interests, whatever they may be, without having to consider alternative choices.[4]

One notion that is very appealing in Cadbury's argument is that if an action is ethical, it will withstand public scrutiny. The Dow Corning code of ethics found at the end of this chapter illustrates this point clearly. Dow Corning recognizes that in the course of doing business overseas, its employees will sometimes be under tremendous pressure

## Table 7-1

## Twelve Questions for Examining
## the Ethics of a Business Decision

1. *Have you defined the problem accurately?*

2. *How would you define the problem if you stood on the other side of the fence?*

3. *How did this situation occur in the first place?*

4. *To whom and to what do you give your loyalty as a person and as a member of the organization?*

5. *What is your intention in making this decision?*

6. *How does this intention compare with the probable results?*

7. *Whom could your decision or action injure?*

8. *Can you discuss the problem with the affected parties before you make your decision?*

9. *Are you confident that your position will be as valid over a long period of time as it seems now?*

10. *Could you disclose without qualm your decision or action to your boss, your CEO, the board of directors, your family, society as a whole?*

11. *What is the symbolic potential of your action if understood? If misunderstood?*

12. *Under what conditions would you allow exceptions to your stand?*

Adapted from Laura Nash, "Ethics Without the Sermon,"*Harvard Business Review* (November-December 1981): 81.

to give bribes to foreign officials to make a sale or to get a job done. While this may be extremely distasteful to the employee in question and a serious violation of his or her personal sense of values and ethics, not to make the offer would probably mean a lost sale or more red tape. Dow Corning recognizes this fact in its ethical code by simply asking the employee to acknowledge publicly that he or she felt compelled to offer, or take, the bribe.

We may argue at length about the painful choice faced by an employee in such a situation and hope that we do not have to make such a choice ourselves. The point here is that if there is public disclosure of the action taken, at least we know exactly what choice was made and *why*. Perhaps one of the outcomes of more such public choices will be pressure to change the sometimes murky rules of international business. As Americans accustomed to fairly open ways of dealing with problems, we have a well-founded national suspicion that any deal made in secrecy in a smoke-filled back room has to be crooked. Cadbury's grandfather, and Cadbury himself, apparently understood this principle well.

Cadbury and Laura Nash seem to be more or less in agreement on such issues. Nash's questions assume that a choice that is well thought through, and that is not wantonly injurious, will withstand the light of day. However, nowhere in her list of questions, or in Cadbury's themes, is there an assumption that any ethical choice is easy, or that it will somehow go away if it is not dealt with. If there is a psychological theme in these articles, it is indeed a tough-minded one: Better sit down and take a good hard look at those choices and be well aware that there is going to be no avoiding conflict in making such choices. This is a philosophy of thinking that by and large has served man well historically, and seems to hold equal promise for the future.

## Self-Esteem: The Bedrock of Ethics

The need to protect our sense of self-worth, or self-esteem, is a powerful one, and one may fairly say it is the very bedrock of ethical choice. In almost every choice involving an ethical or moral problem or dilemma, we see this need at work, sometimes in a healthy and growth-oriented way, and sometimes in a neurotic and defensive way. Either way, we are provided with more evidence that the need of every human being to have a positive self-concept is a major factor in determining the choices an individual makes.

We have examined the defensive processes that persons who have committed crimes or made dubious ethical choices use to justify their actions. They *deny* responsibility for their actions, they *invent* good reasons for bad actions, and they frequently *project* blame onto their accusers. Our normal inclination is to judge these persons harshly because their defensive behaviors are so unpleasant and involve significant distortion of reality. But if we take the judge's hat off for a moment and replace it with the deep-thinker's cap, we can begin to understand the root causes of such behavior, and become less inclined to rush to judgment.

As we pointed out in Chapter 4, the self-defeating protestations of innocence of the truly guilty reveal their need to feel that they are good persons. True human compassion may require that we learn to feel some sympathy for the heaviness of the burden they bear: that they made a series of choices that have indeed caught up with them. Ultimately, sadly, they can no longer go on denying responsibility for their choices.

We believe that to understand these choices and their consequences is a major step toward ethical insight. The old saying, "There but for the grace of God go I," is just a common-sense recognition of the consequences of choice, and how precarious and difficult the whole process can be. Fortunately, many of us have had the good judgment—or good luck—to work for organizations that value and implement ethical decision making, from the top down, which makes the choice process easier.

## Ethical Leadership and Ethical Choice: A Recapitulation

Virtually every business textbook and self-help management book advises us that the chief executive officer, or CEO, is the major catalyst in determining an organization's strategy. "In most firms, particularly larger ones, CEOs spend up to 80 percent of their time developing and guiding strategy."[5] The CEO has an important *symbolic* role in the implementation of strategy: Lee Iacocca's highly visible public role in the early 1980s as a television spokesperson for the "new Chrysler Corporation" is a good example of this symbolic role and its importance to the success of a strategy.

The CEO's role is no less important, as we have noted, when it comes to the ethical standards and practices of the organization. Lee Iacocca was equally visible, as we have already noted, as a spokesman for Chrysler when the odometer-disconnection crisis developed in the late 1980s. James Burke of Johnson & Johnson adopted a similar role when the Tylenol-poisoning episode erupted, and his strong public statements reassured the public about the company's integrity and its commitment to its customers.

If the leadership of Exxon had made a similar choice after the *Exxon Valdez* disaster, one wonders if the subsequent damage to the firm's image and the enormous costs incurred in the cleanup and litigation would have been lessened. The dramatic increase in the number of both small and large oil spills that occurred in the late 1980s and early 1990s has presented the petroleum industry with a serious problem of credibility, and has begun to saddle it with a regulatory burden that will not easily be shed. The tradition of leadership in this industry has been at best defensive rather than proactive, and in the minds of the American public, the industry has not been socially responsible. Possibly only the investment banking and savings and loan industries have a more unsavory reputation at the present time.

## Corporate Culture Revisited

Whatever the woes of specific industries, the example set by an organization's leader or leaders sets the tone for the entire organization and ultimately becomes a major determinant of that organization's corporate culture, which we defined earlier as the values, legends, customs, and system of rewards and punishments of an organization. People employed by the organization often learn about it from working with and watching other employees. It is informal, and it is powerful.

Individual business ethics are often influenced more by corporate culture than by an employee's personal values. Most people use one set of moral standards at home and another at work. They learn what is accepted in the informal corporate culture from their co-workers or their immediate supervisors, and they learn what it takes to be success-ful in their company. The role of people we work with, who are sometimes called *significant others* in organizational and psychological language, is a powerful one indeed.

For decades, psychologists and sociologists have studied the power of conformity in social life, particularly American social life, and they have found that it is virtually an all-encompassing principle of middle-class life. We keep up with the Joneses, buy what they buy, and do as they do. When the Joneses and all the other significant others that we live and work with maintain high moral standards, and we happen to be right next to them, we tend to follow suit. There's no room in an organization for a loose gun. Everyone must abide by the standards of that organization or it can destroy the company.

## Suggestions for Improving Ethical Behavior

Although it would be unthinkable to dictate the ethics of employees (and probably unethical, as well), it is practical and possible to use the knowledge of how personal ethical standards, organizational pressures, and opportunity influence unethical behavior to foster more ethical decisions within the organization. In Table 7-2, we attempt to do just that, offering six suggestions for improving ethical behavior within an organization. While it would be nearly impossible for a company to implement these suggestions quickly, over time an organization can incorporate these approaches into its culture and improve ethical behavior. Rome, let us remember, was not built in a day—that immortal cliché is still true today!

A first and basic step in improving ethical decisions is to sensitize employees to the ethical problems and tough choices they may face in their line of work. One way to accomplish this is to develop training programs that explicitly address ethical issues that are specific to the organization. Many companies, such as Citicorp, have ethical work-shops in which employees work through cases, vignettes, and even multiple-choice ethical alternatives to learn about ethical issues. Train-ing programs are important because they send a signal that ethics is important and that all employees must sometimes make tough choices. These programs can help employees learn to recognize ethical prob-lems and begin to resolve them.

## Table 7-2

## Suggestions for Improving Ethical Behavior

■ *Offer training programs which independently and explicitly address specific treatment of ethical issues.*

■ *Limit the opportunity to engage in unethical behavior by providing a well-developed structure and a system of checks and balances, including explicit penalties for unethical behavior.*

■ *Let employees know what penalties the company imposes on those who engage in unethical behavior.*

■ *Recognize how the behavior of co-workers and superiors can influence the behavior of other employees in the organization.*

■ *Develop a code of ethics or ethical policies that are widely communicated and enforced.*

■ *In larger organizations develop an ethics committee to address new issues and help establish and evaluate existing codes and policies.*

A second step in improving ethical decisions is to limit the opportunities to act unethically. In plain language, this means getting the candy out of reach of the baby. In management language, this can be accomplished through a clear policy and structure and a supporting system of checks and balances. An important aspect of this is clear communication: Organizations should *spell out* what the penalties are for unethical behavior and *enforce* them. When transgressions are discovered, the tough-minded response should be to confront the situation, let the employee know that he or she is violating the organization's ethical standards, and clearly state what will happen if he or she does not rectify the problem. The occasion to reprimand an employee for an ethical infraction can provide a golden opportunity to make other employees aware that the behavior is unacceptable and why. Don Zale, former president of Zale Jewelry, once told us that he got on a plane and flew across the country to personally fire a purchasing agent for taking a bribe from a vendor. He then made sure that everyone in the company knew about this tough-minded action because he wanted to send a message that he would not tolerate such behavior. Don Zale obviously understood the principle of clear communication.

Because the behavior of co-workers and superiors can affect how other employees deal with ethical issues, managers must make sure that good role models are present at all times and at all levels of the firm. To paraphrase an old expression, "To improve the ethical behavior of co-workers and superiors, set a good example." When an employee sees her superior cheating, lying, and stealing, then she may assume this is how you get ahead in the company. But, when an employee sees his manager confront problems in a constructive, tough-minded, and ethical manner, he can also learn that *this* is the best way to get ahead.

Another way to foster more ethical decisions in the organization is to implement policies on ethical standards or codes of ethics. Codes of ethics that are widely communicated and enforced have proven very effective in improving ethical behavior within an organization. However, if a code of ethics is only created to be framed on the wall as a public display, or "window dressing," then employees will soon realize that it lacks teeth and carry on as always, not only with no improvement in ethical behavior, but also with increased contempt for the organization and its hypocrisy. There are many case studies of companies that have unenforced codes of ethics that have slipped into deep ethical trouble. Codes of ethics must be specifically stated, related to decisions and actions within the organization, and *enforced*.

Among Fortune 500 companies, IBM has an enviable reputation for a strong code of ethics. The code of ethics is not only communicated clearly to all managers and employees, it is enforced. Employees and managers who cheat are fired, and this is clearly understood throughout IBM. The code of ethics is not window dressing, it is the company's traditional way of doing business, and it has become deeply imbedded in IBM's corporate culture. Not surprisingly, most IBM employees are proud of the company they work for.

Finally, larger organizations can establish an ethics committee to address ethical issues and to help establish and evaluate existing codes of ethics and corporate policies on ethics. At Motorola, for example, the Business Ethics Compliance Committee is charged with interpreting, classifying, communicating, and enforcing the company's code of ethics.[6] One of the major contributions of an ethics committee is that it provides an opportunity to bring ethical issues and problems out into the open. Discussion and debate of problems and issues help resolve issues to satisfy the company and interested groups. Although everyone will probably not agree on the issues and solutions, discussion and debate encourages open dialogue and allows different viewpoints to be expressed and understood. In the long run, this openness and exchange of ideas can improve ethical decisions.

## Surviving in the Unethical Organization

The manager working for an ethical and proactive organization faces a daily positive challenge: how to uphold the standards of conduct required by the organization. The challenge faced by the individual working for a company that is corrupt, however, is a very different one. This is a problem that is not usually addressed when dealing with organizational ethics. Nonetheless, some sensible observations can be made that may be of value to the person who finds himself or herself in such a dilemma.

First, there simply may not be a conflict. If the person can accept the values of the corrupt organization and maintain a reasonable level of happiness and well-being while accepting employment there, so be it. If the person can say, "Well, in a den of thieves, you've got to be a thief," and not lose sleep over the organization's way of doing business and the behaviors that are required to maintain its business, we should probably leave well enough alone. There are probably hundreds of thousands or even millions of individuals who get along well enough in this fashion, and it is not our purpose to judge this method of coping.

Second, if there *is* a conflict, and an individual has difficulty accepting the values and conduct of the organization that employs him or her, there would seem to be several choices available. One choice that may or may not be practical is *voting with one's feet,* or leaving the organization, which until recently was the alternative of choice for many citizens of Eastern European nations with orthodox communist governments that were simply intolerable for thousands of ordinary persons.

A third choice available to the individual, and one which also involves a high degree of risk and personal courage, is to be *the person who stands alone.* Professors Arvind Bhambri and Jeffrey Sonnenfeld document the case of a 39-year-old manager named Tony Santino who faced a difficult ethical dilemma in his job as director of marketing for a small manufacturing firm. Santino learned of the existence of a fictitious product line that his company was selling. The lower-priced line was "developed" to meet a competitor's price, but in reality was simply an old product line labeled differently and sold only to new customers. Santino objected vocally and in writing to the fictitious line of products. He considered the scheme not only unethical, but illegal. He came under heavy pressure from his superiors, and was threatened with dismissal, to represent the fictitious line as a new product line. He was even asked to make a sales presentation at a company retreat. After eventually leaving this firm, he was hired as a senior executive with a large high-tech manufacturing company whose executives admired his courage in making the choices he had with his previous company.

Bhambri and Sonnenfeld remark that they feel Tony Santino was a success "... because his convictions triumphed over external pressures. Trapped by an ethical dilemma that was very costly in extrinsic terms, he nevertheless purchased a very valuable intrinsic good: personal dignity and professional pride." In facing a situation that compromised his personal sense of morality, he was willing to stand alone. In closing this fascinating article, Santino's comment rings in our ears: "Finally, you have to live with yourself. I spend one-third of my life sleeping and don't want to do anything that will keep me awake nights."[7]

Tony's choice again illustrates in a very concrete and human way that self-esteem is the bedrock of ethics, but it also demonstrates very clearly the terrible risks an individual must take in dealing with senior managers and executives in the unethical organization. In another widely publicized case, black FBI agent Don Rochon, assigned to the Omaha, Nebraska, office in 1983, was the victim of crude incidents of racial harassment there. After receiving no satisfaction from his superiors despite repeated verbal complaints, he eventually sued the FBI and won favorable rulings from both the Justice Department and Equal Employment Opportunity Commission supporting his claim of discrimination and harassment. Don Rochon is another brave American who was willing to assume the risks of standing alone.

## Ethical Training and Ethical Choice

Those of us who work closely with and write about ethical issues and ethical choices sometimes lose sight of an important fact: Many intelligent and thoughtful persons have never had any training in ethics, and sometimes just don't recognize certain types of ethical conflicts. Some of the ethical issues we have dealt with in these pages, such as lying and bribery, are more easily recognized as basic issues in ethics. We have also stressed that fishermen, due to the incredibly stressful nature of fishing and its unbelievably low (real) success rate, have a lifetime exemption from any and all ethical guidelines and considerations! There are other occupations, however, where an ethical situation may arise, and may not immediately be recognized as such. The pizza business presents us with a case in point.

Fast-food giant Domino's Pizza regularly tracks its customers and their pizza orders through a computerized telephone identification system. One of the purposes in establishing the system was to aid the company in identifying fraudulent orders, but the identification system had another payoff for Domino's in that it allowed the company to identify loyal and frequent customers. This fact, and the company's desire to recognize and reward such customers, inadvertently led it into an ethical conflict.

A manager in the Detroit area told us that he once wanted to reward an area customer who ordered a pizza every weekday evening by presenting the man with a gift. When the regional manager agreed with his idea, the manager contacted the customer and was amazed that he was furious about the prospect of being recognized. He was upset that the company would track his eating habits and felt that the attempt to reward him was an invasion of his privacy. The company had simply not thought of this and was upset that its attempt to do good had gone awry.

In a recent seminar, we described the Domino's incident to a group of college juniors and seniors (without revealing the outcome) and asked them, "How many of you feel that this was an ethical situation?" Fewer than a quarter of the hands in the room went up, although one or two of the students *did* recognize the invasion of privacy issue. The case illustrates, among other things, that sensitivity to potential ethical conflicts must sometimes be enhanced by appropriate training.

Much training in the field of ethics, unfortunately, takes the form of heavy-handed and preachy repetition of themes of "Don't Do Bad Things, Be Good," which have a quick and predictable outcome: They turn people off. In each generation, it seems, educators must rediscover the principle that the most effective education teaches people to think for themselves. In the field of ethics education, this is doubly true. Effective training programs tend to focus heavily on case-by-case analysis, involve participants extensively in discussion and interaction, and stress the need for each individual to learn an ethical choice process that is uniquely his or her own.

Manny Valasquez, the director of Santa Clara University's Center for Applied Ethics, believes that college courses cannot teach people to be ethical but can make students aware of the ethical aspects of their business lives and of the consequences of unethical behavior.[8] Valasquez's belief is shared by the present authors: The complex world of ethical choice is best served, we believe, by stimulating each person to think for himself or herself. Our perceptive readers have long since noticed, of course, that this volume has raised far more questions than

# The (ethical) Thinker

"Hmmm . . . What would Laura Nash or Lord Cadbury think?
What do *I* think? Will my decision hurt anyone? How will
the company react? What exceptions might there be . . . ?"

it answers, and long since realized that ethical questions in their lives will continue to arise long after they have finished reading these few pages.

## A Perspective on Ethical Choice, and a Note on Survival

The field of ethics is one where simplistic, preachy, and all-encompassing rules of conduct cannot be handed down from on high. Almost by definition, an ethical choice is complex, often with painful and unpredictable consequences. Yet choices can be made, and indeed must be made, on virtually a daily basis, by managers and ordinary persons everywhere. The authors are reminded of the old saying that begins, "Fools rush in . . . ."

Because choice is inevitable, we are reminded again of the wise words of the English poet Percy Bysshe Shelley who once said, "We look before and after, and pine for what is not."[9] It is precisely this ability to think and choose, and to contemplate the wisdom of our choices, that has placed mankind a notch above any other species. We may indeed pine as we contemplate the consequences of a rotten choice, but in the very process of pining, we are also contemplating wiser future choices. As always, enough said. Man has survived at least in part because man has made good choices.

If there is a perspective that summarizes this slender volume, it is an upbeat one: Because we have no freedom but to choose, then we have complete freedom to make choices. Your outlook can be a completely positive one: When the freedom to choose is accompanied by the ability to make good choices, the outcome will probably be survival, and even success. To the manager agonizing over a tough choice in a tough world, we can only say contemplate your choice, live with it, and go on choosing. As Socrates said, "The life which is unexamined is not worth living,"[10] and life is a situation that presents us with many examinations.

## References in Chapter Seven

1. Laura L. Nash, "Ethics Without the Sermon," *Harvard Business Review* (November-December 1981): 80.

2. Ibid.

3. Sir Adrian Cadbury, "Ethical Managers Make Their Own Rules," *Harvard Business Review* (September-October 1987): 69-73.

4. Ibid.

5. John A. Pearce II and Richard B. Robinson, Jr., *Strategic Management*, 3rd ed. (Homewood, IL: Richard D. Irwin, 1988): 375.

6. Patrick E. Murphy, "Implementing Business Ethics," *Journal of Business Ethics* 7 (December 1988): 909.

7. Arvind Bhambri and Jeffrey Sonnenfeld, "The Man Who Stands Alone," *New Management* 4 (Spring 1987): 29-33.

8. Gary Meyers, "Some Firms Taking Ethics Seriously," Springfield, IL *The State Journal-Register*, September 11, 1988, p. 52.

9. Percy Bysshe Shelley, "To a Skylark," quoted in John Bartlett, ed., *Bartlett's Familiar Quotations* (Boston: Little, Brown & Company, 1980): 468.

10. As recorded by Plato, in John Bartlett, ed., *Bartlett's Familiar Quotations* (Boston: Little, Brown & Company, 1980): 83.

- Laura Nash believes that we can talk about ethics *without the sermon.* She proposed a list of twelve questions that we should ask when examining the ethics of a business decision. Her questions force us to focus on examining the *consequences* of an ethical decision, particularly in the long run.

- Sir Adrian Cadbury believes that the least ethical thing a manager or business can do is *avoid* making a painful decision. He further argues that an ethical decision, even a painful one, will withstand *public scrutiny.*

- When we examine how individuals make ethical decisions, it becomes apparent that the need to protect one's self-esteem is a powerful human need and may even be said to be the *bedrock* of ethical choice.

- For those of us fortunate enough to work for an organization headed by ethical leaders, who have committed the entire organization to ethical ways of doing business, the process of ethical choice is made much easier. The ethical values and practices of the CEO may eventually become part of the corporate culture, which is the informal way it does business. The role of other people we work with in the organization's culture is also important in influencing the ethical decisions we make as individuals.

- There are some ways to foster more ethical decisions in an organization: Offer *training programs* on ethical issues; limit the *opportunity* for unethical behavior through checks and balances; make employees aware of the *penalties* for violating the rules; understand how co-workers and superiors can *influence the behavior* of other employees;

develop a *code of ethics* or *ethical policies* and *enforce* them; and, in larger organizations, develop an *ethics committee* to address ethical issues and formulate and evaluate ethical policies.

■ For those of us who work for *unethical* organizations, there are at least three choices:

1. Accept the organization's way of doing business and try not to lose any sleep over it.

2. Vote with one's feet and leave the organization.

3. Learn to be the person who stands alone, an expression describing the person who attempts to change the unethical organization from within. This is an extremely stressful role, not surprisingly, often requiring great personal courage.

■ In the field of ethical training, one of the surprising realities we sometimes encounter is that some ethical conflicts are not easy to recognize. *Sensitivity* to potential ethical conflicts is often an important need in ethical training.

■ Heavy-handed preaching about ethics ("do good, don't be bad") is a generally ineffective way of teaching ethics because it instantly turns people off. Most effective training programs focus on teaching people to *think for themselves* and use real-world situations that are unique to each organization.

## FORMAL ETHICAL CHOICE:
## A CORPORATE CODE OF ETHICS

*Most large companies now have codes of ethics, as we noted in Chapter 1, and these documents, the basic accountability statements for the companies that developed them, have been printed on fine and glossy paper and distributed widely among manager and employees. Cynics sometimes accuse these codes of being mere "window dressing," and the acid test of a company's sense of morality and propriety is no doubt its behavior. Nonetheless, occasionally a code of ethics comes along that seizes attention because it deals with the real ethical and moral conflicts that the company is going to have to deal with in a particularly open and refreshing way. The Dow Corning code of ethics is a good example.*

## *To Dow Corning Employees:\**

The 1990 revision of Dow Corning's Code of Business Conduct reflects the changes we have perceived in global business practices in recent years. I encourage you to read it, discuss it with others and, above all, practice it.

Every Dow Corning employee knows from the first day on the job that business integrity is a vital and valued part of our culture. Our Code provides guidelines that set general directions for our conduct. It does not, however, always provide clear and precise answers to the many issues we encounter in conducting business across an increasing number of cultures.

So, while the Code serves as a first point of reference, we have learned that living up to our standards of business integrity requires continuing dialogue. That is one reason we have a Corporate Business Conduct Committee — to help stimulate that dialogue and to remind us that good ethics is indeed good business.

I am convinced that international competitiveness and ethical conduct go hand-in-hand. To the extent each employee continues to make legal and ethical business practice part of his or her everyday working life, the more valued a supplier we will become in the eyes of our customers.

Lawrence A. Reed
President and Chief Executive Officer,
Dow Corning Corporation

---

\* ©1990, Dow Corning Corporation. Dow Corning Center, Midland, MI 48640. Reprinted with permission.

# Dow Corning Corporation Code of Ethics

## Dow Corning Values

- INTEGRITY  Our integrity is demonstrated in our ethical conduct and in our respect for the values cherished by the society of which we are a part.
- EMPLOYEES  Our employees are the source from which our ideas, actions and performance flow. The full potential of our people is best realized in an environment that breeds fairness, self-fulfillment, teamwork and dedication to excellence.
- CUSTOMERS  Our relationship with each customer is entered in the spirit of a long-term partnership and is predicated on making the customer's interests our interests.
- QUALITY  Our never-ending quest for quality performance is based on our understanding of our customers' needs and our willingness and capability to fulfill those needs.
- TECHNOLOGY  Our advancement of chemistry and related sciences in our chosen fields is the Value that most differentiates Dow Corning.
- ENVIRONMENT  Our commitment to the safe-keeping of the physical environment is founded on our appreciation of it as the basis for the existence of life.
- SAFETY  Our attention to safety is based on our full-time commitment to injury-free work, individual self-worth and a consideration for the well-being of others.

- PROFIT  Our long-term profit growth is essential to our long-term existence. How our profits are derived, and the purposes for which they are used, are influenced by our Values and our shareholders.

## *Integrity: A Basic Dow Corning Value*

*Fair, legal and ethical business practice is key to maintaining our corporate integrity. Our Code addresses many diverse business situations. Those not explicitly covered can generally be resolved through your own thoughtful judgment or discussion with management or, as needed, a review with the Business Conduct Committee.*

## *Dow Corning's Responsibilities to Employees:*

- *All relations with employees will be guided by our belief that the dignity of the individual is primary.*
- *Opportunity without bias will be afforded each employee in relation to demonstrated ability, initiative and potential.*
- *Management practices will be consistent with our intent to provide continuing employment for all productive employees.*
- *Qualified citizens of countries where we do business will be hired and trained for available positions consistent with their capabilities.*
- *We will strive to create and maintain a work environment that fosters honesty, personal growth, teamwork, open communications and dedication to our vision and values.*
- *We will provide a safe, clean and pleasant work environment that at minimum meets all applicable laws and regulations.*
- *The privacy of an individual's records will be respected; employees may, however, review their own personnel records upon request.*

## Our Responsibilities as Dow Corning Employees

- *Employees will treat Dow Corning proprietary information as a valued asset and diligently protect it from loss or negligent disclosure.*
- *Employees will respect our commitment to protect the confidentiality of information entrusted to us by customers, suppliers and others in our business dealings.*
- *The proprietary information of others will be obtained only through the use of legal and ethical methods.*
- *Employees will not engage in activities that either jeopardize or conflict with the company's interests. Recognizing and avoiding conflicts of interest is the responsibility of each employee. When a potential conflict of interest exists, the employee is obligated to bring the situation to the attention of Dow Corning management for resolution.*
- *Employees will use or authorize company resources only for legitimate business purposes.*
- *The cost of goods or services purchased for Dow Corning must be reasonable and in line with competitive standards.*
- *Employees will not engage in bribery, price fixing, kickbacks, collusion or any related practice which might be, or give the appearance of being, illegal or unethical.*
- *Employees will avoid contacts with competitors, suppliers, government agencies and other parties that are or appear to be engaging in unfair competition or the restriction of free trade.*
- *Business interactions with our competitors will be limited to those necessary for buyer-seller agreements, licensing agreements or matters of general interest to industry or society. All such interactions will be documented.*

## Relations with Customers, Distributors, Suppliers

- *We are committed to providing products and services that meet the requirements of our customers. We will provide information and support necessary to effectively use our products.*

- *Business integrity is a criterion for selecting and retaining those who represent Dow Corning. Dow Corning will regularly encourage its distributors, agents, and other representatives to conduct their business on our behalf in a legal and ethical manner.*
- *The purchase of goods and services will be based on quality, price, service, ability to supply and the supplier's adherence to legal and ethical business practices.*

## Social Responsibilities, Conservation, Environment, and Product Stewardship

- *We will be responsible for the impact of Dow Corning's technology upon the environment.*
- *We will minimize the generation of waste materials from our operations to the extent economically and technically feasible. Reduction at the source and recycling will be vigorously pursued in all facilities. Non-recyclable waste will be disposed of in accordance with applicable standards.*
- *New facilities will be designed and existing facilities will be modified as necessary to optimize the efficient use of natural resources and to conserve energy.*
- *We will continually strive to assure that our products and services are safe, efficacious and accurately represented in our selling and promotional activities.*
- *Characteristics of Dow Corning raw materials, intermediates and products—including toxicity and potential hazards—will be made known to those who produce, package, transport, purchase, use and dispose of them.*
- *The impact of Dow Corning operations and facilities on the communities where they are located—including hazards and the means employed to safeguard against them—will be made known to those who may be affected including employees, contractors, local authorities and members of the community.*

- We will build and maintain positive relationships with communities where we have a presence. Our efforts will focus on education, civic, cultural and health and safety programs.

## International Business Guidelines

- Dow Corning will be a responsible corporate citizen wherever we do business. We recognize, however, that laws, business practices and customs differ from country to country. If there is a conflict with U.S. law or this Code of Conduct, we will seek reasonable ways to resolve the difference. Failing resolution, we will remove ourselves from the particular business situation.
- Dow Corning employees will not authorize or give payments or gifts to government employees or their beneficiaries or anyone else in order to obtain or retain business.
- Facilitating payments to expedite the performance of routine services are strongly discouraged and should be considered only when there is no reasonable alternative. If made, such payments should be the minimum amount and must be accurately documented and recorded.
- No contributions to political parties or candidates will be given by Dow Corning, even in countries where such contributions are legal.
- While encouraging the transborder transfer of technology necessary to support its subsidiaries and joint ventures, Dow Corning expects to receive fair compensation for, and protection of, its technology.

## Financial Responsibilities

- Dow Corning funds will be used only for purposes that are legal and ethical and all transactions will be properly and accurately recorded.
- We will maintain a system of internal accounting controls for Dow Corning and assure that all involved employees are fully apprised of that system.